MW01087187

A PRACTICAL GUIDE TO LEGAL RESEARCH AND ANALYSIS FOR PARALEGAL AND LEGAL STUDIES STUDENTS

Margaret Phillips

WEST
ACADEMIC
PUBLISHING

The publisher is not engaged in rendering legal or other professional advice, and this publication is not a substitute for the advice of an attorney. If you require legal or other expert advice, you should seek the services of a competent attorney or other professional.

© 2020 LEG, Inc. d/b/a West Academic
    444 Cedar Street, Suite 700
    St. Paul, MN 55101
    1-877-888-1330

West, West Academic Publishing, and West Academic are trademarks of West Publishing Corporation, used under license.

Printed in the United States of America

ISBN: 978-1-68328-902-9

For Jonathan, Sam and Lilly.

Preface

The motivation for writing this book has been 17 years in the making—the 17 years I have been involved in legal education, and the changes I have seen in technology, teaching, and the students.

I am extremely indebted to my colleagues—many experienced and creative legal educators from the American Association for Legal and Paralegal Education (AAfPE) from whom I have learned so much—friends, and present and former students who gave generously of their time, provided ideas and inspiration, and suffered through earlier drafts of this book in order to supply me with much-needed feedback.

I would like to thank Leslie Keane (my dear friend to whom I will owe a cocktail to for the rest of my life, for reading drafts and keeping me on task); Nan Lipsitz Haynes (my law school classmate, friend, and long-time Legal Research and Writing faculty at UB Law School, for reading drafts, always being available and having a quick turn-around time); my erstwhile assistants Lynette Boesken and Dana Kelley (for keeping everyone else at bay when I was trying to write); my encouraging colleagues and the supportive administration at Daemen College; my wonderful, patient and hard-working copy editor Mary Trevor (for her hard work, enthusiasm, and eye for detail); and of course my husband Jonathan and my children Sam and Lilly (for listening to me think and complain about "the book" for the last three years).

I am likewise very grateful to West Academic for giving me this opportunity, especially James Cahoy and Jon Harkness, and the West editing and word processing experts Laura Holle, Michele Bassett, and Greg Olson, who were invaluable.

Margaret Phillips

August 2019

Table of Contents

SECTION II. WHEN YOUR LEGAL
ISSUE COMES ALONG: IRAC

**SECTION III. CONCLUSION:
PUTTING IT ALL TOGETHER**

Table of Cases

A PRACTICAL GUIDE TO LEGAL RESEARCH AND ANALYSIS FOR PARALEGAL AND LEGAL STUDIES STUDENTS

Introduction

I hope that you find this book clear, simple, and easy to read. The overarching theme of this book is that legal analysis can be broken down in simple, discrete, and sometimes visual steps. This book is for you: the paralegal or legal studies student. I aim to speak to you directly in clear and simple prose. There is no magic in learning the law and the process of legal reasoning. As a student interested in the law, I am confident you can learn the process for both legal research and legal analysis, and then use those skills to write a legal memo and a motion by the end of the text.

In Section I, Chapters 1–4, you will be introduced to some background information and legal vocabulary (italicized for easy recognition) in order to get you started. You will learn how to recognize different forms of law—statutes, administrative regulations, case law, and constitutions—as well as some basic principles of our legal system: jurisdiction, the difference between criminal and civil law, and how the legal system is put together. You will also learn how to figure out the context for a legal issue by answering some basic legal questions, and even perhaps starting a bit of legal research. Chapter 4 provides in-depth research instruction, building on the fundamental ways to think about legal sources that you were introduced to earlier. Section I also involves a discussion about understanding the legal rule—and what the rule means—by breaking it down into its distinct elements, or separate parts.

The middle of the text, Section II, Chapters 5–9, presents IRAC, the fundamental organizing principle of legal analysis: *Issue, Rule, Application, Conclusion*. The IRAC structure is used to analyze legal issues and necessarily involves both law and the facts to which the law will be applied. Therefore, one of the themes in this second section will be identifying legally relevant facts. You will learn the simple (but not easy) methods to find the legal rule you need, and importantly, the way to determine if the rule you found is really the right one.

Specifically, in Chapter 5 you will learn the building blocks of legal analysis by working through IRAC exercises and case briefing exercises. After this overview comes "I" or "Issue" in Chapter 6, where you will learn about issue spotting and how to articulate a legal issue. Issue spotting is an important skill in legal practice. Clients with problems and questions will have legal issues for you to spot, understand, and resolve with your legal team—under the supervision of an attorney.[1] For "R" or "Rule," in Chapter 7, you will review the sources of legal rules and learn the necessary skill of synthesis. Synthesis is the combination of ideas from multiple sources into one coherent whole and is used when you need to construct a rule from various sources.

The "A" ("Application") follows in Chapters 8 and 9, which focus on the application of the legal rule to facts. The application process involves identifying the legally relevant facts, which then become the focus of your analysis and argument. You will learn how to accurately identify the court's decision, or holding. This means you will be able to describe who won the dispute and why, using the legally relevant facts. For example, you will learn the difference between the substantive holding and the procedural holding, and along with that, learn to

---

[1] The role of a supervising attorney is critical. Throughout the text and the exercises, we will research and analyze the specific ethical prohibition against practicing law if you don't have a law license. Although the practice of law is defined differently in different jurisdictions, a general rule of thumb is that it includes appearing on behalf of a client in court or at a deposition, signing legal documents on behalf of a client, or offering legal advice about how a legal rule applies to a specific factual situation. *See* ABA Model Rule of Ethics 5.3, A Lawyer's Duty to Supervise Non-Lawyers.

understand summary judgment. Understanding the substantive holding is critical to understanding the application or legal reasoning process.

The last chapter in Section II, Chapter 9, deliberately examines patterns of analysis, or rule application. You will have the opportunity to mimic them in your own analysis and argument when you learn how to draft memos and motions in Section III. These fundamental patterns of reasoning include interpreting a legal rule narrowly or broadly; using comparison, such as analogies and distinctions, for legal analysis and argument; and finally, looking to the purpose or the legislative history behind the legal rule for analysis and argument. Synthesis again appears as an important tool for helping construct and interpret rules, and for doing document drafting, another skill covered in Section III.

Finally, in Section III, Chapters 10 and 11—the last two chapters—apply all the skills covered in the earlier chapters to drafting memos and motions. These are typical writing products in the legal profession. Memos are used as internal exploratory documents that present a legal question and resolve it for the supervising attorney as an important step in the development of a case strategy. Some lawyers may claim they never wrote a legal memo after they left law school, but that's not the point. The point is that memos, or problems that require you to write a memo, provide an opportunity for you to practice legal analysis. And you need the skill of legal analysis every day in the legal profession.

Similarly, motions, which are requests to the court for an order, are an opportunity for you to practice legal argument. Motions are usually supported by multiple documents, typically including a notice of motion, supporting affidavit(s) and supporting evidence, and a persuasive memo of law. Typically, memos are deemed "objective" and motions are deemed "persuasive" legal writing. Both use the same legal reasoning tools explained throughout the text, but persuasive legal writing has a different perspective and goal. For that reason, once the book shifts from memos to motions, you will learn about additional features and techniques for putting together a legal argument.

A word about the examples: I searched for easy-to-understand and hopefully somewhat interesting examples for the hypothetical fact situations and the case law situations you will examine. For example, I have used negligence, the bedrock of civil law, and burglary, a rather simple crime. I have also used a variety of U.S. Supreme Court cases on marriage, both because the evolution of our ideas on marriage over the past 60 years is compelling to many, and because U.S. Supreme Court cases give us wonderful opportunities to examine and dissect complex yet interesting legal reasoning. When introducing you to a concept, I have often used a simple example such as the *No Sleeping in the Park* problem. That example is borrowed (with permission) from an esteemed law school educator, Professor Laurel Currie Oates from the University of Seattle School of Law, the founder and former Director of the Law School's Legal Research and Writing program.

Try to remember that ALL the legal skills reviewed in this book are general skills that apply in all areas of law that are useful to students of the law. If you wish to delve further, there are many fine texts devoted solely to legal writing, legal argument, or legal reasoning that provide a much deeper level of instruction.

Good luck, get reading, and onward and upward!

Getting Started

In Chapters 1, 2, and 3 you will be introduced to the basics of the legal system, court structure, legal vocabulary, and how to perform legal research with primary and secondary sources.

Identifying the Rule (What Does a Legal Rule Look Like?)

Legal Skills:
- Identify legal rules
- Identify *sources* of legal rules
- Identify rule-making roles of each branch of government
- Define "*elements*" of a legal rule
- Define secondary *sources*
- Name basic components of a *citation*

PART I. THE LEGAL RULE IS A PRIMARY *SOURCE*

This chapter aims to make it easier to understand, recognize, and find legal rules in all forms. You will examine each *source of law* so that you can begin to recognize the format for each one, as well as some of the visual and substantive characteristics for each form. This examination should help you know what you are seeing on the screen, and later, will help you when doing your research and analysis tasks. So, let's get started.

Let's start with the thing itself. I often start my introductory law class with the question, "What is law?" It is fun to think about for a moment. Inevitably, a student will point out that law is the rules we live by. But rules that we may live by differ from laws that rule society because laws are enforced either directly or indirectly by the government.

This explanation is certainly the foundation, but the next step is a harder one to take—that laws that rule society, legal rules, are created by a variety of *sources* that can be found in a variety of contexts. Most students can quickly learn that there are four "*sources*" of law—*statutes, administrative regulations, case law,* and *constitutions.* This makes sense, and it correlates with the branches of government that create the different types of law: legislative branch (*statutes* and, on rare occasions, *constitutional* amendments); executive branch agencies (*administrative regulations*); judicial branch (*case law*); and with the originator of these branches, *constitutional* conventions (*constitutions*). See Diagram 1, which includes each *source of law* and the branch or originator of government to which it correlates.

Diagram 1:
Primary Sources and Branch/Originator of Government

SOURCE OF LAW	**BRANCH/ORIGINATOR OF GOVERNMENT**
Statutes	**Legislative Branch**
Administrative Regulations	**Agencies/Executive Branch**
Case Law	**Judicial Branch**
Constitution	***Constitutional* Conventions/Founders**
Constitutional Amendments	**Either Congress (legislative branch) passes a proposed amendment by 2/3 vote or a *constitutional* convention is convened by vote of 2/3 of state legislatures**

Further, the legal rules in the different *sources of law* look different from each other. Typically, the first *source of law* many students learn becomes their "go-to," or their model, for recognizing law. For example, generally, first year law students all take courses—contracts, torts, property, etc.—that teach the substance of the law by having them read *case law*. Subsequently, when asked to research, they naturally gravitate to *case law*, and unsurprisingly overlook the other sources of law—*statutes, administrative regulations,* and *constitutions.* It's easy to make that mistake. We all look for the familiar. And it's not easy, initially, to understand that law comes in different shapes and sizes—from different branches of our government, in different formats, and with different looking *citations.*

This chapter will explain and demonstrate each *source of law— statutes, administrative regulations, constitutions,* and *case law*—and offer some visual and substantive cues for identifying each type of *source.* Before we get to that material, however, there are certain things it is helpful to know about *sources of law* and the legal rules in them.

First, let's review the basic nature of legal rules. We all know what rules are—**if** this, **then** that. For example, **if** you stay out past midnight, **then** you will be grounded. We intuitively know that legal rules work the same way—if/then. For example, on the *criminal* side of things, **if** a person knowingly enters a building with the intent to commit a crime, **then** that person has committed burglary and is guilty of a crime. Or, on the *civil* side of things, **if** a driver violates the duty to drive at a safe distance and rear-ends you, causing injuries, **then** that driver is negligent and liable for your injuries. Rules are rules.

Second, legal rules typically have multiple parts. The legal term we use to describe the separate and distinct parts of a legal rule is "*element.*" According to Black's Law Dictionary (11th ed. 2019), an *element* is a "constituent part of a claim that must be proved for the claim to succeed." In subsequent chapters when we discuss researching a legal rule and using a legal rule as the basis of analysis, we will focus more on identifying and working with the separate *elements* of a legal rule. For now, you need to know that each legal rule has separate and distinct parts, or *elements.*

Third, the *sources of law* are identified (and found) by legal *citations.* By *citation*, we mean how we refer to these *sources of law*—the identifying name, volume number, page number, section number, and year. Legal *citation* is a peculiar breed, and there is no other system of *citation* like it. Don't be discouraged if *citations* look strange to you or if it takes a while to master them. For now, at the outset, let them serve as a tool to help you figure out the *source of law* (eventually, citations will be tools that also help you figure out *jurisdiction*, and for *case law*, the weight of the precedent.)

In general, *citations* for all the *sources of law* have the same components: 1) an indication (often abbreviated) of the type of source—*statute, administrative regulation, constitution,* or *case law*; 2) the geographic *jurisdiction* of that source (federal or a particular state or locale); and 3) a relevant date. *Jurisdiction* is another one of those fundamental legal terms that has many different layers. According to Black's Law Dictionary, *"jurisdiction"* means "A court's power to decide a case or issue a decree" or, in other words, the specific geographical place or court in which the authority applies. When we talk about *jurisdiction* with respect to a *citation*, we are referring to the place (such as the federal or particular state or municipal locale) where the *source of law* comes from and where it applies.[1]

For a thorough guide that walks you through *citations* and shows you how to use them to identify your legal *source*, see Appendix A. This text relies on The Bluebook: A Uniform System of Citation (Columbia Law Review Ass'n et al. ed., 20th ed. 2015), but individual *jurisdictions* may rely on different *citation* guides or conventions, especially in the legal practice (as opposed to academic) arena. The descriptions below of each type of *source* will include a basic description of its *citation.*

---

[1]   In Chapter 2, we will look at another type of *jurisdiction*—subject matter—in addition to geographical *jurisdiction.*

Hopefully, learning, observing, and reviewing the different characteristics of each source, as well as its *citation*, will help you to distinguish one source from another when you are looking at the computer screen.

Fourth, a word about ***primary*** *sources of law* versus ***secondary*** *sources of law*. In law, the different types of *sources of law* that have been discussed here are *primary sources*. A *statute* is a *primary source*, a *case* is a *primary source*, a *regulation* is a *primary source*, and the *Constitution* is a *primary source*. In other words, a *primary source* is THE LAW itself—in any format—because each *source of law* is a form of legal rule. This will be important to remember when we start researching to solve problems.

In contrast, *secondary sources* are **NOT** THE LAW. *Secondary* sources are *sources* where someone—other than a branch of the government—is explaining, discussing, or questioning the law, but not creating it. As you start doing even basic research, you will run across *secondary sources*, and it is important that you know you are looking at a *secondary source*, **not** THE LAW. Some examples of *secondary* sources include legal encyclopedias, treatises, form books, and periodicals like law reviews or law journals. Because their purpose is to explain the law, these sources are often a great place to start your research. For example, all states have a state law encyclopedia that contains outlines and explanations of that state's law.

You may see *secondary sources* referred to in *case law* or included in the *annotations* following the text of a *statute*. (*Annotations*, addressed below in the discussion of *statutes*, are the cross-references to *primary* and *secondary sources* that accompany *statutes* in some publications.) You will also see *secondary* sources among the results when you do searches either on free legal sites or on subscription legal databases. Again, it's important to know what you are looking at—*secondary sources* are supremely helpful in assisting you to understand the law, and to find other relevant *sources of law*, but alas, *secondary* sources are **not** THE LAW. *Secondary sources* are more fully explained and discussed in Chapter 2, Part II.

The balance of this chapter will focus on *primary sources*, looking in more detail at each of the four *sources of law* already described. Part of your initial look at these *primary sources* will include learning how to distinguish them from *secondary sources*. Fortunately, visual and substantive clues help distinguish one from the other.

As an example, one hallmark of *secondary sources* to keep in mind is the idea of personal authorship. With *secondary sources*, whether written by a group of lawyers that are managed by an editor, like an encyclopedia, or written by one scholar or expert practitioner, such as a practitioner's resource or a treatise, generally authorship is personal. In other words, people acting as people author *secondary sources*—not people acting as a branch of government.

Therefore, when you look at a *statute, regulation,* or *constitution,* there will not be lawyers' or judges' names listed as authors. Slightly trickier is *case law,* because court decisions often (not always) list the name of the judge who wrote the opinion. But with such *cases,* the judge who wrote the opinion is considered to be acting as the court, not as an individual.

Now, we will look at each *source of law.*

A. *Statutes* (Legislative Branch)

Statutes can be short and simple, like the one used as an example below, or long and complex, with many definitions and subparts. Unlike *case law,* a *statute* is ALL RULE—there is no need to separate the relevant from the irrelevant, and there is no opportunity to observe legal reasoning (the application of a legal rule to the facts). Like *case law,* a *statute* can be about *civil* matters, such as laws spelling out the requirements for getting a divorce, or the requirements for different types of contracts, or a *statute* can be about a *criminal* matter. Also like *case law, statutes* can be from the federal or state *jurisdictions. Statutes* are the laws that are passed by legislatures (whether state legislatures or federal legislatures).

Here is a sample state *criminal statute*, starting with its title:

Third Degree Burglary

A person is guilty of burglary in the third degree when he knowingly enters or remains unlawfully in a building with the intent to commit a crime therein.

* * *

What are some readily observable characteristics of this *statute*?

- The heading or title (in bold) indicates the subject matter—***Third Degree Burglary***.

- A *statute*, like any legal rule, can be divided into *elements*, or parts. The *elements* of this rule are *person; knowingly enters* OR *remains unlawfully; building; intent to commit a crime therein.*

- A *statute*, like any legal rule, has the "if/then" quality— IF this, THEN that. Here, IF you enter a building with the intent to commit a crime, THEN you have committed burglary in the third degree.

- The *statute* does not include facts—unlike a *case*, which usually tells a factual story, the *statute* is just a rule waiting to be applied;

- In other words, the *statute* is ALL RULE;

- AND, therefore, within the text of the *statute* is nothing but *statute*. Unlike a case, which can include multiple *citations* to all the different sources of law (*statutes, administrative regulations, constitutions* and *case law*), a *statute* is just a *statute*, and does not itself usually directly reference any other legal sources.

- Publications of *statutes* can be *annotated* or *unannotated*. *Statutory annotations* add cross-references and links to related *primary* and *secondary sources* after the statute. (The verb "annotate" means to add explanatory notes, and that is what the cross-references to other legal sources are supposed to do.) For example, when you look up a *statute* in a volume of *annotated statutes*, there may be a TON of annotations after it: references to other *sources*, including an explanation of the *statute* by a noted legal scholar, *citations* and blurbs of *cases* that have interpreted the *statute*, cross-references to similar topics and helpful *secondary sources*, links or references to legal databases, and plain old *citations* of multiple sources.

• If you have a choice, you always want to use *annotated statutes* when you are looking up a *statute*; *unannotated* publications include only the language of the statute itself. Remember, you don't want to do work you don't have to—make sure you take advantage of all the legal research that's already been done for you!

• Although the *statute* in this example is a short declarative statement, which can be typical of well-written *statutes*, *statutes* can also be long and complex. A full version of such a *statute* usually includes separate sections laying out the definitions of statutory terms, for example, as well as the legal rule or rules. There can be paragraphs, sub-paragraphs, sub-sub paragraphs, and sub-sub-sub paragraphs (usually indicated with alternating letters and numbers).

For the example statute, a sample *citation* might be: State Crim. Code § 111.222 (1980). This *citation* has all three components: 1) the *jurisdiction;* 2) the type of source; and 3) the year. Often, words in citations are abbreviated.

State	Crim. Code § 111.222	(1980)
Jurisdiction (in reality, would use a specific state's abbreviated name)	*"Code"* indicates —or at least hints at— **type or *source of law:* statute**	**Year** of the book's edition (for versions in print) OR **currency date** of the database (for online versions)

You can recognize the *source of law* by the word *"code."* Other cue words—*statutes*, revised *statutes*, laws, consolidated laws, annotated *statutes* (or *statutes* annotated), or compiled laws—are also used to refer to *statutes*. The word *"code"* is often used to refer to *statutes* because after a law is passed by the legislature, it is then "codified"—organized (usually by topic) to fit in with the existing statutes in the jurisdiction. According to Black's Law Dictionary, "codification" means "The process of compiling, arranging, and systematizing the laws of a *jurisdiction* . . . into an ordered *code.*" Note also the inclusion of the section sign (the "§ "), which you often see in *statutory citations*.

The geographical *jurisdiction* "State" would be a reference to a specific state, and "1980" is the year the book you found the statute in was published. According to The Bluebook, what to put in the parenthetical part (the end part, between parentheses) of the *code citation* is different depending on whether you are looking at a book version or an electronic version of the *code* (*see* Bluebook Rules 12.3.2 and 12.5; *see also* Appendix A for a full explanation). Both Westlaw and Lexis (subscription legal databases) indicate a "currency date" for the electronic database in which a *statute* is found, which can be the date included in the parenthetical.

In summary, a *statute* is passed by a legislature in a particular jurisdiction (state or federal) and lays out legal rules that can be simple and short, or lengthy, with multiple paragraphs, sections, sub-sections, and sub-sub-sections.

B. *Administrative Regulations* (Executive Branch)

An *administrative regulation* is another type or form of law that is adopted by an administrative agency in the Executive Branch. *Regulations* can have a similar look to *statutes*—both tend to come in sections with numbers, letters, and section signs. Both *administrative regulations* and *statutes* also commonly use the words "Title" and "Chapter" for ordering themselves, as if they are books (and yes, the

"Title" of a regulation or statutory series is the main idea, and the "Chapter" is simply a section of the overall "Title").

There are two major distinctions between *administrative regulations* and *statutes*: many times, *administrative regulations* will be more detailed than *statutes*, and all of the time, *administrative regulations* derive their authority from a *statute* and amplify the idea of the *statute* with the necessary details. Another distinction is the author—the legislature writes and passes *statutes*; the proper administrative agency then composes the *administrative regulations* that explain or fill in the details regarding that *statute*. Like statutes, however, *administrative regulations* can come in annotated form.

For example, for those of you who drive a car and have obtained your driver's license, you may recall the agency called the Department of Motor Vehicles. It is this agency's job to regulate and administer the process for obtaining a driver's license. It is the legislature's job to determine that a person must have a driver's license in order to drive.

Here is a sample motor vehicle regulation for driver's licensing loosely based on the New York *Code* of Rules and *Regulations*:

General Driver Licensing Procedure.

(a) *Original licensing.*

The provisions of this subdivision shall apply to a person who is not the holder of a valid or renewable driver license.

(1)   An appropriate learner's permit shall be issued upon passage of a vision test, submission of all documentation required with respect to age, identity and fitness, payment of all fees required by section 503 of the Vehicle and Traffic Law, the taking of a photo image, and passage of a knowledge test appropriate for the license for which application is being made. An applicant shall be entitled to make an appointment to take a skills test upon submission of evidence of completion of the required prelicensing driver training and highway safety course as provided in Part 7 of this Title.

* * *

In general, how would you describe this section of an *administrative regulation*? What characteristics does it have?

- The heading or title indicates the subject matter—General Driver Licensing Procedure.

- A *regulation*, like any legal rule, can be divided into *elements*. Here, the *elements* are: *passage of a vision test; submission of all documentation required; payment of fees;* and *passage of a knowledge test.*

- A *regulation*, like any legal rule, has the "if/then" quality—IF this, THEN that. Here, IF you submit all the items listed, THEN you are entitled to receive a learner's permit.

- We see that this regulation gives directions on how people can obtain driving licenses, such as the tests that have to be passed and the documentation that has to be submitted.

- The directions may seem detailed—and if you cannot imagine elected members of a legislature setting out this type of detail, your instincts are right. Instead, the authors of this rule were employees of the Department of Motor Vehicles agency.

- There is a reference to another law—note that section (1) the regulation refers to "section 503 of the Vehicle and Traffic Law." "Section 503 of the Vehicle and Traffic Law" is a reference to a *statute*. Remember, this regulation exists or "serves" the *statute* passed by the legislature. So one way to identify regulations is the reference to the *statute* or law (usually when we say "law" we mean a *statute* that has been passed by a legislature).

- In addition to the reference to the *statute* ("section 503 of the Vehicle and Traffic Law"), we see references to a "subdivision," and "Part 7 of this Title." These terms indicate that the *regulation* has difference parts and different sections. As with a *statute*, these segments and divisions make it different from *case law*, which usually tells a factual story. Also as with a *statute*, a *regulation* is just a rule—ALL RULE—waiting to be applied.

A sample *citation* to a regulation might be: State Admin. Code R. 1234 (1990). This *citation* has all three components: 1) the *jurisdiction*; 2) the type of *source*; and 3) the relevant year.

State	Admin. Code R. 1234	(1990)
Jurisdiction (in reality, would use a specific state's abbreviated name)	"Admin. Code R." indicates—or at least hints at—**type or** *source of law: regulation*	**Year** of the book's edition (for versions in print) OR **currency date** of the database (for online versions)

The type of source is indicated by "Admin. Code R." which stands for Administrative *Code* Rule. The geographical *jurisdiction* is indicated by "State," which would include the name of the actual state, and the relevant year is in the parenthetical. (See Appendix A for a more complete discussion about the *citation* rules for regulations, including the proper year to put in parentheticals).

Remember, an *administrative regulation* is a detailed set of directions, laid out, similar to a *statute,* in sections and subsections. It provides the detail needed to implement a *statute*'s directives.

C. *Constitutions* (Constitutional Conventions)

We all probably think we know the U.S. *Constitution*—free speech and the founding fathers, for example. But how many of us have ever actually read it? Would we recognize it if we were to see an excerpt? Keep in mind, too, that there are state constitutions in addition to the U.S. *Constitution* that perhaps even fewer of us are familiar with.

Constitutions are unique documents. Their main purpose is to set up how government will work. Our state and federal *constitutions* organize our government in three branches so that no single branch has all the power. That is what is meant by "checks and balances"— each branch can "check" the other branch (read: stop/overturn/ thwart)—so power is "balanced" between branches and no one branch has all of it. State *constitutions* cannot take away rights and privileges provided by the U.S. *Constitution*; they can, however, offer more rights and privileges. Thus, the U.S. *Constitution* applies to both state and federal governments, and it offers a floor of basic rights guaranteed to all citizens.

Many people do not know that the U.S. *Constitution* is not just the Bill of Rights, which consists only of the first ten amendments to the *Constitution*. Many people also would not recognize the Preamble, do not know there are multiple "Articles" in the first part of the *Constitution*, and do not know that there are multiple amendments to the *Constitution* beyond those in the Bill of Rights.

Here is an excerpt—the first part of an Article from the U.S. *Constitution:*

Article II

Section 1, Clause 1. The executive Power shall be vested in a President of the United States of America. He shall hold his Office during the Term of four Years, and together with the Vice-President, chosen for the same Term, be elected, as follows.

Here is the second clause of Article II, Section 1:

Each State shall appoint, in such Manner as the Legislature thereof may direct, a Number of Electors, equal to the whole Number of Senators and Representatives to which the State may be entitled in the Congress: but no Senator or Representative, or Person holding an Office of Trust or Profit under the United States, shall be appointed an Elector.

* * *

How is this excerpt from Article II of the *Constitution* different from the above two sources of law—*statutes* and *administrative regulations*? What do you observe both in format and in substance about this excerpt?

- A *Constitutional clause*, like any legal rule, can be divided into *elements*. Here, the *elements* of the first sentence of the first clause of Section I of Article II are: *Executive Power, shall be vested, in President*. The second sentence provides: *He, shall hold his Office, during Term of four Years, and together with Vice-President, chosen for the same Term, be elected, as follows*. Then, the *elements* of the second clause of Section I go on to state: *state, shall appoint; Number of Electors; equal to the whole Number of Senators and Representatives*.

- Note that a *Constitutional clause*, UNLIKE other legal rules, DOES NOT necessarily have the "if/then" quality. This is because the *Constitution* primarily lays out the duties and structure of our three branches of government, not the consequence(s) of certain actions or events. For example, the above clauses set out the terms of the President and Vice President and the structure of the Electoral College. This information organizes the government by providing term limits and explaining a representative body like the Electoral College.

- However, note that other clauses of the *Constitution*, such as the Due Process Clause and Equal Protection Clause provisions of the Fourteenth Amendment, do indeed have the "if/then" quality. For example, the clause from the Fourteenth Amendment that contains those provisions states: *[N]or shall any State deprive any person of life, liberty, or property, without due process of law; nor deny to any person within its jurisdiction the equal protection of the laws*. So, IF you deny anyone life, liberty or property without Due

Process, THEN you have violated the *Constitution*, specifically, the Fourteenth Amendment. Or, IF you deny any person equal protection of the laws, THEN you have violated the *Constitution*, specifically, the Fourteenth Amendment.

• The *Constitution* is a unique legal document because it includes both information about the structure and exercise of power in the branches, and, in the Amendments, "if/then" rules protecting people's rights.

• On a superficial level, we can notice that the capitalization in the U.S. *Constitution* is not conventional for today's usage—many items that do not seem like proper nouns are capitalized. What might this be evidence of? Hint: this *Constitution* was written at a time when the usage and capitalization rules were different. (In other words, this *Constitution* was written a long time ago.)

• Like a *statute* and an *administrative regulation*, the U.S. *Constitution* is ALL RULE—there is no extraneous or irrelevant factual information that you need to sift through like you do for *case law*.

• Try to identify what the section of the U.S. *Constitution* we started with pertains to. Because it refers to how a president gets elected, the Electoral College, and how we select the delegates to the Electoral College, you can observe that a *constitution*—or at least, this *Constitution*—describes the process of governing.

The U.S. *Constitution* is therefore a form of law fundamentally distinct from a *statute*, which can be civil or criminal and can range in topic from making burglary illegal to governing the issuance of driver's licenses. For future reference, remember that much of our *Constitution*, such as the Commerce Clause or the Bill of Rights, impacts our daily lives but is only generally (although eloquently) stated. As a result, many parts of the *Constitution* have been brought before the courts, which then clarify and explain the provisions in *case law* for today's audiences. The U.S. Supreme Court is the final and authoritative word on the meaning of the U.S. Constitution.[2]

A sample *citation* to a *constitution* might be: State Const. art. X, § 3. This *citation* has only two of the three components: 1) an indication of the type of source, and 2) the *jurisdiction*. The Bluebook does not require us to include a parenthetical with the year. We have an easy reference here to "Const." for *constitution*, and "state" indicates the *jurisdiction*.

Here is a visual depiction of the *citation*:

State	Const. art X, § 3	
Jurisdiction (in reality, would use a specific state's abbreviated name)	"Const." indicates the **type or *source of law: constitution***	**Year** The U.S. *Constitution* does not include the year in the citation, although state *constitutions* do

Remember, in addition to our U.S. *Constitution*, each state has a *constitution*, and all *constitutions* are ratified at *constitutional* conventions and provide our governmental framework.

D. *Case Law* (Judicial Branch)

This section will examine *case law*, found in judicial opinions. Don't be confused by the legal profession's use of the word "case" to mean multiple things. For example, legal professionals use "case" in the statement, "Here at our law firm we've got a new case," to mean a new client and the corresponding legal problem. But "case" also means a

---

2   The official U.S. Supreme Court website says it well when it states: The Court is the highest tribunal in the Nation for all cases and controversies arising under the Constitution or the laws of the United States. As the final arbiter of the law, the Court is charged with ensuring the American people the promise of equal justice under law and, thereby, also functions as guardian and interpreter of the Constitution.

court opinion, written by a judge. And to make matters worse, the following terms are used interchangeably: *case, decision, court opinion, judicial opinion,* and *case law.*

A *case,* by definition, contains a legal rule. Unhappy parties bring their legal issue to a court, asking how a specific legal rule applies to their problem. The court discusses and then applies that legal rule. Most court opinions you will read are from appellate courts because appellate court opinions are published more frequently and carry precedential value. An *appellate court* (a panel of appellate judges) is more apt to write an opinion; a *trial court,* with one judge, is not as likely to write a lengthy decision or to submit a decision for publication. Because a *case* is the application of a legal rule to facts, we can always count on a *case* to contain at least one legal rule; often they contain more than one.

There are roughly two types of *cases* in the state law world: 1) *cases* that interpret or apply a legal rule that comes from another *source of law,* such as a *constitution,* an *administrative regulation,* or a *statute*; and 2) *cases* that rely on, and develop, legal rules solely from another *case* (or multiple *cases*).

When that legal rule comes from other *cases,* or *case law,* and not a *statute, administrative regulation,* or *constitution,* we call the legal rule *common law.* Students of the law may call this "judge-made law." *Common law* is the body of law based on judicial opinions or *cases.* We call our American legal system a *common law* system, and *common law* courses still form the bulk of the first year law school curriculum. So this is a term with a rich definition. You will explore the different types of *cases* more fully in Chapter 3, Part I, Section C.

Here is a sample civil case in a state court. This example is a case about someone named Phyllis Carr who was injured in an auto accident and brought a lawsuit against Arlo Buss. As you will see, this case relies on a legal rule that is in another case and is therefore *common law.* In state law, negligence is usually a *common law* topic. Can you spot the legal rule? Look for it.

State Mid-level Appellate Court

Phyllis Carr, Plaintiff, v. Arlo Buss, Defendant

Opinion.

Memorandum by the Court.

J. Denman, J. Jackson and J. Dillon.

Plaintiff sued for damages for personal injuries suffered as a result of a two-car collision in which the aqua Volkswagen bus owned by the defendant, Arlo Buss, rear-ended plaintiff's red Chevrolet Malibu sedan. The Plaintiff, Phyllis Carr, suffered a broken sternum, whiplash, and various bruising. The accident occurred on May 5th, 2019, on Elmwood Avenue, in Buffalo, New York.

A rear-end collision with a stopped automobile establishes a prima facie case of negligence on the part of the operator of the moving vehicle and imposes a duty on the operator of the moving vehicle to explain how the accident occurred. See <u>Gambino v. City of New York</u>, 205 Official State Reporter 583, 613 Unofficial/Regional State Reporter 417 (1990).

Here, although the defendant Buss had the duty to explain how he rear-ended the plaintiff in order to avoid the conclusion that he was negligent, he was not able to do so. According to the police report, Buss simply told the officer that he was "grooving to the music" and lost track of where he was. In the absence of any reasonable explanation, the rear-ending vehicle is negligent. Therefore, the trial court's grant of summary judgment to the plaintiff, Phyllis Carr, is affirmed.

* * *

Did you spot the legal rule? It is the long sentence in the second paragraph:

> A rear-end collision with a stopped automobile establishes a
> *prima facie* case of negligence on the part of the operator of
> the moving vehicle and imposes a duty on the operator of the
> moving vehicle to explain how the accident occurred.

The first part of this sentence—"A rear-end collision with a stopped automobile establishes a *prima facie* case of negligence on the part of the operator"—means that a driver whose car runs into a stopped car in front of it is assumed to be negligent, or at fault. The Latin phrase *"prima facie"* can be roughly translated to mean "at first sight" or "on the face of it."

The second part of the rule "and imposes a duty on the operator of the moving vehicle to explain how the accident occurred" simply means that the driver of the offending car must give an acceptable explanation for what happened to avoid being held at fault. In other words, unless the driver of the offending car has a very good reason for smacking into the rear-end of the stopped car in front of it—perhaps the offending car was hit from behind itself—the driver of the offending car is negligent.

One way to recognize a legal rule from a case is by the *citation*, or reference, to the case, because whenever a court mentions a legal rule in its decision, that rule must be followed by a *citation*. You can see in the body of the case that this rule was followed by a *citation* to the Gambino v. City of New York *case*.

In addition to recognizing a *case citation*, it is also important to be able to distinguish a case from other types of legal sources. Look again at the *Carr v. Buss* case. Observe. Evaluate. What characteristics does the case have? What can you say about it?

- First we see the *"caption"* or heading with the *parties'* names at the beginning.

- Like the other legal rules, case holdings can be divided into *elements*, or parts: *rear-end collision* plus *stopped automobile = prima facie negligence*.

- Like all other legal rules, this rule has an "if/then" quality—IF you collide with the rear end of a stopped vehicle THEN you are *prima facie* negligent.

- This case is just one decision issued by a court resolving one dispute between two *parties*. At least part of a *case* may resemble a story: where it lays out facts about what happened to cause one of the *parties* to initiate a lawsuit.

Remember, this is the only *source of law* that includes facts!

- Given the extent of information, it may be hard to tell what facts are important. In other words, you may have to separate the relevant from the irrelevant.

- There is a lot of information here, which can make it difficult to read.

- A *case* might have vocabulary you don't understand, especially procedural information, which includes the specific legal mechanism the court used to resolve the case. In our *case* example of *Carr v. Buss*, the *plaintiff's* case was resolved by summary judgment—something the *plaintiff* would have requested in a motion. However, typically a summary judgment motion is made by a *defendant*, after the discovery process (exchange of information between both sides), in order to get rid of—dispose of—a case. The *defendant* basically argues that there is no way the plaintiff can win at trial. For a more legal and technical definition, see <u>Black's Law Dictionary</u>.[3] Additionally, the opinion mentioned the term *prima facie* case. As noted above, *prima facie*, Latin for "at first face" or "at first appearance," means that on the first try, without looking at the other side's evidence, the party has enough evidence to establish its claim.[4] Procedural information can also include the way a *case* got to that particular court.

---

[3]   <u>Black's Law Dictionary</u> defines summary judgment as "a judgment granted on a claim or defense about which there is no genuine issue of material fact and on which the movant is entitled to prevail as a matter of law."

[4]   <u>Black's Law Dictionary</u> defines *prima facie case* as "a party's production of enough evidence to allow the fact-trier to infer the fact at issue and rule in the party's favor."

Finding all these characteristics together usually means you are reading a case (although perhaps the last two bullet points about encountering challenges can be true for other primary sources as well).

A sample case *citation* would be: *Carr v. Buss*, 123 Official State Reporter 456, 789 Unofficial/Regional State Reporter 111 (1990). This *citation* has all three components: 1) the *jurisdiction*; 2) an indication of the type of source; and 3) the relevant year. The *jurisdiction* is sometimes indicated by the name of the *reporter*—when the name of the *reporter* indicates the state. (*Reporters* indicating only the region do not show the specific state jurisdiction.) One indication of the type of source is the reference to the "Official State *Reporter*" and the "Unofficial State *Reporter*." Here, a *reporter* is a book that *cases* are published in (not a person with a note pad!). *Cases* can be "*reported*" (published in one or two *reporters*), by different publishers; if it's an "official" *reporter*, that means the publication is by the government; if it's an "unofficial" *reporter*, that means it's published by a private company.

The most obvious indication of the type of source is the first piece of information—a name versus another name. The "v." stands for versus, and that should make it clear that this is the resolution of a dispute, unlike the other sources of law, which are all law. The relevant year is in the final parenthetical. Some *citations* have additional information about the specific level of state court deciding the issue within that same parenthetical.

Here is a visual depiction of the *citation:*

123 Official State Reporter 456, 789 Unofficial/Regional State Reporter 111	*Carr v. Buss*	(1990)
Jurisdiction The name of the State *Reporter* indicates the state (or indicates that it's federal). Remember, in reality, an abbreviation for the specific state, such as New York, would be in the place of "State."	Names of the *parties* plus the "v." for "versus." Indicates the **type or source of law: case.** Remember, only *cases* involve people and the application of law to facts.	**Year** This is the year the decision was made.

Remember, a *case* is decided by a court, which applies a legal rule to a dispute between two or more *parties*. See Chapter 3 for a thorough discussion of the court structure.

Remember that all the *primary* legal *sources* we have reviewed exist in both the federal and state worlds, and likewise exist in all subject areas, including *civil* and *criminal*.

Congratulations on finishing your introduction to primary legal sources.

CHAPTER 1 LEGAL SKILLS

- **Identify legal rules**
- **Identify *sources* of legal rules**
- **Identify rule-making roles of each branch of government**
- **Define "*elements*" of a legal rule**

- **Define secondary *sources***
- **Name basic components of a *citation***

CHAPTER 1 VOCABULARY

- Administrative agencies
- Administrative regulations
- Annotations
- Appellate court
- Caption
- Cases (synonyms: judicial opinions, case law, court decisions, judicial decisions, court opinions)
- Cause of action
- Citation (also called: cite)
- Civil
- Code
- Common law
- Constitution (Articles, Bill of Rights)
- Criminal
- Defendant
- Element
- Jurisdiction
- Official versus unofficial
- Party/parties (in a case)
- Plaintiff
- Prima facie
- Primary source
- Reporter
- Secondary source
- Source of law
- Statute
- Trial court

SKILLS DEVELOPMENT

Tips on Improving Reading Comprehension

It can be difficult to read dense material with a lot of new words in any discipline. Law is no exception. The writing can be archaic, inflated, or positively cryptic. To gradually improve your reading comprehension, try these tips:

1. Preview: figure out what you will be reading. What type of source? How many items? What is the date? What is the historical context? Where is the material placed according to any table of contents?

2. Skim: provide yourself with an outline of the material by reading just the topic sentences first. That way, you familiarize yourself with the basic subject-matter.

3. Active Reading: read through carefully, highlighting key words, visualizing events, and annotating the text (or taking notes in a separate notebook) with questions and comments that come to mind.

4. Review: review all the information you have learned and try to summarize what you have read in your own words. Try summarizing in writing, or verbally in class.

CHAPTER 1 RESEARCH AND ANALYSIS EXERCISES

(Can Use Westlaw, Lexis, free legal internet sites, or the Books)

Research skills introduced:

- Use simple key word searches
- Make sure the results of your searches are up-to-date and current
- When you search most databases using quotes around words, you will find those specific, literal words
- Follow the trail of a case that relies on another case
- Use state legal encyclopedias to find background on a specific legal topic

- **Use online legal dictionary or key word searches on
  internet search engines to find definition of legal
  terms (* Do NOT rely on non-legal sources)**
- **Draft a summary**

Directions:

Before diving in to these exercises, acquaint yourself with your
databases and/or your library. Do the basic tutorial, get a tour from the
librarian, and listen to your professor's introduction to your available
sources. If you are using free databases, investigate their search techniques
(full-text or key word) if you can. For online sources, when you find a
source that looks applicable, try to ensure that it is up-to-date by ensuring
there is no red flag or red stop sign (Westlaw, Lexis), or checking to see
how recently the website was updated. One of the most important things
for legal research is making sure that your source is up-to-date.

Because these exercises are basic ones to introduce you to different
sources, simple key word searches should work. A simple "key word"
search means you use the basic terms or names you are looking for to
search a database. Here, we are not trying to solve legal problems, but
rather, just trying to find basic legal resources. So it is fine to search for
these sources by name. Try a variety of key word searches, see what you
get, and make sure if you are using a subscription database that you have
chosen to search the correct jurisdiction and/or database with the sources
you need. Remember that you can use an online legal dictionary for any
terms you don't know, and that you can also use key word searches on
internet search engines to see what trustworthy and reliable legal sources
you can find that may provide basic explanations or definitions for term
or subjects. Be sure to review the Appendix to see some examples.

Remember that Appendix 1 includes much more detail about the
differences in citation form for each source, as well as sample citations for
some states and federal sources, so refer freely to this Appendix to help
you.

I. Investigating your state jurisdiction:

To help you identify and become familiar with the different sources
of law in your state, with the help of your professor:

1.   Find an example of each primary source from your state from a non-subscription source in order to acquaint yourself with free online sources and state-specific online sources such as court websites and legislative websites.

2.   Find the following primary sources and answer the questions about each source:

  a.   **Constitution:** Constitution for your state. Use simple key word searches such as "(your state) constitution"; "last modification of (your state) constitution." On free and subscription databases, there may be lists of all the primary and secondary sources available for your state.

  i.   How long is it?

  ii.   When was it written? Last modified?

  iii.   Can you find a secondary source comparing one (or many) aspect of your state constitution with the U.S. Constitution?

  iv.   How many different ways can you find your state constitution? List each successful pathway to your state's constitution using free internet sources, the books, and the subscription databases available to you. (Note: this exercise can be done for each source you find here).

  v.   List the three main components of a citation to your state's constitution: an indication of the type of source (or its Bluebook abbreviation), the jurisdiction, and a relevant date.

  b.   **Statute:** Your state's general burglary statute (any degree). Use simple key word searches such as "(your state) burglary statute." In order to answer the questions, be sure to review the pages in the chapter that discuss statutes and that define annotations.

i.   Does your state have an annotated version of its statutes? Does it have a version of statutes without annotations?

ii.   Does your state have a version of its statutes that are published by the state and is therefore considered an "official" version? Is that version annotated or unannotated?

iii. Summarize, in your own words, the general meaning of the statute.

iv.   List the three main components of a citation to this statute: an indication of the type of source (or its Bluebook abbreviation), the jurisdiction, and a relevant date.

c.   **Case law—common law:** Since negligence tends to be a common law topic across states, try searching negligence cases that cite the basic elements of negligence—duty, breach of duty, causation, damages—and therefore relies on another case.

You can try simple key word searches such as "(your state) highest court in the state and common law negligence," or various combinations of that search.

i.   Does your state have official reporters AND unofficial reporters?

ii.   Summarize, in your own words, the factual problem that occurred in this case and the court's decision. We will learn how to "brief" a case in Chapter 8 (this is an organized way to analyze a court decision), so for this exercise try to do a basic summary

iii. List the three main components of a citation to this statute: an indication of the type of source (or its Bluebook abbreviation), which for cases means the name of the reporter, the jurisdiction (your state and the name of your state's highest court), and a relevant date.

d.   **Administrative Regulation:** Your state's Department of Motor Vehicle regulations on the criteria to get a driver's license.

Again, use simple key word searches. If you search "(your state) and driver's licenses" you should probably pull up, among other things, the relevant state regulations.

> i.   Does that regulation refer to the statute it is based on? If not, try searching for "statutory basis for (your state's) driver's license regulations," or any variation of that, to see if you can find the statute that seems to correspond to the regulation you are looking at.
>
> ii.   Summarize, in your own words, the meaning and requirements of this regulation.
>
> iii.   List the three main components of a citation to this statute: an indication of the type of source (or its Bluebook abbreviation), the jurisdiction, and a relevant date.

> e.   **Compare:** Develop a chart that lists each source of law and the characteristics of each form of law. Include one column in the chart with the basic three components of a citation for each source: the name of the source, the jurisdiction, and the relevant year.

3.   **Common law:** Investigate the root of common law, a primary source, and with the case you found in #1, note the case that your case relies on, and continue to do that as you follow the trail of cases back to the English common law. In an electronic database, usually you can do that by simply clicking on the hyperlink for the case the court is relying on. Hint: use decisions from your state's highest court for this exercise, and be ready for the trail of cases to go back to the 1800s.

> a.   As you identify the trail of cases, keep track of each case by noting the name of each case, the name of the court that decided it, and the year the case was decided.
>
> b.   How many cases are in your trail to English common law (or the "first" case to come up with the rule in your state)?
>
> c.   What is the name and date of the English common law case (or the "first" case to come up with the rule in your state)?

4. **Secondary source—state legal encyclopedia:** You were introduced to the concept of secondary sources in this chapter. Secondary sources explain the law, and are often a good place to begin your research. For state law issues, practitioners may start with the state law encyclopedia, which virtually every state has. These are available in book form and on subscription databases.

    a.   What is the name of your state's legal encyclopedia?

    b.   Using the index or a key word search, find out whether your state has social host liability. Use the internet to supplement your search. If your state has a social host liability statute, find the summary and explanation of this area of law in your state encyclopedia.

    c.   If your state does NOT have social host liability, find the summary and explanation of your state's dram shop statute and how courts have interpreted that statute. You can start by using a law dictionary and/or internet search engines to get an idea of what "social host" or "dram shop law" means in YOUR STATE.

    d.   Note the central components of a citation to your state encyclopedia—the name of the source, the jurisdiction, and the relevant year.

    e.   Identify some differences in appearance, style or substance between this secondary source and the primary sources you investigated above in #1.

II. Now, the same with the Feds:

1.   Find the following primary sources using a combination of internet search engines, books, and subscription databases if they are available to you.

    a.   **Constitution:** Find the U.S. Constitution.

    b.   **Statute:** This time you will use the citation for this well-known and oft-used federal civil rights statute in free legal databases, using your favorite search engine, or using your subscription database.

  i. Find and compare 42 U.S.C. § 1983 (official U.S. code—this is the version that should be cited) and 42 U.S.C.A. § 1983 (the "A" indicates "annotated").

  ii. What is the difference between the unannotated and the annotated? Remember there should be NO difference in the text of the code. However, looking at the end of the statutory text, what is the difference in what follows? What are some of the things you can find out using an annotated version?

  iii. List the required citation components for the citation—the name of the source, the jurisdiction, and the relevant year.

  iv. Read the statute and list some observable qualities about the test: is it short or long? Does it have subsections? What type of vocabulary does it use? Can you understand the purpose of the statute?

c. **Case law:** Since you haven't learned about federal jurisdictions yet, you will now find out how easy it is to locate a U.S. Supreme Court case. If you use a simple key word search in your internet search engines or subscription databases "Supreme Court cases" your search should pull up Supreme Court cases in your subscription database, and on the internet this basic key word search should pull up several websites that have summaries or the full text of Supreme Court opinions. You can also go to the Supreme Court website (see Appendix F).

  i. Based on the blurbs or the names of the cases, choose a Supreme Court case that interests you.

  ii. List the necessary components for the citation: an indication of the type of source, which for cases means the name of the reporter, the jurisdiction, and the year of the decision.

iii.   Look at the decision and observe its characteristics: is
it long or short? Multi-sections? Sub-headings? How does
it compare to the statute above?

d.   **Administrative Regulations:** Take a look at the federal
regulations, formally known as the Code of Federal Regulations
(C.F.R.). Again, if you do a basic key word search on an internet
search engine, such as "code of federal regulations" or
"interesting federal regulations" you will pull up a number of
government sites and free legal research sites that include the
C.F.R.

i.   Find a regulation pertaining to the Endangered
Species Act, a federal statute, using basic key word
searches. Specific federal regulations are more difficult to
find than U.S. Supreme Court cases, so you will have to dig
a little, and may have to learn about some specific terms to
search. Hint: try using the keyword "title," since the C.F.R.
is organized by titles, and throwing that into your search
might help.

ii.   Once you find a regulation, make some observations
of its characteristics. Is it long, short, complicated,
straightforward, easy or complex vocabulary? How does it
compare to a statute, a case, or a constitutional provision?

iii.   List the three required components for a citation: an
indication of the type of source (here, the Code of Federal
Regulations should do it), the jurisdiction, and the relevant
year.

III. Oral presentation for groups:

You can do these exercises in your state jurisdiction or the federal
government.

1.   State government processes: Find free legal resources that
explain the three different processes of our three government branches,
executive, legislative, and judicial, and, without copying and pasting ANY

material from your sources, prepare a 5–10 minute presentation that explains and teaches the process to your classmates.

    a.   Executive:

        i.   Who is your top executive, and what parts of the government are in the executive branch?

        ii.   What source of law can the executive branch create?

        iii.   How do they do so? What are the different stages in the process?

        iv.   Provide an example.

        v.   Provide visual aides to explain the process.

    b.   Legislative:

        i.   What are the legislative bodies in your state called?

        ii.   What source of law can this branch of government create?

        iii.   How do they do so? What are the different stages in the process?

        iv.   Provide an example.

        v.   Provide visual aides to explain the process.

    c.   Judicial:

        i.   What is the highest court in your state called?

        ii.   What source of law can this Court create?

        iii.   How do they do so? What are the different stages in the process?

        iv.   Provide an example.

        v.   Provide visual aides to explain the process.

IV. Sources of law for ethics:

    1.   Identify the specific statute(s) that prohibits the unauthorized practice of law in your state and which would apply to paralegals or lawyers without a license.

    a.   List the three main components of a citation to this statute: an indication of the type of source (or its Bluebook abbreviation), the jurisdiction, and a relevant date.

2.   Identify your state's ethical code for attorneys. Investigate whether there is a separate state ethical code for paralegals.

    a.   Identify the source of law for this code (statute, common law, administrative regulations, or constitution).

    b.   List the three main components of a citation to this statute: an indication of the type of source (or its Bluebook abbreviation), the jurisdiction, and a relevant date.

3.   Using a legal dictionary, find out what a model code or model rules are.

    a.   Explain the difference between model codes and primary sources.

    b.   Find a model ethical code for lawyers.

    c.   Find a model ethical code for paralegals.

Whose Rule Is It? (Sorting out Subject Matter and Jurisdiction in the Legal Mess and Finding a Direction for Your Research)

Legal Skills:

- Identify subject matter and *jurisdiction* for your legal problem
- Find, recognize, and use *secondary* sources
- Distinguish between *primary sources* and *secondary sources*

PART I. THE LEGAL MESS

What is context and why is it so important when sorting out the "legal mess"? In any topic, context is the surrounding environment and facts, which contribute to meaning. Of course, we are only aiming for a beginner's context. An expert's context can take years, not to mention a Juris Doctorate.

Much of the context you need here is simply ordinary civics—how our government is set up and how it functions. You have already learned about the four sources of law in Chapter 1: statutes, administrative regulations, constitutions, and case law. In Chapter 1 you were also reminded about the branches of government: judiciary (responsible for case law), legislature (responsible for statutes), and executive (responsible for administrative regulations). Some of the context you need is also legal vocabulary, which is introduced as needed and available for review in the Glossary at the end of the book.

Based on all that legal knowledge, you are now ready to become a bit more familiar with the various contexts in which legal *issues* can be raised. First, let's define legal *issue*. A legal *issue* is completely distinct from other types of issues, such as having an issue with a friend, or arguing about a political issue. Legal *issues* always revolve around a legal rule. But even that is not enough—in legal analysis we are even more specific when we discuss legal *issues*. Not only must there be a legal rule, but there must be a question about whether or how the legal rule applies.

When you have a legal *issue*, in addition to thinking about the branches of government and the source(s) of law that might apply, you should ask yourself three important questions:

A.   Think first about jurisdiction: what is the geographical *jurisdiction*? As we learned in Chapter 1, *jurisdiction* can be geographical—e.g., the geography or location of the dispute is part of *jurisdiction*. We can also think of *jurisdiction* in a broader sense as whose laws would apply to a legal question or *transaction*. Both components are important; the power of a court to hear a dispute, for example, depends on both the geography and the subject matter of the dispute. To determine geographical jurisdiction, ask yourself:

      1.   Where am I?

      2.   Whose law governs? Local, state, federal, or a combination?

      3.   Which courthouse would I go to?

B.   Think about subject matter: Is this a civil or a criminal *issue*?

C.   Think some more about subject matter: is this a *transaction* (an exchange or agreement between two *parties*, such as a real estate purchase or a contract) or a dispute (a conflict between two *parties* that needs to be resolved with *litigation*)? Or both?

Knowing the answer to these questions can serve you well in the legal research and problem-solving process. These questions are fundamental and systemic and will help you sort out where your legal *issue* is in our legal system. Think of it as the "YOU ARE HERE" message that you look for on maps. Understanding where you are is the first step in figuring out law. Once you are oriented on the legal map (see Diagram 2), you will be better prepared to understand the nature of your legal *issue*, your legal research path, and even the path to finding the right rule (see Chapter 3). At the very least, knowing the right questions to ask will help you sort through the legal questions.

So let's get started with your legal orientation.

A. Thinking About the First Question: What Is the Geographic Jurisdiction for Your Legal Issue?

The starting point for legal issues is jurisdiction. Before we start applying the law, we have to know which law to apply—federal, state (which state?), or local (county, village, city). Remember, geographical jurisdiction refers to the geographical limits of the court's authority.

1. Where Am I?

The law you apply depends in part on where your legal *issue* is: the locality, the state, and the country. Often, there are parallel or relevant legal rules from all three levels of location. When in doubt, check all three levels. The main determination you will often have to make is whether the legal *issue* is governed by state or federal law—or both.

Of course, sometimes the question of "where am I?" includes the question of the parties' location and the location of the dispute or conflict—the accident, the land, the adoption, or the contract (for example).

2.   *Whose Law Governs? State Law, Federal Law or Both?*

Just remember—check them all. To figure out this aspect, we need to harken back to the fundamental structure of our system. It is easy to forget that we have parallel legal systems—one is federal, and one is state. We wanted it that way—at least our Founding Fathers did. Our country's founders purposely wrote the U.S. Constitution to set up a dual federal and state system, and they wanted a dual system because they wanted to avoid a "kingly" assumption of powers by any one all-powerful government (especially a central one). Remember, our country was started in part by people fleeing a monarchy that restricted their religious freedom. Once you are bossed around by a king, it is only natural that you want to avoid that. You also want to avoid a government structure built on a bossy central authority.

Hence, *federalism*. What is *federalism*? *Federalism* is the brilliant power-sharing arrangement our founders came up with in which the parts share power with the whole. That means the states (the "parts") share power with the federal government (the "whole"), and the two have roughly equal status. *Federalism* is often referred to as having "parallel" systems—state legislature/federal legislature; state judiciary/federal judiciary; state executive branch and administrative agencies/ federal executive branch and administrative agencies.

So, we have two of everything. No wonder people are confused. Contrary to what you may have heard, the important stuff is not necessarily federal. There is an old saying, "Don't Make a Federal Case about It," which implies that if something IS a big deal, it is federal. In fact, generally, most people's day to day legal issues—speeding tickets, DWIs, divorce, child custody/support, real estate *transactions*, wills, car accidents or other injury-related claims—are governed by local or state law. You could easily live your whole life and experience several legal issues (such as writing a will and purchasing real estate) and not even one of those issues would be federal.

You may be curious about the legal issues that are grounded in state law versus the legal issues that are federal. It would be nice if we could give you a list. But like many things in law, it is not that easy. Indeed, there are some issues that are governed by *both* state and federal law. Remember, the two parallel systems have roughly equal power. And there has to be at least some consistency on some issues, which is one of the functions our Constitution serves.

When it comes to overlapping federal and state jurisdiction, there is one fundamental principle to keep in mind. For our U.S. Congress to have jurisdiction, or the authority, to pass a federal statute, there has to be an underlying federal concern, which means that the concern has to extend in principle beyond one state's boundaries. An underlying concern that extends beyond one state's boundaries includes federal Constitutional issues. Some of the most common federal *issues* are found in the first Ten Amendments (the Bill of Rights), such as the First Amendment (freedom of assembly, religion, and speech); the Fifth Amendment (you can't be compelled to testify against yourself); and the Fourteenth Amendment (due process and equal protection of the law).[1] Constitutional *issues* are necessarily federal issues because the federal Constitution applies to everyone everywhere. (In such cases, there may be related state Constitutional questions in addition.)

Another example of an underlying concern is railroads; as railroads necessarily extend beyond one state's boundaries, the law governing railroads is almost solely federal.[2] As you might expect, you can sometimes look to the Constitution, the ultimate set of directions for how to run a parallel state and federal system, to determine exactly when Congress can pass a federal law.

Yet another well-established basis for federal statutes is the Constitution's *commerce clause*, which gives the federal government

---

[1]   U.S. Constitution.

[2]   *See, e.g.*, Federal Railroad Safety Act, 49 U.S.C. §§ 20101 et seq. (1994). Section 20106(a)(1) provides: "Laws, regulations, and orders related to railroad safety and laws, regulations, and orders related to railroad security shall be nationally uniform to the extent practicable." *Id.*

authority to regulate interstate commerce.[3] The *commerce clause* has been used as a basis for everything from legislating about railroads to legislating protections for civil rights.[4] In fact, our Constitution provides numerous bases for federal statutes—too numerous to list here.

Although the authority from the *commerce clause* is quite broad (some would argue too broad), it nevertheless gives us a tool for how to think about whether a legal *issue* is state or federal. Does the *issue* have possible ripple effects beyond the state boundaries? So, in an easy example, a divorce between two people living in the same city most likely does NOT have ripple effects outside of that state. However, for the regulation of pension funds, since pension funds typically exist in every state and are owned by multi-state companies, you would want to look at both federal and state law. For law governing railroads, you would look to federal law.

So, to help you determine the context of a legal problem, in considering the first question you should ask whether the *issue* concerns federal or state law. You need to think about the nature of the problem and whether it is typically resolved within a state's boundaries, whether it has ripple effects beyond the state's boundaries, or, finally, whether it necessarily involves travel between states or issues that can exist nationally (including Constitutional issues).

3.   *Which Courthouse Will I Go to?*

In the old days, a lawyer or paralegal had to physically go to the courthouse to start a lawsuit—either that or get a very reliable delivery service to deliver the summons and complaint. Now, most courthouses

---

[3]   Kenneth R. Thomas, The Power to Regulate Commerce: Limits on Congressional Power (Cong. Res. Serv., May 16, 2014) (stating that more than 700 statutory provisions on a range of issues are explicitly based on interstate or foreign commerce).

[4]   In *Katzenbach v. McClung*, 379 U.S. 294 (1964), the Court held that Congress acted legally and within its power to outlaw race discrimination by enacting the Civil Rights Act of 1964 because race discrimination was a burden on interstate commerce. In *Katzenbach*, the statute was applied to Ollie's Barbecue in Alabama to stop the practice of discriminating against African Americans.

have e-filing (electronic filing via the internet), so you no longer have to physically walk into the courthouse. In thinking about "which courthouse will I go to"—you are really thinking about whether the legal conflict would be tried in state court or federal court. Why is this important? Because the procedural rules are different in each court, and because knowing whether you will be in state or federal court can be an important part of jurisdiction.

Maybe it should be easy—state law issues get resolved in state court, and federal law issues get resolved in federal court. But it's not. Thinking about state versus federal court, you should remember that federal court is reserved for a couple of unique or special situations. Indeed, federal court is a *court of limited jurisdiction,* while state courts are courts of *general jurisdiction.* (See Diagram 2, which illustrates how state jurisdiction is larger than federal jurisdiction). *Limited jurisdiction* means that federal court is empowered by specific legal authority—the Constitution—to hear only certain types of cases, as explained below.

Black's Law Dictionary provides a helpful quote from a venerable source on federal courts, Charles Alan Wright:

> It is a principle of first importance that the federal courts are courts of limited *jurisdiction* . . . . The federal courts . . . cannot be courts of general *jurisdiction.* They are empowered to hear only such cases as are within the judicial power of the United States, as defined in the Constitution, and have been entrusted to them by a *jurisdictional* grant by Congress.

Charles Alan Wright, The Law of Federal Courts § 7, at 27 (5th ed. 1994). In other words, the ability of federal courts to hear cases depends on a specific grant of power from the Constitution.

On the other hand, state courts are courts of *general jurisdiction.* This means their jurisdiction is much broader than that of federal courts (see Diagram 2), and instead of being based on a specific grant of authority from the Constitution, is based on general geographic jurisdiction. *General jurisdiction* is defined in Black's Law Dictionary as "A court's authority to hear a wide range of cases, civil or criminal, that arise within its geographic area."

Here is a visual depiction of how state compares to federal jurisdiction. The diagram below demonstrates that federal jurisdiction is limited as compared to state jurisdiction—as explained above, most issues that affect us are state law issues. The diagram also shows *concurrent jurisdiction*. The diagram also shows that both state and federal courts handle both civil and criminal matters.

Diagram 2:
Whose Law Governs? State and Federal Jurisdiction

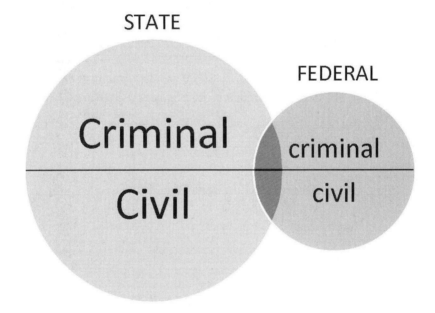

Let's take a look at federal and state jurisdiction more specifically.

Federal Jurisdiction: Federal courts are *courts of limited jurisdiction*. To establish federal jurisdiction you need 1) a *federal question*; 2) *diversity jurisdiction*; or 3) the United States as a party to the lawsuit.

Federal question jurisdiction arises when the plaintiff is asking for enforcement of a federal statute or a Constitutional right. Federal courts are the "experts" in federal law, so even when there is *concurrent jurisdiction* (meaning that a plaintiff can bring the claim in either federal or state court), many times the plaintiff will choose a federal court for a federal issue because of the court's expertise.

Diversity jurisdiction is when you have a dispute with someone from another state. If the matter is worth a lot of money (in the federal jurisdictional statute we call this the "amount in controversy")— currently $75,000 or over—AND the two parties (people having the dispute) are from different states, the plaintiff can file in federal court even if the claim is governed by state law.[5] Through *diversity jurisdiction* we can bring to federal court everyday matters such as car accidents or other common causes of action.

You can remember the concept of *diversity jurisdiction* if you can remember the reason we have a dual system. When the country was established, in addition to the desire to avoid a kingly power, the individual states had very specific and strong identities. If citizens from two different states were in an accident, each citizen would likely fear that a trial in one of those states would favor the citizen of that state. Individuals had a very strong allegiance to their states and states had a strong allegiance to their citizens. So the founders had to figure out how to resolve disputes in a way that would not favor one citizen over the other. Although state courts would be fine for almost everything, they would not be fine to resolve disputes between people from two different states (for matters over a certain amount).

Lastly, the U.S. (through its attorneys, such as the U.S. Attorney's Office) can enforce its civil and criminal laws in federal court, just as we can enforce our federal rights in federal court.[6] Specifically, according to the Federal Judicial Center, "Article III of the Constitution states that the judicial power of the United States extends 'to Controversies to which the United States shall be a Party.'"

---

[5]　28 U.S.C. § 1332 (2011).

[6]　Federal Judicial Center, Jurisdiction: Civil, United States as a Party, https://www.fjc. gov/history/courts/jurisdiction-civil-united-states-party (last visited May 7, 2019).

State Jurisdiction: Unlike federal courts, state courts don't have a specific grant of jurisdiction from a federal or state statute or constitution. Rather, state jurisdiction in trial courts is generally based on the location of the parties or the cause of action. There may be specific state *courts of limited jurisdiction*, such as when an individual court's jurisdiction is limited to a specific topic—Surrogate's Court, Traffic Court, Domestic Violence Court, Drug Court, Veteran's Court, or Family Court, to name a few examples. There is typically also a state trial *court of general jurisdiction* where a wide variety of issues can be tried, based on the geographical *jurisdiction*, and usually limited only by the amount in controversy.

Concurrent Jurisdiction: As stated above, *concurrent jurisdiction* means that a cause of action can be tried in either state or federal court. Again, when it comes to federal law, many federal law *issues* can be tried in either state or federal court.

However, unlike federal law *issues*, when it comes to state law, those *issues* are almost always litigated in state court, and a federal court can only hear the case if the diversity rules are met and the party filing suit chooses federal court. Again, as we learned in Section 2, most of our daily legal *issues* are state law *issues*, and those *issues* will usually be tried in state court.

In addition to *concurrent jurisdiction*, another common wrinkle is when a legal problem presents both federal and state issues. If the federal issues are the core issues to be resolved, the state issues can piggyback on them and both sets of issues can be resolved in federal court. The federal court then has *"pendent"* jurisdiction (think "dependent"—the state issues are "dependent" on the federal issues for federal jurisdiction) over the state law issues.

Here is a visual depiction of the difference between state and federal jurisdiction:

Diagram 3:

Comparison of State Versus Federal Jurisdiction

State jurisdiction	Federal jurisdiction
State trial courts are *courts of general jurisdiction*. With some exceptions, any type of claim can be filed.	Federal courts are *courts of specific jurisdiction*. Only claims that meet certain requirements can be filed.
Basis for state jurisdiction: 1. Location of *parties,* or 2. Subject of dispute. Specific state rules govern the amount of money that has to be in controversy for a specific state trial court or state *courts of limited jurisdiction* (such as Family Court or Traffic Court).	Basis for federal jurisdiction: 1. Diversity jurisdiction (parties from 2 different states) PLUS $75,000 in dispute, or 2. Federal question (legal *issue* based on Constitution or federal statute) or 3. United States is a party.
Many causes of action are subject to *concurrent jurisdiction*—that means they can be brought in **either** state or federal court	Many causes of action are subject to *concurrent jurisdiction*—that means they can be brought in **either** state or federal court

Jurisdiction can be a complicated subject, and one that law students can study in multiple classes. There are fine points, and there are questions not only of *subject matter jurisdiction* (jurisdiction over the legal issues), but also of *personal jurisdiction* (*jurisdiction* over the particular people involved). This chapter is not a scholarly treatise on the subject, but rather, simply an introduction. At this point in your legal career, it should be enough to know that this is an important question that you can resolve by figuring out whether the issue involves state or federal law and by determining where the parties are located.

B. Thinking About the Subject Matter: Is This a *Criminal Law* or *Civil Law Issue*?

As a society we don't know enough about the difference between *civil* and *criminal law*. As with our analyses above, there are always gray or overlapping areas. But still, if we are painting with a broad brush, there are some fundamental differences, and knowing about them can help you think about legal issues and how to research them.

To be sure, perhaps the most basic difference is one that will seem obvious: the idea behind *civil law* is making someone whole, while the idea behind *criminal law* is punishment or rehabilitation. Therefore, a conflict or a violation of *civil law* is governed by a concern for providing a *remedy*, while a violation of *criminal law* is governed by a concern for punishment.

In the *civil law* world, the *remedy* is often compensation, typically money, usually called damages. In the *criminal law* world, the punishment can be a fine (monetary) or loss of liberty (like landing in jail or prison). Compensation versus punishment: the contrasting effects of *civil law* violation versus *criminal law* violation.

Another type of *remedy* in *civil law* cases is an *equitable remedy*. Remedies called *equitable* were developed in England for situations where the legal remedy under common law—damages—was not enough, or was not flexible enough. A common *equitable remedy* is an *injunction*, which is a court order to either refrain from or to do a certain action. Sometimes called a "stop-order," an example of an *injunction* in a *civil law* case would be when a court stops an activity, such as a parade, protest, or building demolition.

But what is the difference between these two vast areas of law when we are *not* talking about compensation or punishment? We can look at the goals of each area and surmise that *civil law* orders our relationships, our ownership and use of things, and takes care of people in the case of accidents. By ordering our relationships, *civil law* keeps us together. On the other hand, *criminal law* keeps us safe. Because we fear criminal punishment, we don't usually intentionally hurt people or steal their things. *Civil law* keeps us together; *criminal law* keeps us safe.

Typical *civil law* areas include the law of accidents, or *negligence*, where someone was careless and hurt someone else, an area many people are familiar with (or see advertisements about). *Negligence* is a type of *tort*, which is a legal word for an act that results in injury. In addition to *negligence*, there are intentional *torts*, such as assaults. Other types of *civil law* include property law (real property—land or buildings—or intellectual property, such as patents or copyrights); contract law; employment law; and family law, to name a few. *Civil law* also includes the exciting matters, like Constitutional Law, which is one of the major vehicles for civil rights and anti-discrimination law. Remember, both the federal and state systems include *civil law* (see Diagram 2).

For typical *criminal law* areas, all you have to do is look at daily life and your own personal experiences or the experiences of those around you, in your neighborhood or in the news. *Criminal law* penalizes acts of violence, such as assault, murder, kidnapping, and sexual violence, as well as harm or theft of property, from burglary to pickpocketing to embezzlement.

Don't worry, it's not that simple: there is a great, gray overlapping area. You may have wondered, when reading above about assault as an example of *civil law*, why assault would not be under *criminal law*. You may next have noticed that assault, indeed, was listed as an example for *criminal law*. So why is it listed in both areas? Because assault can be a matter of both *criminal* and *civil law*. You can sue someone for assaulting you to get the compensation to make you whole, and that person can likewise be criminally prosecuted if there was *criminal* intent to harm. Two results—compensation and punishment—are sometimes warranted by one act.

There is one more important difference between the worlds of *civil* and *criminal law*: the *burden of proof*. The *burden of proof* means what it sounds like it means—how heavy a burden does the party seeking to prove the case have to carry? In other words, how convincing does the proof from that party have to be? The *burden of proof* comes up in the context of proving a case in court, whether a violation of a *civil law* or a *criminal law*, but the weight of the burden varies. Many of us are familiar with the criminal *burden of proof: beyond a reasonable doubt*. It is important to know that that this is a **very heavy** *burden of proof* that applies **only** in *criminal law*. It makes sense to have a strict or hard-to-meet *burden of proof* in criminal matters because the punishment is so severe—usually loss of liberty (whether it's probation or imprisonment). You would not want to put someone in jail for committing a crime that you were only mostly sure, but not convinced, that the person committed.

In all other matters, whether it is our employment or our injuries or our property, the *burden of proof* is **not** the same as the *criminal burden of proof*. Rather, the *burden of proof* in *civil law* matters is less heavy. There are several different proof measures for *civil law* matters, and the terms all sound less serious and less weighty than *beyond a reasonable doubt*. Two common ways of describing the *burden of proof* in *civil law* matters are *preponderance of the evidence* and *clear and convincing evidence*.

Here is a visual reminder that subject matter jurisdiction—civil versus criminal—and choosing the right courthouse—state versus federal—need to both be considered. This chart combines the considerations of Questions 3.—Which Courthouse Should I Go to? and B.—Thinking About the Subject Matter: Is This a *Criminal Law* or *Civil Law Issue*?

Diagram 4:

Which Courthouse Will I Go to? State and Federal Jurisdiction

	FEDERAL COURT	STATE COURT
CIVIL LAW	YES Federal *civil law* statutes	YES
CRIMINAL LAW	YES Federal *criminal law* statutes	YES
U.S. CONSTITUTIONAL LAW	YES	YES *Concurrent jurisdiction*
STATE LAW ISSUES	YES In cases of *diversity jurisdiction*	YES Most state law issues are decided in state courts
FEDERAL LAW (OTHER THAN CONSTITUTIONAL) ISSUES	YES	MAYBE Some federal statutes can be tried in either state or federal court because there is *concurrent jurisdiction*

C. Thinking More About the Subject Matter: Is This a *Transaction* or a Conflict?

When the law gets a lot of press, it is often because of courtroom drama. We imagine the setting of the courtroom as the scene of the ultimate confrontation between right and wrong. However, very few of our conflicts make it all the way to the courtroom, and many of our everyday dealings with law are not based on the violation of a legal rule at all.

Many of our legal dealings are really about *transactions*. A *transaction* is either an exchange between people (parties) or a relationship-defining event. An exchange could include a sale or a lease of something simple, like a car or an apartment, or something more complex, like municipal bonds of a city or stock of a company. An exchange can deal with objects (cars and apartments) or people, such as an employment contract or even an adoption. On the other hand, a relationship-defining event can be something as simple as a marriage, or something more complex, like the formation of a company with owners, partners, and shareholders.

Understanding whether your legal issue concerns a conflict or *transaction* helps you understand what kind of legal sources to check out. For example, if the matter is NOT a conflict that will result in *litigation*, then you may want to start with statutes and regulations. You at least want to make sure you don't forget those sources. On the contrary, if you know your legal issue IS a conflict (two neighbors have threatened to sue each other over the use of their shared driveway and the easement), then in addition to reviewing any applicable statutes, you want to make sure you have checked the case law to see if a similar matter has been *litigated* before, and whether the courts have issued any decisions that affect your issue.

So now that you know all the questions to ask in order to gain context, how do you find out the answers? We are going to take a look at some research strategies and some legal sources that will get you started.

PART II. STARTING YOUR RESEARCH: KEY WORD SEARCHES AND SECONDARY SOURCES

You do not need to figure out the answers to the three "sorting the legal mess" questions in Part I on your own. Rather, the idea is that you now know what questions to ask, and you can ask these questions when you begin your research. The questions will focus your research.

Remember, your end goal is to find the applicable legal rule in your jurisdiction. Since every legal rule has component parts, or elements, you also want to make sure that you find a complete statement of the rule that includes all the elements.

Although the conventional wisdom for a research strategy with "book" research is to start with secondary sources, that approach doesn't take into account today's advantages of being able to use one database that very quickly retrieves all types of relevant sources, including primary AND secondary sources. In today's world, beginning legal students should think more about their reading strategy when they are researching. As the next section advocates, you should integrate both primary and secondary sources from the databases or libraries you have available in order to answer the three questions. Make sure you read *both* types of sources, especially more general secondary sources, so you can start to develop a general background knowledge for your research question.

A. Key Word Searching and Reading Strategy

You all know how to research with word searches on incredible databases like Google or Google Scholar. Much to the surprise and consternation of sophisticated and experienced researchers, word searching sometimes works on at least a beginner level—meaning you get some "relevant enough" websites and sources. A danger of getting some easy and accurate results, though, is that you stop looking, because you think you are done. Another danger is that you could think every search will be like this. This "quick fix" mentality can lead to complexities missed, inaccuracies, and lack of depth. Of course, quick, accurate results have a benefit—there is simply so much information online and the databases are sophisticated and fast. Moreover, as undergraduate students studying the law, many of you will have a version of a legal database available to you, whether it's a professional package (geared toward practitioners) for paralegal students or whether it's a more academic package for all undergraduates. Regardless of your database, this section will advocate that you take care and stand wary of this "quick fix" approach to research.

Using words to search databases is often called *"key word" searching.* This is the easiest and least sophisticated way to search a database, because this type of searching does not require any knowledge about the services or information categories provided by the database. Rather, you simply take a few relevant *key words* from your research question and plug them in to the search bar. All you really need to do is to carefully read your research question.

It is not necessarily wrong to search for relevant *key words* or specific legal terms. It is a good start. Just be aware of the limitations of the "quick fix" approach, and stand strong against the seductive feeling that you are a great researcher and can be finished quickly. Also, remember that results from *key word searching* vary depending on the database. For example, when you use the Google or Google Scholar database, you are not searching the full text of the items in the database. However, in a subscription database like Westlaw or Lexis, you ARE searching the full text of EVERY item in the database, so general and broad *key word searches* can produce WAY TOO MANY results to sift through and read. With legal research, sometimes the strategy of a few *key word searches* might work if the question is simple and if you are lucky enough not to get too many sources.

Let's look at the traditional advice given to beginner researchers: start with secondary sources. As explained above, secondary sources are legal *encyclopedias, commentaries, hornbooks,* practitioner's *treatises,* and articles from legal *periodicals* such as trade magazines (bar association magazines, paralegal magazines, or other publications aimed at the legal profession), law reviews, and law journals.

The idea behind starting with secondary sources is to gain context, specifically, to gain a basic understanding of the legal topic you are exploring so you do not go way off track in your research. Gaining a basic understanding includes learning the basic legal rules, when and how they are applied, and some key vocabulary or terms of art that are used in that legal topic. Having this understanding and vocabulary, and thus a little background, is ultimately thought to help you in both the short run and the long run by being a more accurate and focused researcher who is more likely to identify a complete and accurate answer.

So we have the old (and arguably more time-consuming) way, finding and reading secondary sources on the general topic of your research question, and the so-called new way, doing a speedy word search, reviewing the list of primary and secondary sources you pull up, and locating a snippet of information from a source that appears to answer the question.

We will use a hybrid solution: doing both in a careful and organized way using the three "legal mess" questions (from Part I) and a variety of *key word searches* on internet search engines, Google Scholar, a subscription legal database, or free legal databases that include both primary and secondary sources. Remember, you should also review BOTH primary and secondary sources in order to answer the three questions. The goal should be not only to answer the three questions accurately, but also to learn additional vocabulary, and hopefully even concepts that can help you with additional and more advanced word searches. In answering the questions, you should come up with both primary and secondary sources.

B. Different Types of Secondary Sources

Like all other sources, secondary sources can be found in book form in a law school or courthouse library. Even tech-savvy attorneys sometimes prefer the book form for secondary sources because physically browsing an index, the subjects on a spine, or an outline at the beginning of the subject can really assist with the search. Browsing through pages can actually be quicker than clicking through them. One of the easy things about going to a physical library is that secondary sources are arranged by topic, so you can easily see a number of sources on one topic.

Of course, secondary sources—along with primary sources—will come up with a key word search on Lexis or Westlaw in whatever jurisdiction you choose to search in. In both databases you can also choose to search ONLY secondary sources. Keep in mind that because those searches are full-text searches, you will probably get too many sources, and many of those will not be relevant or helpful. Secondary sources are also included on some free legal databases such as FindLaw, Justia, Legal Information Institute, and Google Scholar; indeed, those websites and others provide their own explanations of many legal topics and are secondary sources in their own right.[7] As long as it's not the ONLY thing you do, it is even fine to start off with a Google search just to see the types of sources that are out there. Sometimes, with a specific enough search that is narrow because of unusual search terms, a Google search can expedite the process of solving the three "legal mess" questions.

Sometimes references to secondary sources are integrated into primary sources, especially in the case of annotated statutes. Therefore, once you find the relevant statute you also often find relevant links to secondary sources to help you understand the statute, including practitioner's materials, *treatises, hornbooks,* or even an expert's *commentary* on a specific statutory section.

Below we have a list of each type of secondary source, as well as some specific examples of each source and the need that each source could fill. As a beginner legal researcher, your goals should be to distinguish between the various types of secondary sources, and to begin trying to develop a sense about which type of source will be most helpful for which questions. You should also make it a point to identify the secondary source(s) for the jurisdiction and topic you are looking for. For example, if you are trying to solve a question on the interpretation of the Federal Rules of Civil Procedure, you would be remiss not to look at Moore's Federal Practice (Bender 2015) or Wright's The Law of Federal Courts. Or, for a federal criminal trial,

---

[7] See the Bibliography for a list of legal websites.

you would want to be sure to review the <u>Pattern Federal Criminal Jury Instructions</u> for your federal jurisdiction or circuit (see below for explanation of pattern jury instructions).

Consulting secondary sources is an important part of your research because these sources can save you a great deal of time. As you begin to explore the relevant secondary sources for your jurisdiction and your area of practice, begin to keep mental notes about their differences, their similarities, and their utility. For example, note the author (law student, judge, practitioner, or scholar?), how current the citations are, and how general or in-depth the explanation is. Understanding the range of secondary sources available to you, and learning which ones you should use for particular purposes, are great strategies for fighting that overwhelmed feeling that comes with being a beginner legal researcher.

Of course, secondary sources are available online as well as in print. As previously noted, when you run basic keyword searches in any jurisdiction in Westlaw and Lexis, the system will automatically search for secondary sources as well as primary sources. You can also choose to search only in secondary sources.

Legal *Encyclopedias*: *Encyclopedias* are made up of entries that each provide descriptions of the law in a given area and include citations to relevant primary sources. *Encyclopedias* typically have an editorial team made up of lawyers who write the entries. The entries tend to be broad and easy to read. Therefore, *encyclopedias* can be a good place to start your research. They are organized alphabetically by main topic, and each main topic starts with a detailed outline of the sub-topics included. The benefit of *encyclopedias* is that you can easily find an easy-to-read explanation of your topic, along with helpful citations; the drawback can be that the entries' citations to sources may not be to the most recent cases due to the publication schedule.

One example of a national legal *encyclopedia* is <u>Corpus Juris Secundum</u> (C.J.S.) which covers both state and federal law on as many as 430 topics. Another example of a national legal *encyclopedia* is

American Jurisprudence (Am. Jur.), which also covers both state and federal law. They are considered comprehensive *encyclopedias* and contain references to cases, statutes, and law review articles on point. (As you will read below, "law review" is a general term that covers legal journals published by law schools.) Both Am. Jur. and C.J.S. are owned and published by West. Am. Jur. also provides references to the American Law Reports (see below), and other Am. Jur. publications such as Am. Jur. Trials, Am. Jur. Proof of Facts, Am. Jur. Pleading and Practice Forms, and Am. Jur. Legal Forms. C.J.S. refers its readers to relevant West topics and key numbers (you will learn about key numbers later).

Each state also has its own legal *encyclopedia*, which typically includes the title word "Jurisprudence," such as California Jurisprudence, New York Jurisprudence, or Illinois Jurisprudence.

You would use an *encyclopedia* if you were given a legal research assignment in an area of law that was new to you in order to gain a basic understanding of the principles, the potentially applicable legal rules, and the vocabulary for that area. *Encyclopedias* are great for imparting general principles.

American Law Reports: The American Law Reports (ALR) are known for their "annotations"—articles—about emerging areas of the law; each annotation is written by a different legal scholar. The annotations are more in-depth than an *encyclopedia* entry and explore nuances and opposing arguments on *issues*. The ALR is really its own category; it is not like an *encyclopedia* because the annotations are based on cases that present emerging issues in the law and are more complex than *encyclopedia* entries, yet it is also unlike a *treatise* (described below) because it is a compendium of articles on selected topics rather than a comprehensive source for one area of law. In addition to an in-depth analysis, an ALR annotation provides citations to every case—in every jurisdiction—that discusses the *issue* it covers. Therefore, it is a great source for case citations in multiple jurisdictions on a single *issue*.

You would use the ALR if you needed a detailed and in-depth look at a particular area. For example, if you wanted to write about how multiple states were handling a legal *issue*, or to get an idea on the difference between state and federal law on a particular topic, or to get a sense what the majority view is on a legal *issue*, you would consult the ALR. Consulting the ALR is great for multi-state research, especially academic research.

__Treatise:__ A *treatise* is simply a book (or multiple books) devoted to one legal topic and can range in type from a practitioner-oriented book with practical pointers for solving a legal problem to a multiple-volume set of books written by a legal scholar explaining an area in depth. Sometimes a *treatise* is written by an expert practitioner who is also a scholar. *Treatises* go much more in depth than *encyclopedias*, typically providing analysis, context, and tips, and like all the secondary sources discussed so far, they include citations to the relevant primary sources. The author can be anyone from a renowned legal scholar like William Blackstone, who wrote an 18th century *treatise* on the common law of England,[8] to the oft-cited Weinstein's Federal Evidence, written by Senior United States District Court Judge Jack B. Weinstein.[9]

Some examples of famous *treatises* referred to in law school classes and used by courts are Prosser and Keeton on Torts, 5th Edition (West 1984), Corbin on Contracts, Rev. Edition (Bender 1993) and Page on Wills, 3rd Edition (Anderson 2003)—all multi-volume sets of books. As noted above, *treatises* aimed at lawyers who practice in federal court include Moore's Federal Practice and Federal Practice and Procedure by Wright and Miller.

A *hornbook* is also a type of *treatise*—authored by a legal scholar and dedicated to one topic—that is specifically aimed at explaining the law to law students. *Hornbooks* are geared toward law school curriculum and

---

[8]   William Blackstone, Commentaries on the Laws of England (Clarendon Press at Oxford, 1765–1769).

[9]   As of August this writing, this notable jurist was 97 years old and still taking a full docket. *See* United States District Court, Eastern District of New York, Article III Judges, https://www.nyed.uscourts.gov/content/judge-jack-b-weinstein (last visited May 7, 2019).

to explaining the subtleties of the legal topics that are commonly explored by law school faculty.

Remember, you would use a *treatise* to get an in-depth explanation of a legal topic that is goes beyond an *encyclopedia* entry's coverage.

Form Books: As indicated by the name, *form books* provide templates for practitioners so they have a starting point for drafting a legal submission—whether it's a *litigation* document, a contract between two parties, or a submission to a government agency. Like all sources, form books are available in print and online. Form books can be organized by topic or by jurisdiction. Be on the lookout for citations to forms in annotated statutes, regulations, or other secondary sources (e.g., American Jurisprudence Legal Forms).

The advantage of using a form is that it can alert you to necessary elements for your legal document and help make your drafting quicker and easier. Forms help educate beginner researchers on what should be in the form, as well as what the form typically looks like. The potential disadvantage is that you could be tempted to have a false sense of security and fail to make the necessary alterations for your particular research question or your jurisdiction. So a word to the wise: NEVER, EVER, EVER use a form from a *form book* without carefully reviewing every aspect of the form for conformity with YOUR jurisdiction and your specific legal question.

Sample forms are available from many different publishers and are available for every legal topic and every legal practice. Forms can even be available for free on websites of your state court, state government, state department of state, or FindLaw. Additional examples include Bender's Federal Practice Forms, or the free forms available on www. uscourts.gov under the link to Federal Court Forms (which includes multiple practice areas).

You would want to locate a sample form in a *form book* anytime you need to draft a legal document, and especially if you are doing so in a legal topic that is relatively new to you. Again, the sample form could provide ideas, applicable legal rules, and possible issues to consider. Remember, the sample form does not provide a wholesale answer to your legal drafting problem. It just gets you started.

Continuing Legal Education (CLE) materials: The category of *Continuing Legal Education (CLE) materials* is broad and includes materials written by lawyers for lawyers, usually in conjunction with a seminar or class presentation. The term is also used for materials specific to paralegals. Most states require practicing lawyers to continue their legal education after law school, and specifically require a certain number of hours of course work to maintain their license to practice. Courses include a lecture and printed or digital materials. Once a course has been presented, the materials, along with a video of the accompanying lecture, are available through local, state, or national bar associations, paralegal associations, or private companies.

The advantage of *CLE materials* is that they are specifically aimed at the nuts and bolts of legal practice, and they come in a variety of shapes, sizes and prices. Well-written *CLE materials* can provide step-by-step instructions as well as useful caveats. Many paralegals and lawyers find that regular *CLE* seminars are an efficient way to stay up to date on a particular practice area—*civil law* and procedure in your state, federal employment law, state or federal *criminal law*, etc.

Most *CLE materials* are purchased from a bar or paralegal association, and they are not typically available from free or on subscription databases. They may, however, be available without cost in law school or government law libraries. Usually, these materials give you a practical overview of the subject area, as well as tips and precautions in that area of practice.

Pattern Jury Instructions: *Jury instructions* are easily overlooked by beginner researchers—if you are not preparing for an imminent jury trial, jury instructions don't sound that relevant. Moreover, we may know from television that the most boring part of any trial is when the judge reads the jury the legal instructions on how to apply the law to the evidence presented.

However, *pattern jury instructions* can really aid you in understanding the law because they contain a straightforward and short recitation of the elements of the legal rule, and are followed by an explanation of that rule. The explanation of the rule is well-researched, correct, and based on case law. Therefore, it is a great source and tends to be comprehensive. *Pattern jury instructions* are typically written by a number of appellate judges. Some examples include the <u>Federal Jury Instructions</u> which are available for each federal circuit, the <u>Modern Federal Jury Instructions</u> by *LexisNexis*, and the <u>Federal Jury Practice and Instructions</u> by West.

You would refer to jury instructions either as a beginning point, to help you find the right legal rule, or even better, after you have identified the legal rule, as a confirmation of the rule's elements and a resource for a thorough discussion of the case law.

Legal *Periodicals:* The word *periodical* refers to anything that is published serially, like a magazine. Thus, a legal *periodical* can be a legal magazine like the <u>American Bar Association Journal</u>, the National Federation of Paralegal Association magazines, or the National Association of Legal Assistants magazine.

In addition, a legal *periodical* can be a law review or law journal, which are usually published by and through law schools. Most law reviews include in-depth and heavily footnoted articles written by law students and by today's legal scholars. Some law reviews may be dedicated to specific topics, such an environmental law or human rights, and some law reviews may be known for publishing practical articles that are relevant to practitioners in their state. Other law reviews have no predetermined topic focus and publish a wide range of articles. Law reviews tend to be run by law students, and law students choose and edit the articles. Because most undergraduate colleges, graduate programs, and professional programs like law schools require their professors to publish scholarly articles in order to obtain tenure, there are many, many scholarly articles in the world.

Some examples from among the many include the <u>Buffalo Law Review</u> (published by the University at Buffalo Law School), the <u>Human Rights Law Review</u> (published by Oxford Academic), and the <u>Journal of Law, Medicine and Ethics</u> (published by the American Society of Law, Medicine and Ethics).

You would consult a legal *periodical* (magazine) from a bar or paralegal association in order to stay abreast of current legal issues in your jurisdiction and your area of practice. You would consult a law review or law journal if you needed an in-depth look at a particular issue, or if you needed background for an academic paper. A law review or law journal article may also provide great background to a legal issue, including a synthesis of relevant case law.

Now that you have been introduced to the "legal mess," let's walk through an example.

C. Trying It out: Beginning Your Research

For example, let's say your professor or supervisor presents you with this scenario to research and analyze:

Billy Blye is an itinerant college drop-out who goes from city to city in the U.S. and Canada and dances for a living. Usually, he sleeps at a friend's apartment when he travels; since he is really friendly, sometimes he meets other dancers or artists and stays with them. While at a music festival in Boston, Massachusetts, he decides he wants to experience sleeping under the stars. (Plus, his friends from the festival have told him they have no more room in their apartments.) At around 10 p.m., while Billy is asleep in his sleeping bag under a picnic bench on Boston Common, a local police officer arrests him for sleeping in the park.

If you are representing Billy, what should you do first? An initial question would be what law he violated. This information would normally be available from the police officer, but we will look into it here for demonstration purposes.

Let's start with the first of the three "legal mess" questions from Part I:

1. What is the jurisdiction?

    a. Where am I?

    b. Whose law governs?

    c. Which courthouse would I go to?

2. Is this a *criminal law* or a *civil law issue*?

3. Is this a *transaction* (an exchange or agreement between two *parties*) or a dispute (a conflict between two *parties* that needs to be resolved with *litigation*)?

Let's start with the first question, *What is the jurisdiction*, and the first step, *a. Where am I?* According to the hypothetical, "you" (the client) are in Boston (are Boston ordinances relevant?); Massachusetts (are Massachusetts laws relevant?); and the United States (are federal laws relevant?). There is no other party or property for which we need to investigate the location.

Next jurisdiction step: *b. Whose law is it?* Based on what you have learned, you need to ask yourself whether you see any conduct or potential conduct that crosses state lines. One hint is that the arrest was made by a local police officer; this suggests that the law violated was in the police officer's jurisdiction. Another hint is that the conduct—sleeping on Boston Common—is not an activity that crosses state boundaries or exists across state boundaries.

If you want to explore or double-check this issue with a little bit of research, you could try a variety of *key word searches* in your legal subscription database (Westlaw or Lexis), a free legal database, or Google or Google Scholar. A *key word search* is a search that includes specific terms such as the cause of action and the specific facts that are particular to your problem. For example, you can try searching for:

- Law against sleeping in a park in Boston (and try "sleeping in a park" in quotes; also, try "Boston," "Boston Massachusetts," and just "Massachusetts")

- Prohibition against sleeping in a park in Boston, Massachusetts

- Arrested for sleeping in a park in Boston, Massachusetts

When searching Westlaw or Lexis, be mindful of the jurisdiction you have selected. You have the option of selecting the jurisdiction for the search, and you can choose one state, multiple states, one state and the corresponding federal jurisdiction, or one state and the entire federal jurisdiction.

Here, you have been provided with the pretty specific location of Boston, Massachusetts, so the broadest database selection would be the state of Massachusetts and the corresponding federal jurisdiction (First Circuit—appellate court—with corresponding District Courts), and the narrowest selection would be the state of Massachusetts. You could also do these searches on the free statute database for Massachusetts statutes,[10] or on another free legal database such as FindLaw.

When you do the variety of searches, what do you find? You may pull up a lot of irrelevant information, especially on your legal subscription database. Remember, the information in your legal database is so voluminous, and the search mechanism so thorough, that there will likely be too many matches with many irrelevant results. You will probably find articles and cases on Occupy Boston, which was a movement in 2011 in which some protesters camped out in public areas. If you are careful to check the search terms that match, you will see that sleeping in the park as a political expression may be protected by the First Amendment. Interesting, but not our issue here.

On the other hand, in your Google search, one of the items you should pull up will be "Parks Rules & Regulations/City of Boston" at

---

[10] *See* Commonwealth of Massachusetts, General Laws, https://malegislature.gov/Laws/GeneralLaws (last visited on February 26, 2019).

the handy source of CityofBoston.Gov.[11] Sound relevant? Correct. These are Boston's City Ordinances. After reviewing these, you will see that our friend Billy Blye did indeed violate a local ordinance by sleeping on Boston Common.

The last step of jurisdiction to be resolved is *c. What courthouse do I go to?* For the answer to this question, we would have to look at the court structure in Massachusetts, as well as the relevant ordinance for Bill Blye, in order to determine which court would hear violations of this ordinance. If you investigate in your database or ask this simple question in Google, you will find that the court with jurisdiction over violations of Boston ordinances is the Massachusetts District Court.

Which brings us to our next question: 2) Is this a *criminal law* or a *civil law issue?* At this point, since we are just determining context, we can rely on the arrest as an indication of a *criminal law issue.* Further down the researching trail, we would have to make sure that violation of a local Boston ordinance is indeed a criminal violation.

Lastly, we have question 3): *Is this a transaction or a dispute that will be litigated?* Again, we know from the arrest that the matter is being treated as a criminal one, in which case there will be a criminal court proceeding. Because there are no federal law issues or diversity of citizenship, the jurisdiction would likely be state jurisdiction. To research the precise court in Massachusetts that would hear a violation of a park ordinance, we would research Massachusetts court jurisdiction. (Note the answer to question 1(c), above.) Again, since we are just determining context here, we do not have to delve any further. So now you have some important context for the issues in the sleeping in the park hypothetical, and you are ready for the next steps in research and analysis.

Remember that working through a problem methodically prevents you from getting lost in the weeds. For example, if you had just done a

---

[11] *See* City of Boston, Parks Rules and Regulations, https://www.boston.gov/departments/parks-and-recreation/parks-rules-and-regulations (last visited on February 25, 2019).

word search in a legal database you might not have found the Boston ordinances so easily. Having come up with initial answers for the "legal mess" questions, you now have a direction for going forward.

CHAPTER 2 LEGAL SKILLS

- **Identify subject matter and *jurisdiction* for your legal problem**
- **Find, recognize, and use *secondary* sources**
- **Distinguish between *primary sources* and *secondary sources***

CHAPTER 2 VOCABULARY

- Burden of proof
- Burden of proof in civil cases: preponderance of evidence, clear and convincing evidence
- Burden of proof in criminal law: beyond a reasonable doubt
- Civil law
- Commentaries
- Commerce clause
- Concurrent jurisdiction
- Continuing legal education (CLE) materials
- Court of general jurisdiction
- Court of limited jurisdiction
- Criminal law
- Diversity jurisdiction
- Encyclopedias
- Equitable remedy
- Federal question
- Federalism
- Form books
- Hornbooks
- Hypothetical (fact situation, fact scenario, legal problem)
- Injunction
- Issue
- Key word searching

- LexisNexis, Lexis Academic
- Litigate, litigation
- Negligence
- Pattern jury instructions
- Pendent jurisdiction
- Periodical
- Personal jurisdiction
- Remedy
- Subject matter jurisdiction
- Tort
- Transaction
- Treatises
- Westlaw, Westlaw Campus, WestlawNext

CHAPTER 2 RESEARCH AND ANALYSIS EXERCISES

I.   Investigating your state jurisdiction:

Find an example from your state for each of the secondary sources explained in this chapter. (You may not find examples for all of them at the state level.)

II.   Now, do the same with the Feds:

Find an example in federal sources for each of the secondary sources explained in this chapter.

III. Compare sources from your state:

Look up negligence in three (3) different types of state-specific secondary sources, choosing from among the following:

1.   a legal encyclopedia

2.   a treatise

3.   a form book

4.   continuing legal education materials from your local bar association

5.   pattern jury instructions

6.   a legal periodical

7.   a restatement.

For each of the sources you used, make one (1) observation about any notable characteristics of the source, such as whether it is easy or hard to read; how much detail is included; how many citations and how current the citations are; or the amount of explanation.

III. Try sorting through the "legal mess" with these hypotheticals:

1.   Professor Alden, a professor at the State University Law School, decided to have a party at her house for all the law students in her Contracts class, a required class for first year students. She intended to host the party after fall final exams, and to welcome the students with a bonfire and a keg of locally brewed beer. Because her first year class is so large, about 100 students, she posted the party invitation and directions to her house on Facebook. She wants to know if she faces any liability in the event any of the law students drinks too much and gets into a car accident.

a.   Is this a federal or state law issue? Explain your answer.

b.   Is this a civil or criminal issue? Explain your answer.

c.   Is this is a potential transaction or conflict? Explain your answer.

d.   Review your state encyclopedia and two additional secondary sources. Explain which source was the most useful, and why.

e.   Now that you have thought through these questions, find the relevant case law with the help your instructor.

2.   Dr. Castro walked inside his apartment building at about 1:00 in the morning and was quickly approached by the apartment superintendent's wife, Mrs. Trenton. She told Dr. Castro that she thought her husband was ill and asked him to take a look at him. Dr. Castro followed Mrs. Trenton into their apartment, and found Mr. Trenton sitting in his easy chair, looking pale, and gasping for breath. Mr. Trenton

complained that his left arm hurt. Dr. Castro immediately knelt by his side, took his pulse, and explained to Mrs. Trenton that her husband was very sick and should go to the hospital immediately. He then whipped out his cell phone and called 911 for an ambulance for Mr. Trenton. Dr. Castro then left the apartment. In the ambulance on the way to the hospital, Mr. Trenton had a heart attack and died. Mrs. Castro wants to sue Dr. Castro "for not doing more" to prevent her husband's death and wants to know if she has any viable cause of action.[12]

a.   Is this a federal or state law issue? Explain your answer.

b.   Is this a civil or criminal issue? Explain your answer.

c.   Is this is a potential transaction or conflict? Explain your answer.

d.   Review your state encyclopedia and two additional secondary sources. Explain which source was the most useful, and why.

e.   Now that you have thought through these questions, find the relevant case law with the help of your instructor.

3.   Mr. Cheechy and Ms. Chongy have a small local business in Colorado selling marijuana, and they would like to go on a road trip to several different states with marijuana "samples" to see if they can start more stores in other states. Cheechy and Chongy have not set their route yet, but they want to know if it's legal to transport marijuana over state lines.

a.   Is this a federal or state law issue? Explain your answer.

b.   Is this a civil or criminal issue? Explain your answer.

c.   Is this is a potential transaction or conflict? Explain your answer.

---

[12]   This fact scenario is based on *Rodriguez v. N.Y.C. Health & Hosps. Corp.*, 132 Misc. 2d. 705, 505 N.Y.S.2d 345 (Kings Co. 1986).

d.   Review your state encyclopedia and two additional secondary sources. Explain which source was the most useful, and why.

e.   Now that you have thought through these questions, find the relevant case law with the help of your instructor.

IV. Ethics: secondary sources and a hypothetical:

1.   Find and identify three (3) different types of secondary sources devoted to legal ethics. Legal ethics can include judicial ethics. Consider the following sources:

a.   Restatements

b.   Practice materials (such as desk books or CLE materials)

c.   Treatises

2.   Try sorting through some of the "legal mess" with this hypothetical:

a.   Attorney Michael Walt represents a not-for-profit organization called Vets for Life, a local organization started in his town, which pays him a yearly retainer so that the Board of Directors can get his advice on legal issues pertaining to the organization whenever they need it. As required by his state's ethical rules, Michael deposited this sizeable retainer in a separate account called a client trust account. Michael began having financial difficulties due to a gambling problem, and in order to make his mortgage payments he started taking money out of the client trust account, thinking he was just "borrowing" the money. Michael "borrowed" a total of $20,000. However, he was unable to pay it back, and when Vets for Life dropped him as an attorney and asked for the retainer back, Michael could not supply it.

b.   Is this a federal or state law issue? Explain your answer.

c.   Is this a civil or criminal issue? Explain your answer.

d.   Is this is a potential transaction or conflict? Explain your answer.

e.   Review your state encyclopedia and two additional secondary sources (that you did not use in the above two problems). Explain which source was the most useful and why.

f.   Now that you have thought through these questions, with the help of your instructor, find the relevant case law.

What You Need to Know About Court Structure, Case Law, and Our Three Branches

Legal Skills:

- Recognize which court rulings are authoritative
- Identify different types of case law (*common law* cases vs. cases applying other sources of law)
- Demonstrate understanding that multiple sources of law may be necessary to solve a problem
- Demonstrate understanding that legal sources can be interrelated

PART I. UNDERSTANDING LEGAL RULES IN THE COURT SYSTEM

A. The Three-Tier Court System

All cases are not created equal. The federal judicial system, and most state judicial systems, can be thought of as a triangle with three tiers, or levels, of courts: the lowest level, the *trial court* level, typically with numerous trial courts; the mid-level, typically with one or more *mid-level appellate courts*; and the top level, with a single court, known as the *court of last resort*, with *discretionary jurisdiction*.

The farther up a court is on this triangle, the more *precedential value* its decisions have. *Precedential value* is simply the weight we give the past decisions of that court, on a scale from lower value, just *persuasive* (later decisions can but don't have to follow), to higher value, or *mandatory* (later decisions must follow). So, in general, the *precedential value* of cases corresponds with where the deciding court falls on the triangle, that is, cases decided by lower level courts have less *precedential value* than those decided by higher level courts. In other words, in order to understand which cases are more valuable—which *precedent* is *mandatory* and which is just *persuasive*—you have to understand the basic structure of the courts in the *jurisdiction* (state or federal) where the cases were decided. Take a look at Diagram 5 to get a visual sense of court hierarchy.

Additionally, courts at different levels have different powers of jurisdiction. In this context, jurisdiction means the power of a given court to address or act on a legal issue. (As you know from Chapter 2, courts have different types of *jurisdiction*—such as *geographic jurisdiction* and *subject matter jurisdiction*.)[1] If a court does not have *jurisdiction* over your case, the court cannot act.

In general, the lowest level courts, the *trial courts*, have the broadest jurisdiction. As discussed in Chapter 2 (Part I, Section A) in the discussion about the jurisdiction of state courts, this is "general jurisdiction," which more or less means a *trial court* has jurisdiction over a variety of matters. We also call the *trial court's* jurisdiction *original jurisdiction*, because typically this court is the first court to exercise jurisdiction over a case. Additionally, for *trial courts* to exercise jurisdiction, there must be a minimum "amount in controversy" (money amount sought) that must be alleged in order to gain entry to the court.

As explained in Chapter 2, Part I, within the *trial court* system, there are also *trial courts* of limited, or specific, jurisdiction that handle special topics. In a state system, these special topics might include Surrogates, Veterans, Housing, Domestic Violence, Family, and Small Claims. In

---

[1]   As noted in Chapter 2, this text is not covering *personal jurisdiction*, which looks at the question of whether a court has power over a particular person or entity (such as a corporation).

the federal system, courts of limited jurisdiction include the Bankruptcy Courts and the Tax Courts.

Diagram 5:
Triangle of Court System Hierarchy

Court of Last Resort
(discretionary jurisdiction, sets its own agenda, novel questions or questions of first impression, resolution of disputes between appellate courts, AND all of the below traits of a mid-level court)

(mid-level) Appellate Court
(panel of judges, oral argument by attorneys, questions of law, appellate briefs)

Trial Court
(findings of fact, testimony, witnesses, juries, evidence, application of law to facts, jury instructions)

The next level of court is the *mid-level appellate court.* The first appeal of a *trial court* decision is to this appellate court. The *mid-level appellate court* also has broad authority (jurisdiction) to act. State and federal courts may have different rules of exactly what can be appealed from the *trial court.* Generally, the aggrieved—hurt—party can appeal from a final disposition or result. (However, some states may allow appeals from specified types of non-final orders of *trial courts* as well.) A final disposition can come in the form of a final decision by a judge in a non-jury trial, a final decision (verdict) by a jury in a jury trial, a final decision by a judge overturning a jury verdict, or a final decision by a judge on a *dispositive motion*—a *motion* that "disposes" of a case—like summary judgment. We will fully explore summary judgment in Part III of Chapter 7—what it is and how to recognize and describe a court's summary judgment *holding.* For now, all you need to know is that summary judgment is a way to resolve a case by *motion* without a trial.

The last, or top level, court is the *court of last resort.* As discussed in Chapter 2, all the states and the federal governments have a top court, often (but not always) called a supreme court. The top court has *discretionary jurisdiction.* This means that cases don't automatically go to this court. While a losing party may be able to appeal "as of right" (automatically allowed) to the *mid-level appellate court,* there is no appeal as of right to the top court. The parties—through their lawyers—have to request to be heard.

For example, you may have heard of "cert petitions"—the petitions for *writs of certiorari* that get filed with the U.S. Supreme Court. A "writ" is an order from a court requiring a specific act. The term "certiorari" literally means "to be more fully informed." A petition for *a writ of certiorari* is a request to the higher court to review an order (and the supporting record) of a lower court. The *court of last resort* does not have to grant each—or any—of these requests, because this highest of courts is not required to hear every appeal. Rather, the highest court gets to decide, by a vote of the judges on the court, which controversies are important enough, or have generated enough disagreement among the *mid-level appellate courts,* to warrant a resolution by the highest court.

The *court of last resort* in your state, like the U.S. Supreme Court, has specific rules about how many votes of its judges are needed to grant a petition for a *writ of certiorari*.[2]

Remembering that parties need to ask permission to be heard, and that this process has a Latin name, will hopefully help you remember that the highest court has limited *discretionary jurisdiction*.

Another aspect of the three-tier hierarchy to understand is that, for both state and federal courts, different levels of court resolve different types of questions. It is often explained in a black and white way: trial courts decide questions of fact, and appellate courts decide questions of law. Of course, it is not really that simple, but that notion is a good place to start. It's true that at the trial level, questions of fact are decided—either by the jury or a judge sitting without a jury. But there is more to it than that. When a jury will decide the case, for example, the judge, with advice and/or argument of counsel, first prepares jury instructions, which contain an explanation of the law and the factual decisions that have to be made in order to know how to apply the law. In fact, decisions about both law and fact are made at the trial court level, and some decisions involve a mix of both.

Of course it's true that the *mid-level appellate courts*, whether state or federal, decide strictly legal questions, like whether the trial court did, indeed, provide the correct jury instructions, whether the admissibility of evidence was properly decided, or whether the quantity and quality of evidence was sufficient to support the verdict.

At the very highest level, although some of these "mixed law and fact" questions may make it to the top, the questions that successfully make it through the hoops of *discretionary jurisdiction* tend to be more strictly legal. Of course, at the U.S. Supreme Court level, the question is often—but not always—whether a given statute, regulation, or case decision is Constitutional. The Supremes also look at other types of

---

[2]   *See* Supreme Court of the United States, Rules of the Supreme Court of the United States (2017), https://www.supremecourt.gov/filingandrules/2017RulesoftheCourt.pdf (last visited on February 27, 2019).

questions, especially when there is a disagreement among the federal *mid-level appellate courts* as to such matters as the interpretation of a statute, regulation, case decision, or Constitutional provision.

Similarly, for the top courts of states, the questions are also usually more strictly legal. Believe it or not, issues of both federal and state Constitutionality can be litigated in state courts. Remember, we learned in Chapter 2 that there are some areas, including the Constitution, where federal and state courts both have jurisdiction, which is called concurrent jurisdiction.

Understanding the court structure helps us with our research because it helps inform us as to the precedential value of the cases that we find. To assist you in your research, learn the names of the reporters for each level of the federal courts and the courts in your state. Remember, we learned in Chapter 1 that reporters are the books with the cases. Once you know how the citations to each level of court look, and how to distinguish one from the other, you can then easily judge the precedential value of a particular case by looking at the citation.

For example, with many federal court decisions, the parenthetical with the year will also include the abbreviation for the specific district (*trial court* level) or circuit (*mid-level appellate*) court that decided the case. A citation to the Supreme Court, however, will include only the year in the parenthetical. Therefore, the citations would look like this:

District Court citation:

- *Standish et al v. Law School*, 123 F. Supp. 3d 456 (D. Mass. 2016). We see from the reporter—F. Supp., which stands for Federal Supplement—that this is a federal case. We also see from the parenthetical that this case comes from the district court—*trial court*—in Massachusetts, which has only one federal district.

Court of Appeals citation:

- *Standish et al v. Law School*, 789 F.3d 100 (1st Cir. 2018). We see from the reporter—Federal Reporter 3rd Series—

that this is a federal case. We see from the parenthetical that this case comes from the First Circuit Court of Appeals—a *mid-level appellate court* in the federal system.

Supreme Court citation:

• *Standish et al v. Law School*, 101 U.S. 200 (2019). We see from the reporter—U.S.—that this is a federal case, and because the United States Reporter contains only cases from the U.S. Supreme Court, we know that this case is from the United States Supreme Court, the *court of last resort* in the federal system.

You will also find and learn the reporter names and citations for the different levels of courts in your state. That way, you will know which court your case comes from, and therefore, its precedential value.

B. *Precedent* and *Stare Decisis*

One of the reasons we turn to case law when we research is because of the tradition of *stare decisis* that we imported from England. *Stare decisis* literally means "it stands decided," and the term represents the idea that we don't decide cases in a vacuum. Rather, the judiciary looks at past cases and follows such *precedents* whenever possible. This system of relying on *precedent* means that courts don't start from scratch every time they are handed a dispute. General principles of fairness mean that case law should yield fairly consistent and predictable results. Therefore, in the decision-making process, courts always look to past cases addressing the same legal issue to get guidance on how to decide issues.

Though in general all *precedent* has some value, all *precedent* is not created equal. As discussed earlier in this chapter, court decisions can either be *persuasive precedent* or *mandatory* (must follow) *precedent*. You have to consider two things when looking at case law and determining its precedential value:

1.   The level of court it comes from—in general, the higher the court, the more valuable the precedent; and

2.   The jurisdiction, meaning, in this context, not only the geographical area in which the issue is being raised, but also whether you are in state or federal court.

Perhaps it's obvious that when you are researching a legal issue in your state jurisdiction, the cases with the most precedential value will come from the *court of last resort* in YOUR state, not some other state. Just like it's obvious that *precedent* coming from the U.S. Supreme Court is generally *mandatory precedent* for all Constitutional questions.[3] In other words, the top court is the boss.

It's when you are looking at the *mid-level appellate courts*, in either the federal court system or your state court system, that you have to pay special attention to the geographical jurisdiction. The *mid-level appellate court* decisions that have the most precedential value, or are known as *mandatory precedent* that a lower court must follow, are those in your geographical jurisdiction.

For example, let's look first at the federal system and those *mid-level appellate courts* (circuit courts). In the map below, Diagram 6, find your state and the federal circuit in which it is located. The Court of Appeals in that circuit is the *mid-level appellate court* for your jurisdiction. Therefore, if you are researching federal legal issues, the *mandatory precedent* in your jurisdiction will come from your circuit court. Decisions by courts from other circuits are only persuasive authority for your jurisdiction. This concept has a corollary in your state system. Only cases from the *mid-level appellate court* in your jurisdiction are *mandatory precedent*; *mid-level appellate* cases decided by courts outside of your jurisdiction are only *persuasive* for your jurisdiction.[4]

---

[3]   *Marbury v. Madison*, 5 U.S. (1 Cranch) 137 (1803). This is a famous case read in the first year of law school in which the Supreme Court held that it had the power to declare a law unconstitutional (otherwise known as judicial review).

[4]   Note that not all states have mid-level appellate courts. At the time of this writing, 40 of the 50 states had mid-level appellate courts. *See* National Center for State Courts, Appellate

Remember, part of what you learned in Chapter 1 is the importance of the citation, and that a citation almost always includes an indication of the jurisdiction of the court in question—the geographical area in which it exercises power. A citation to a case from a *mid-level appellate court* will include an abbreviation for the court that indicates its geographical jurisdiction. For example, some states may have only one *mid-level appellate court*, and thus one geographical jurisdiction (the whole state) at that level. But highly populated states will have more than one *mid-level appellate court*, each covering a different geographical jurisdiction within the state, and the citation will indicate the specific geographical jurisdiction by referencing a region of the state. For the federal system, as suggested by Diagram 6, the geographical jurisdiction is indicated by, mostly, circuit numbers. Therefore, once you know the citation indicators of the court level for your jurisdiction, you can tell at a glance whether you have found *mandatory* or *persuasive precedent* for your legal issue.

Procedure Resource Guide, https://www.ncsc.org/Topics/Appellate/Appellate-Procedure/Resource-Guide.aspx (last updated March 4, 2019).

Diagram 6:
Map of Federal Circuits for Federal Courts of Appeal

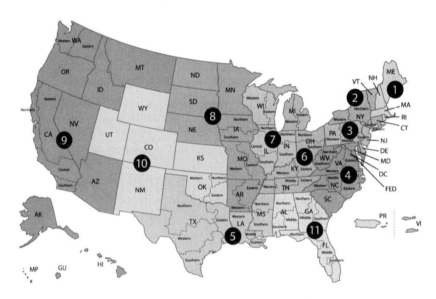

C. Understanding Legal Rules in Case Law

It is easy to focus your legal research on case law, because case law is a treasure trove of legal rules. Essentially, if you can find a relevant case for your legal *issue*, that case will contain at least some of the relevant legal rules and even explain them. Cases are also important because ideally (not always) the court's opinion shows the legal reasoning process. Reading the court's reasoning gives us examples of the types of legal arguments that courts find persuasive.

Relevant case law is potentially a source for three different types of legal rules. First, remember that, in terms of legal rules, we learned in Chapter 1 that there are generally two types of cases in state law: 1) cases that interpret and apply another source of a legal rule, such as a constitution, an administrative regulation, or a statute; and 2) cases that rely on and develop legal rules contained only in case law, which we call judge-made law or common law.

In addition, the case itself—the court's decision in the case, or the case *holding*—is yet another form of legal rule. A case *holding* provides a court's conclusion about how a legal rule applies to a factual situation, and a full statement of the court's *holding* necessarily references the law and the facts.[5]

Let's review here the three different categories of cases so that when you research, you have a better idea of what you are looking at, and you can recognize the three sources of rules available in case law. Since case law is the one area in which we can observe the legal reasoning process—i.e., our judiciary branch applying the law and coming to conclusions—we will carefully examine all three types of legal rules found in case law.

Diagram 7:
Types of Case Law

CASE LAW	
A court's decision on how a legal rule applies to a set of facts	
COMMON LAW	Applies legal rule from past case *State law only
CASE LAW	Applies legal rules from statutes, administrative regulations, or constitutions, as well as case law that likewise applies rules from those sources
CASE *HOLDING*	The decision of a specific court on how the legal rule applies to a set of facts.

1. *Common Law: Judge-Made Law*

According to <u>Black's Law Dictionary</u>, common law is the rules and customs that do not rely whatsoever on the legislature. Some

---

[5]   For practice in recognizing and articulating a case holding, take a look at Chapter 8.

common law dates as far back as English case law that was transported to the colonies.[6] Common law concepts were imported into and adopted by individual states, and state law typically governs the issues that common law deals with (see Chapter 2, Part I). Common law can be either civil or criminal (although most states have codified their criminal law); it is decisional law, or "judge-made law," that relies on prior court decisions. One typical area of civil common law is negligence. Each state has its own, albeit similar, body of law around negligence.[7]

To determine whether the case law you are reading is common law, ask yourself:

1.   Am I reading a state law case?

2.   For the issue you are looking at, does the case SOLELY rely on past court decisions, with no reliance on statutes, regulations, or the Constitution?

If so, then the decision is most likely common law.

Another way to identify whether your case is relying on common law for the issue you are looking at would be to familiarize yourself with the common law topics in your state. (Hint: The idea of the first year of law school education has traditionally been to teach primarily common law subjects—such as contracts, property, and torts—so the law students will get the experience of reading and understanding courts' legal reasoning.)

---

[6]   Black's Law Dictionary defines common law as "The body of law derived from judicial decisions, rather than from statutes or constitutions."

[7]   Although scholars have debated this, *see, e.g.*, Jeffrey A. Pojanowski, Statutes in *Common Law* Courts, 91 Tex. L. Rev. 479 (2015), currently there is not a body of up-to-date federal *common law*. Federal case law applies and interprets federal statutes, the Constitution, and, when dealing with diversity *jurisdiction*, state law. (For a review of federal *jurisdiction*, including diversity *jurisdiction*, see Chapter 2, Section I.A.)

Let's look again at our fictional common law case from Chapter 1:

New York State Mid-level Appellate Court

Phyllis Carr, plaintiff, v. Arlo Buss, Defendant

Opinion.

Memorandum by the Court.

J. Denman, J. Jackson and J. Dillon.

Plaintiff sued for damages for personal injuries suffered as a result of a two-car collision in which the aqua Volkswagen bus owned by the defendant, Arlo Buss, rear-ended plaintiff's red Chevrolet Malibu sedan. The Plaintiff, Phyllis Carr, suffered a broken sternum, whiplash, and various bruising. The accident occurred on May 5th, 2017, on Elmwood Avenue, in Buffalo, New York.

A rear-end collision with a stopped automobile establishes a prima facie case of negligence on the part of the operator of the moving vehicle and imposes a duty on the operator of the moving vehicle to explain how the accident occurred (See <u>Gambino v. City of New York</u>, 205 Official State Reporter 583, 613 Unofficial/Regional State Reporter 417 (1990)).

Here, although the defendant Buss had the duty to explain how he rear-ended the plaintiff in order to avoid the conclusion of his negligence, he was not able to do so. According to the police report, Buss simply told the officer that he was "grooving to the music" and lost track of where he was. In the absence of any reasonable explanation, the rear-ending vehicle is negligent. Therefore, the trial court's grant of summary judgment to the plaintiff, Phyllis Carr, is affirmed.

We can determine that this case is indeed a common law case by answering the instrumental questions.

First question:

1. Is this a state law case? Yes, the *caption* (heading in a legal document that contains the names of parties and the name of the court) indicates that the court is a New York state court—"New York State Mid-level Appellate Court."

Second question:

2.   For the issue you are looking at, does the case SOLELY rely on past court decisions, with no reliance on statutes or the constitution? Yes, the only authority the case relies on is another case—we know this because the citation contains two names (*Gambino v. City of New York*), as well as references to the state reporters.

2. *Other Types of Case Law*

You will also see cases that are applying another type of legal rule—whether it's a statute, an administrative regulation, or a constitution. The courts' interpretation and application of legal rules is important, and you should never go forward with applying a legal rule without checking to see how the courts in your jurisdiction have done so. You always want to be able to say that *precedent* supports your interpretation of a legal rule.

Let's take a look at the same common law case from above, *Carr v. Buss*, with some additions, and see if you can spot the court's reliance on an additional rule.

New York State Mid-level Appellate Court

Phyllis Carr, Plaintiff, v. Arlo Buss, Defendant

Opinion.

Memorandum by the Court.

J. Denman, J. Jackson and J. Dillon.

Plaintiff sued for damages for personal injuries suffered as a result of a two-car collision in which the aqua Volkswagen bus owned by the defendant, Arlo Buss, rear-ended plaintiff's red Chevrolet Malibu. The Plaintiff, Phyllis Carr, suffered a broken sternum, whiplash, and various bruising. The accident occurred on May 5th, 2017, on Elmwood Avenue, in Buffalo, New York.

A rear-end collision with a stopped automobile establishes a prima facie case of negligence on the part of the operator of the moving vehicle and imposes a duty on

the operator of the moving vehicle to explain how the accident occurred (see <u>Gambino</u>
<u>v. City of New York</u>, *205 Official State Reporter 583, 613 Unofficial/Regional*
State Reporter 417 (Mid-Level Appellate Court 1990)).

    Here, although the defendant Buss had the duty to explain how he rear-ended
the plaintiff in order to avoid the conclusion of his negligence, he was not able to do
so. According to the police report, Buss simply told the officer that he was "grooving
to the music" and lost track of where he was. Based on New York Civil Practice
Law and Rules, Rule 3212, after plaintiff made the motion for summary judgment
asking the court for a judgment against the defendant, in order to defeat that motion,
the defendant had to submit proof that he was not negligent. In the absence of any
reasonable explanation, the rear-ending vehicle is negligent.

    Therefore, we hold that due to the defendant's negligence, he is liable to the
plaintiff and the trial court's grant of summary judgment to the plaintiff, Phyllis
Carr, is affirmed.

As you can see, our sample case now has one additional rule in it.
The reference to "New York Civil Practice Law and Rules, Rule 3212"
is a reference to another rule, specifically, a statute that lays out the
procedure for a specific type of *motion*, a summary judgment *motion*. A
motion is a request to a court for something, and a *motion* for summary
judgment is a request to a trial court to make a final decision on an issue
in favor of the *movant*. Whenever a party wants a court to make a
decision or grant some type of relief, the party makes a *motion*, or moves
the court, for the specific relief.

In the above case, the *movant* (party making the *motion*) is the
plaintiff, and she made a *motion* for summary judgment which asked the
court to decide the case in her favor. In other words, she asked the
court to decide that she wins the case, without any need for a trial. She
(the plaintiff, Phyllis Carr) made this *motion* because she was simply in
a stopped car, doing nothing wrong, when she was hit from behind by
someone who was "grooving to the music" AND there is *precedent*
establishing that summary judgment is appropriate. So, in short, in the
above example there are two rules within the case: the common law

rule, and the statutory procedural rule called Civil Practice Law and Rules, Rule 3212.

The application of case law, instead of a procedural rule, might look something like this in our *Carr v. Buss* case:

Based on New York Civil Practice Law and Rules, Rule 3212, after plaintiff made the motion for summary judgment asking the court for a judgment against the defendant, in order to defeat that motion, the defendant had to submit proof that he was not negligent. According to Giulia v. Alfa, 690 Official State Reporter 94, 98 Unofficial/Regional Reporter 18 (Mid-Level Appellate Court 2011), such evidence can consist of sworn testimony that defendant driver was also stopped and rear-ended, which forced the car forward to hit the plaintiff's car. However, here, in the absence of any reasonable explanation, the rear-ending vehicle is negligent.

You should be able to spot the added sentence:

According to Giulia v. Alfa, 690 Official State Reporter 94, 98 Unofficial/Regional Reporter 18 (Mid-Level Appellate Court 2011), such evidence can consist of sworn testimony that defendant driver was also stopped and rear-ended, which forced the car forward to hit the plaintiff's car.

This is an example of the court relying on a case that explained an aspect of a statute, in this case, the type of evidence that defendant could have introduced to meet the requirement of the Civil Practice statute and defeat the summary judgment *motion*. The court is referring to *Giulia v. Alfa* in order to provide a rule and an example of what defendant could have, but did not, do. *Giulia v. Alfa* gives us another legal rule.

When reading case law, you can see many, many rules that the court discusses and relies on. Therefore, when you are researching a legal question, be sure to pay attention to which rules cited by the court are potentially relevant, and be sure to check them out.

3. *Case* Holdings

Finally, the court's *holding* in each case is another source of a legal rule. In both common law cases and other types of case law, the *holding* is the final decision of the court that you are relying on. Therefore, when reading a case, you have to be able to discern when the court is engaged in reasoning and discussing other cases, statutes, or administrative regulations, and when the court is pronouncing its final decision in the case before it. We will work on recognizing and specifically articulating the legally relevant facts and the court's holding in Chapter 8, but let this serve as your introduction to a case *holding*.

A *holding* is a court decision. There can be *holdings* on different issues. There can be substantive *holdings* (who won and who lost), and there can be procedural *holdings* (how did that party win or lose). It can be tricky to fully understand and articulate a *holding*. For now, you should simply remember that the *holding* from each individual case is another form of legal rule.

With our *Carr v. Buss* case, how do you think you would recognize a *holding*?

The first step is simple: does the court clearly announce its *holding*, using the word "hold" or "holding" at the beginning or end of the decision? In *Carr v. Buss*, we see the last sentence of the decision give us a pretty clear statement of the court's *holding*:

> *Therefore, we hold that due to the defendant's negligence, he is liable to the plaintiff and the trial court's grant of summary judgment to the plaintiff, Phyllis Carr, is affirmed.*

The court conveniently tells us *"we hold,"* so we know that what follows is probably the court's *holding*. Since this is the *holding*, this is a rule, and it can then be used in future cases as a legal rule because of our system of relying on precedent.

So, case law can be a source of common law, a source of other primary legal sources, and a source of a rule by itself.

PART II. ADVICE FOR RESEARCH— INVESTIGATING VARIOUS SOURCES OF LAW

As you begin to delve into actual research, you will have to remember the interplay between the different sources of law, and how one event can have results in multiple subject areas of the law (for example, civil and criminal) and multiple sources of the law (for example, statutes and case law, or statutes and regulations). In short, you will have to remember to check multiple sources, and not to quit researching after you found one statute on point, or one case; rather, you will need to continue checking in all sources of law: statutes, administrative regulations, constitutions, and case law.

A. *Separation of Powers*

The need to check different sources of law is a product of our legal system, which has three branches of government responsible for three different sources of law. Remember, the idea of the separation of powers laid out in our U.S. Constitution was for the law-making to be divvied up three ways, so that no one branch of government had all the power. That way, the framers avoided the problems of having a king who made all the decisions.

Another fundamental and related concept in our legal system is the idea of *checks and balances*. Not only is the power divided among three different branches, but each of those branches has a way of "checking" or stopping the power of the other branches. For example, a court (judicial branch) can declare a statute (legislative branch) unconstitutional. If a court (judicial branch) interprets a statute (legislative branch) in a way the legislature did not intend, the legislature can amend or change the statute. The President of the United States (executive branch) can veto a bill (legislative branch), and that veto can be overridden by a 2/3 vote of Congress (legislative branch). The President (executive branch) can issue an Executive Order, but that order can be declared unconstitutional by the courts (judicial branch).

Similarly, an administrative regulation (executive branch), which should be based on a statute, can be found unconstitutional or outside the bounds of the statute (judicial branch). By giving power to each branch to "check" another, the Constitution ensures that there is a balance of power among all three branches.

Diagram 8:
Checks and Balances

BRANCH OF GOVERNMENT	HOW IT CHECKS
LEGISLATURE Passes statutes	Can amend statutes declared unconstitutional Can amend or pass new statutes if it disagrees with court's interpretation
JUDICIARY Interprets and applies all types of legal rules	Can rule executive order is invalid or unconstitutional Can rule a statute is unconstitutional
EXECUTIVE Enforces legal rules Amplifies statutes by promulgating administrative regulation	Can issue executive orders Can veto legislation

Because of the divvied-up power and the power of one branch of government to "check" another, researchers should remember that the sources of law overlap and are interrelated: that is why researchers should check all sources of law. For example, you will see the judiciary branch applying other sources of law, such as statutes, regulations, and a constitution. Similarly, when you get the facts from a client, or a hypothetical from your professor, you should investigate various sources of law for possible solutions.

As you will see in Chapter 4, when using comprehensive subscription databases such as Westlaw or Lexis, your search will bring up multiple sources of law. However, it bears repeating that you should be sure to actually check and read all these sources, and to revise your search process or follow a research trail until you can be sure that you have adequately checked all sources.

B. General Research Strategies to Check All Sources of Law

In thinking about investigating all sources of law, and to accurately answer our three "legal mess" questions from Chapter 2, there are some specific choices you can make that qualify as research strategies. These research strategies will help ensure that you check all interrelated sources.

Check out multiple key word searches: Remember, we learned about key word searches in Chapter 2. Key word searches are searches that include specific terms rather than broad legal concepts (instead of negligence think: rear-end collision, or slip and fall—in other words, how does your case law refer to the cause of action?) and facts that are unique to your problem. It's worth emphasizing here again that the important thing about key word searches in legal research is (1) to make sure your key words include some or all of the legally relevant facts (we will discuss what constitutes a legally relevant fact in the next chapter, Chapter 4), and (2) to try multiple key word searches. We will continue to learn how to refine our key word searches, and how to keep ourselves from JUST doing keyword searches and thinking our research is complete. In Chapter 4, we will review more complex and deliberately strategic searches, including Boolean searches.

Check multiple *jurisdictions:* We learned in Chapter 2 that one of the threshold questions you have to determine is the jurisdiction for your legal issue. Therefore, you have to be mindful when you are using a subscription database and have the option to search multiple jurisdictions. If you are completely new to a legal issue, you could try searching first in your state database; and second in your state PLUS your federal circuit database. Starting with only your state jurisdiction is a way of starting with what is probably a smaller database, which means you will probably be starting with fewer results. In other words, starting with a smaller or more limited jurisdiction means you are starting with a narrower search. The advantage of a narrow search is that you have fewer results, which you can read through in a shorter amount of time. When you know you are doing a narrow search, you should balance this with a wider (yet still relevant) search. One example is adding the federal circuit database to your state search; this is one way of making sure you are not overlooking any federal legal issues.

Take a look at the above circuit map, Diagram 6, to refresh your memory as to what circuit you are in. For example, if you are in California, your state jurisdiction is California, and your federal circuit is the Ninth. Choosing to search your federal circuit jurisdiction means that you will pull up federal cases in your circuit. These federal cases will include cases at the trial level and the federal mid-level court of appeals.

Check out multiple secondary sources: You had your introduction to secondary sources in Chapter 2. As you know, secondary sources provide context, general outlines of legal rules, important vocabulary, and citations to relevant primary and secondary sources. One key strategy with secondary sources is to make sure you read them when you do your background research to answer the "legal mess" questions. Another key strategy, as advised in the end-of-chapter questions, is to try to find the most-relied on or well-known secondary source(s) for the topic that you are researching. Finally, be sure to peruse more than one secondary source, especially as you are learning legal research. For example, for state law questions, you could make it a habit at the start of your legal researching career to always check your state law encyclopedia, and to explore at least one other type of source, such as an expert's treatise aimed at practitioners or a form book.

C. Examples of Inter-Related Sources in Legal Problems

Let's read through some hypotheticals involving multiple sources of law so you can see some examples of how the sources of law interrelate. One thing to note: with subscription databases, your searches will automatically generate results for most primary sources—statutes, administrative regulations, case law, and constitutions—as well as all different types of secondary sources. For example, in both Lexis and Westlaw, on the search results screen there is a sidebar which lists the number of sources in each of those categories for every search. The ease of uncovering all these sources is a wonderful thing. However, it's not really wonderful UNLESS you actually review and read these other sources when they are available to you. For the examples below, remember that secondary sources would likely provide very helpful guidance in each instance.

<u>Example 1</u>: (state criminal law and civil regulations) If Cindy Lou got stopped by a state trooper for speeding, and then the trooper discovered that she had been driving while intoxicated, Cindy Lou most likely would have violated two statutes—the statute requiring a certain speed limit, and the statute forbidding driving while intoxicated.

Let's say, however, that Cindy Lou refused to take a breathalyzer test. She could still be in trouble for violating the speeding statute. But how do you find out if there are any repercussions to refusing the breathalyzer test? You would have to check the relevant driving-while-intoxicated statute. Hopefully, you would have annotated statutes to help, and could look at the helpful "stuff" at the end of the statute, such as cross-references to any applicable regulations, or perhaps some citations to helpful secondary sources. In annotated statutes, you would also have a selection of case citations and blurbs describing the cases, and you could review those for any cases that dealt with a refusal to use the breathalyzer.

If you don't have statutes, annotated or otherwise, you would still have to check the regulations and the case law for refusal of a breathalyzer test. Perhaps it's somewhat obvious that you would check the case law in your jurisdiction, since that is the source of law that could lead you most easily to other applicable sources of law. In addition to developing a habit of checking all three sources of law, you should also be thinking of hints about what sources of law might be involved. For example, since you know that rules about driving come from the Department of Motor Vehicles, which is an agency, then you should also suspect that there could be administrative regulations from that same agency that would apply to bad behavior while driving—like driving while intoxicated.

Therefore, for a speeding violation and refusal to submit to a breathalyzer test, you would check state statutes, case law, and administrative regulations.

Example 2: (federal and state employment statutes, regulations, case law, and state criminal law) What if Evan, a manager, had a highly unfortunate tendency to physically assault (push, shove, and hit) women colleagues at work and then dock their pay or refuse to promote them if they complained?

For starters, the word "assault" probably triggers the idea of criminal law, so you would check state criminal law, which is usually codified, so that means state statutes. Then, because there are employment consequences, you would check both federal and state employment law—statutes, administrative regulations, and case law. Although initially you might not know that there could be overlapping discrimination statutes in both state and federal law, if you followed the research strategy above of including both your state and your federal circuit in your database, you would quickly discover references to both state and federal employment statutes. The statutes and case law would reference regulations that lay out the administrative process an employment discrimination plaintiff must go through.

Therefore, for a workplace assault, you would check state and federal employment statutes; case law interpreting, and regulations implementing, those statutes; and state law for criminal assault.

Example 3: (state common law and possibly state statutes and administrative regulations) Suppose Juan tripped on one of the outdoor stairs of his friend's apartment building and fell, breaking his leg. Suppose that the steps of the staircase had not been repaired and were unevenly spaced. Suppose also that the landlord that owns the apartment building, Oliver Hazard III, knew that two other visitors had tripped on the same step.

Since you already know that negligence is a state common law topic, you could research your state common law to find examples of liability in cases such as Juan's. Your key word search might include fall, steps, and injury. After looking at some of the cases, you might notice (in some states) references to state statutes and regulations that spell out details about the landlord's duty, including details about steps and staircase construction.

CHAPTER 3 LEGAL SKILLS

- **Recognize which court rulings are authoritative**
- **Identify different types of case law (*common law* cases vs. cases applying other sources of law)**
- **Demonstrate understanding that multiple sources of law may be necessary to solve a problem**
- **Demonstrate understanding that legal sources can be interrelated**

CHAPTER 3 VOCABULARY

- Appellate court
- Caption
- Checks and balances
- Circuit
- Citation
- Court of last resort
- Discretionary jurisdiction
- Dispositive motion

- Geographic jurisdiction
- Holding
- Mandatory precedent
- Mid-level appellate court
- Motion
- Movant
- Original jurisdiction
- Persuasive precedent
- Precedent
- Precedential value
- Separation of powers
- Stare decisis
- Subject matter jurisdiction
- Summary judgment motion
- Trial court
- Writ of certiorari

CHAPTER 3 RESEARCH AND ANALYSIS EXERCISES

I. Investigating your state jurisdiction:*

To help you identify and become familiar with the different courts in your state and federal jurisdiction, find the following with the help of your professor:

1.   A map of your state's appellate jurisdictions, if more than one, and, if this exists for your state, a map of your state's trial court jurisdictions.

2.   Based on the above map(s), draw a triangle (or vertical flow chart) of your state's court system which identifies the trial court, the mid-level appellate court, and the highest court in the state for your specific jurisdiction.

---

*   Can be done in-class as a group if there are computers and internet access.

a. For the trial court in your jurisdiction, which appellate courts issue mandatory precedent? (Hint: Remember that there are usually two levels of court above the trial court).

b. For the trial court in your jurisdiction, which appellate court(s) issue(s) persuasive precedent?

c. What is the name of the court of last resort in your state, and what type of precedent does it issue with respect to state law issues?

II. Now, do the same with Feds:*

1. Locate the map in this chapter of the federal circuits (Diagram 6).

2. Based on the above map, draw a triangle (or vertical flow chart) of your jurisdiction's federal court system which identifies the trial court, the circuit court number, and the highest federal court in the United States for your specific jurisdiction.

a. For the federal district court in your jurisdiction, which federal circuit issues mandatory precedent?

b. For the federal district court in your jurisdiction, which federal circuits issue persuasive precedent?

c. What is the name of the court of last resort in the federal system?

d. Within the federal system, which court has the final say (i.e., issues mandatory precedent) with respect to federal issues and with respect to district and circuit court decisions?

III. Investigating the interrelationships between primary sources:

To help you understand how different sources of law interrelate and overlap, and to reinforce how important it is to check all your sources of law when doing research, work on the following:

1. Find a simple criminal statute in your state that interests you. Be sure to look in the annotated code. If your state's statutes are not

---

* Can be done in-class as a group if there are computers and internet access.

annotated, then look in the annotated code for the United States statutes: United States Code Annotated (U.S.C.A.).

a.   Note the collection of decisions that follows the annotated statute, typically organized by topic, and choose a decision that interests you.

b.   Write a paragraph that describes the relationship between the case and the statute. Consider some of the following questions: which came first, the case or the statute? Does the case assist in your interpretation of the statute, and why or why not?

2.   Review the list of subjects for your state's administrative regulations. Choose an area that interests you; then choose a simple regulation. Review the regulation carefully to identify the authorizing statute.

a.   Review the authorizing statute, and briefly summarize the purpose of the statute.

b.   Describe how you identified the authorizing statute. How was it referenced? Where was it located in relation to the regulation? What was the citation?

c.   Review and summarize the administrative regulation you identified (Hint: most agencies have a web page for the public.)

d.   Write a short paragraph explaining the relationship between the statute and the regulation.

3.   Let's say you live in a state that has a specific state statute, enacted in 1985, that states the following:

State Code § 100 (Warren 1985): It shall be against the law in this state to burn any size of an official American flag. This section does not apply to replicas of the American flag in the form of clothing.

Your firm's client, Sam Jackson, was arrested when he was burning an American flag at a beach bonfire. Your supervising attorney, Juan Alden, has asked you to do some preliminary research to determine the following. Write a paragraph for each question explaining your answer:

a.   Do we have any argument that the statute is not valid? For example, is this statute Constitutional?

b.   Can we argue that Sam was simply disposing of a worn and tattered flag in a respectful way? For example, is there any federal law on the proper way to dispose of an American flag?

4.   Your supervising attorney Ashley Fuller has been asked to pinch hit for a friend, now on maternity leave, who had agreed to develop a presentation on pregnancy discrimination law for the local bar association. Ashley does mostly commercial litigation, so she has asked you to spend several hours gathering some basic information on pregnancy discrimination law. Ashley wants you to get started by asking the following questions. Write a paragraph for each question explaining what you have found:

a.   What is the case holding and citation for the U.S. Supreme Court case *General Electric Company v. Gilbert*? (Hint: for a review of case briefing and identifying substantive case holdings, see Chapter 8.)

b.   When and why did Congress amend Title VII, the federal anti-discrimination statute, to include the Pregnancy Discrimination Act? (Hint: try using your internet search engine to get some background on how to answer the question; then, to find the amending statute and when it was passed, look at the "Credits" at the end of the annotated statute.)

c.   Have there been any U.S. Supreme Court cases in the last 10 years that have dealt with the issue of pregnancy discrimination?

d.   Identify two (2) law review or journal articles that would be helpful in understanding the development of federal law in the area of pregnancy discrimination, and briefly explain why.

IV. Understanding mandatory versus persuasive precedent:

To help you understand that whether precedent is mandatory versus persuasive depends on level of court and jurisdiction, and to help you remember that federal courts are experts in federal law and state courts are experts in state law, work on the following:

1. **State:**

a.   Identify the name of the mid-level appellate court and the top court in your state whose decisions would supply mandatory precedent for the state trial courts.

b.   Identify the name of any mid-level appellate court in your state whose decisions would supply persuasive precedent for a trial court of your choice in the state.

>   i.   If you only have one mid-level appellate court in your state, identify a different source of persuasive precedent for the trial court of your choice.

>   ii.   Identify a source of persuasive precedent that the trial court in your jurisdiction has explicitly relied on. List both the trial court decision and the persuasive precedent.

c.   Find two (2) cases that would provide **mandatory precedent** for the trial court you have chosen and that outline the elements of the intentional tort of assault and battery.

d.   Find two (2) cases that would provide **persuasive precedent** for the trial court you have chosen and that outline the elements of the intentional tort of assault and battery.

2. **Federal:**

a.   Identify the federal district court in your geographic jurisdiction and the federal circuit in which it is found.

b.   Find a recent case from your circuit explaining the statute of limitations for filing a claim of employment discrimination with the Equal Employment Opportunity Commission.

>   i.   Check to make sure the case is still good law on this topic.

>   ii.   Is this mandatory or persuasive precedent for the federal district court in your jurisdiction?

c.   Find a recent case from another circuit of your choice or a neighboring circuit on the same issue.

    i.   Check to make sure the case is still good law on this topic.

    ii.   Is this mandatory or persuasive precedent for the federal district court in your jurisdiction?

3.   **Mixed federal and state law:**

a.   Federal holdings on state negligence law (automobile accidents): Your supervising attorney in the general practice firm that you work for has a meeting with a prospective client in the hospital tomorrow. The client has reported that he was injured in a car accident caused when some large logs fell off of a commercial truck right in front of his car when he was driving on the interstate.

    i.   Find a case from the mid-level appellate court in your jurisdiction that provides the common law rule on a truck driver's duty to secure cargo safely.

    ii.   What kind of precedent is this? Mandatory or persuasive?

    iii.   Find a case from the federal district court in your jurisdiction that provides the common law rule on a truck driver's duty to secure cargo safely.

    iv.   What kind of precedent is this? Mandatory or persuasive?

    v.   In doing this research, did you come across any federal rules? Cite and explain.

b.   State holdings on federal law (First Amendment): Your supervising attorney was contacted by the principal of a local public high school who wants to know whether there is any legal authority to support stopping a planned protest at the high school over gun control in which students in favor of greater gun control plan to wear black armbands. The supervising attorney wants you to help him get a head start on figuring out whether the First Amendment allows the principal to stop the protest.

    i.   Find a U.S. Supreme Court case on public school protests where students wore black armbands.

    ii.   What kind of precedent is this for your state? Mandatory or persuasive?

    iii.   Find a case from the top court in your state that is applicable—either on protests in public high schools and the First Amendment, or with facts that are analogous or similar.

    iv.   What kind of precedent is this? Mandatory or persuasive?

    v.   Which source of law would you prioritize in your legal analysis?

    vi.   What jurisdiction would you search for additional recent cases that further interpreted and applied the First Amendment in the context of public school protests? Be specific about whether you would look in state or federal, or both, and what level of court you would be looking for.

V.   Researching ethical issues:

    1.   Complaints about a lawyer's representation: Your supervising attorney heard through the grapevine that one of her clients was unhappy with her because, he claimed, she was not returning his calls. Apparently, the client stated he was "going to write a letter to the authorities." Your supervising attorney wants to be prepared and asks you to research to whom the letter would be sent. The attorney vaguely remembers from law school that it might be the bar association, but it might be an agency of an appellate court, or it might be another authority. The questions you should research are:

a.   Which organization(s) or governmental body in your jurisdiction has the authority and role to review client complaints about dissatisfaction with attorney representation?

b.   What actions can those bodies take in response to a complaint?

c.   Is there a primary source of law in your state that governs attorney and client relationships and communication? If so, summarize the main idea from the specific relevant part of the primary source and explain whether this rule could apply if indeed the attorney was not returning the client's calls. (Hint: remember that some sources have a table of contents and/or an index.)

Finding the Legal Rule

Legal Skills:

- Find and identify the applicable legal rule
- Identify the *elements* of a legal rule
- Identify the *legally relevant facts*
- Employ a variety of search strategies
- Ensure that the applicable legal rule is still good law

In Chapter 1, you were introduced to the basic nature of a legal rule: <u>if</u> this, <u>then</u> that. You were also introduced to elements—the components of a rule that must be fulfilled in order to apply the rule. Here, we will build on that foundation, as well as the legal research foundation in Chapters 2 and 3, where you learned introductory fundamentals for how to begin legal research, including identifying the legal context by using the "legal mess" questions, identifying the most authoritative rule from the court system, and checking for rules in a variety of primary sources. Remember that focusing on the elements of the rule will help you focus on which facts are relevant. Understanding which facts are relevant to your legal analysis is a key part of legal research and analysis.

When deciding whether a legal rule you have found is applicable, you will have to identify the elements of the rule and make sure your facts fit the elements of the rule. This chapter will further guide you on various strategies when looking for legal rules, identifying their elements, and identifying the corresponding facts. When facts pertain to a specific element of a rule, then the *facts* are *legally relevant*. If you are not sure whether the facts pertain to the legal rule, ask yourself: would it make a difference in fulfilling the element if the facts were different? If it would, then the *facts* are usually *legally relevant*. If you find a rule and none of your facts pertain to any of the elements, you have found the wrong rule. So, finding the applicable rule means carefully looking at and remembering your facts.

One helpful tool is to envision the rule with its different parts—*elements*—lined up with different facts, as in Diagram 9.

Diagram 9:
Rule with Elements and *Legally Relevant Facts*

RULE		
Element 1	Element 2	Element 3
Legally relevant facts for Element 1	*Legally relevant facts* for Element 2	*Legally relevant facts* for Element 3

This diagram shows that your facts have to fit into one of the rule's elements; if you can't draw a diagram where at least *some* of the facts line up with the elements, then you should question whether you have found the correct rule.

PART I. ELEMENTS OF THE RULE, ISSUES, AND THE *LEGALLY RELEVANT FACTS*

So, when you start looking for the legal rule, how will you know when you have found it? In other words, how do you recognize the legal rule as the right one?

First, you have to look for the legal rule that helps you resolve your issue. Remember, in Chapter 2 we learned that an issue is defined as whether a legal rule is met. Now we will see how a legal issue can be narrower, because it can pertain to a specific element in a legal rule.

You will also see how finding a rule may reveal that there are actually multiple issues to be resolved. You discover issues when you are taking that first step of legal analysis and fitting the facts to the elements—and you see where the question(s) are. (See Diagram 9 above).

The concept of an issue is an important part of our legal vocabulary. An issue is a question of mixed law and fact. In other words, it's when we have a question about whether certain facts fulfill one of the elements in our rule. In any given fact situation, there can be an issue for one of the elements of the rule, or an issue for multiple elements. By keeping track of the rule's elements, and the facts that are relevant to each element, you will also keep track of your issues. Articulating and identifying issues is discussed more in depth in Chapter 6.

For example, look again at the common burglary statute that we used in Chapter 1: *[A person is guilty of burglary in the third degree] when he knowingly enters or remains unlawfully in a building with the intent to commit a crime therein. State Code § 111.222 (1980).*

The first part, in brackets, specifies the crime; the rest of the statute spells out how that crime is fulfilled. The *elements* that must be fulfilled for the crime of burglary in the third degree to occur are:

1) **(a) knowingly enters; OR (b) remains unlawfully;**

2) **in building;**

3) **intent to commit a crime therein.**

Keep track of these elements to prevent confusion, and that will provide the foundation for a clear and complete analysis.

For example, what if the question is whether Franklin committed burglary in the third degree when he purposefully entered a gazebo because he intended to steal the picnic table in the gazebo? Using the above list of elements, here is a visual depiction of how we would decide which element would be at issue:

Diagram 10:

Example Showing Rule with Elements and *Legally Relevant Facts*

RULE		
Element 1 **Knowingly Enters OR Remains Unlawfully**	**Element 2** **Building**	**Element 3** **Intent to Commit a Crime Therein**
Legally relevant facts According to the question, Franklin was "purposeful"	*Legally relevant facts* Is a gazebo a "building"? Is this the issue? On one hand, it is a structure with a roof, but on the other hand, it does not have walls, could be characterized as decorative, and could be impermanent	*Legally relevant facts* Franklin "intended to steal a picnic table" that was located in the gazebo

If all the elements are met, then Franklin would be guilty of third degree burglary. If even one element is not fulfilled, then he did not satisfy the elements of this crime and he cannot be guilty. Because there is an issue in this case about whether the gazebo qualifies as a "building" under the statute, it would be hard to say whether Franklin is guilty of the crime.

The way you would resolve this issue is to perform legal research to look for precedent in which courts have defined that same element at issue, as well as any other instances in which a court in the relevant jurisdiction may have resolved the same question about a gazebo or a similar sort of structure.

SKILLS DEVELOPMENT

Steps for Identifying Elements and Legally Relevant Facts

Step 1: Set out (writing or typing) the complete rule.

Step 2: Identify the elements by parsing out the minimum number of words that can be met by a fact; when in doubt—more elements are better than fewer elements.

Step 3: Develop a chart showing each separate element so you can line up the potentially relevant facts.

Step 4: List the applicable facts under each element.

Step 5: Look for confirmation of how you divided the rule as you research—do you see case law that discusses a different or more narrow element? Be open to revising elements as you research.

By looking at the facts in light of each element, you can easily identify where you have a legal issue. And, if you see that at least one of the elements is fulfilled by the facts, then you know you have a relevant legal rule that applies to your situation. (Remember, as discussed in Chapter 3, there can be more than one legal rule that applies, and those multiple legal rules can come from multiple sources of law.)

But what if your facts (note: in legal education and practice, we might call the "facts" a fact situation, factual situation, fact pattern, or hypothetical) about burglary were different: instead of having a man named Franklin and a gazebo, you have two children named Claudia and Jamie who decide to run away from home and skip school to take the train from their suburb to New York City so they can visit the Metropolitan Museum of Art. The children plan on—and do—live in the museum for a few nights.

In the famous story and children's book by E.L. Konigsburg, From the Mixed-Up Files of Mrs. Basil E. Frankweiler (Athenaeum 1967), that's exactly what happens. Claudia and Jamie spend several nights in the museum by hiding in the bathroom during closing time, bathing in the fountain, and finally, sleeping in an antique bed in one of the exhibits. What crime, if any, have they committed? Are they guilty of violating the burglary statute above? (Please assume for the sake of the problem that the children are old enough to be charged with such a violation).

Let's apply the burglary statute element by element:

1. (a) Did Claudia and Jamie **knowingly enter** or,

    (b) **Unlawfully remain** in the Metropolitan Museum of Art?

From our facts above, we know that Claudia and Jamie purposefully went into the museum, and therefore *knowingly entered*. Unlike Franklin entering someone else's gazebo, it is not a crime for Claudia and Jamie to enter the Metropolitan Museum of Art—at least as long as the Museum is open. However, as you can imagine, staying overnight at the Museum is not okay, or legal, and therefore Claudia and Jamie have **unlawfully remained** (fulfilling the first element).

2. Did the children enter or remain in a **building**?

It seems clear that the Metropolitan Museum of Art would qualify as a building. In fact, it's a very large building that takes up several city blocks. Of course, an art museum is much different than an outdoor gazebo because it is large, has walls, has multiple rooms, and is built to last.

And finally, for the third and last element:

3. Did Claudia and Jamie have the **intent to commit a crime**?

Here, according to the facts recited above, we don't actually have any evidence of the children's intent to commit a crime. Unlike Franklin and the gazebo, the facts do not indicate that Claudia and Jamie intended to steal anything. Without satisfying this last element, if the children committed a crime, it is not this one, the crime of burglary. Perhaps the crime of trespassing would match, but not the crime of burglary that we are working with.

So you have seen an example of a fact pattern (Franklin and the gazebo) in which there is an issue based on one of the elements, and a fact pattern (the children and the museum) in which one of the elements is simply not met.

Here is another fact pattern in which all of the elements are met, but which might provoke a tendency for us to "add" another element (even though we are not the legislature and we can't really amend a statute just because we want to).

Consider the oft-used hypothetical statute:[1]

It is unlawful for any person to sleep in the picnic area of a state-owned park. N.Y. Penal Law § 1420 (McKinney's 1992) (this is a hypothetical citation, too).

First, the elements: **1) person 2) sleep 3) picnic area and 4) state-owned park.** Then the fact pattern: what if Mark Savage, a local bank employee, walked to New York State Park, Beaver Island, one summer day during his lunch hour. He sat down at a picnic table in one of the park's picnic areas, ate his bag lunch, and then promptly put his head down on the table and took a nap. When he was arrested, Mark told the policeman that he didn't "mean" to sleep, he just got drowsy after eating his pastrami sandwich because he was sitting in the sun.

Has Mark violated the hypothetical statute? Let's see:

1) **Person:** He is certainly a person.

2) **Sleep:** According to our facts, he did sleep.

3) **Picnic area:** Again, according to our facts, he slept in a picnic area.

4) **State-owned Park:** Mark Savage slept in the New York State Park, Beaver Island.

Therefore, Mark violated the statute. Because the act of Mark's lunchtime snooze seems harmless, you might be inclined to argue that

---

[1] This hypothetical was developed by Laurel Oates, J.D. and Professor of Law at University of Seattle School of Law. Many thanks to her for allowing its use.

he shouldn't be liable for violating this statute—**because he didn't really mean to do so!**

However, nowhere in the statute is there a requirement for intent. There are some minor crimes that have developed as protection for the public, or for public resources, that do not require intent.[2] Therefore, that fact—that Mark didn't intend to take a nap in the park—doesn't come in to the legal analysis. An attorney representing him could argue the equities (i.e., fairness) in court, and could certainly do research to see if this statute had ever been applied to bankers taking noonday naps in broad daylight. An attorney might even do research to uncover the legislative intent behind the statute to see if there is any evidence that it was aimed at a much different event than Mark's nap. Indeed, it seems likely that the statute was not intended to cover naps in the afternoon.

But the fact remains that Mark still technically violated the statute. This is just one of many examples when a student might want to argue about a fact although it is not legally relevant because there is no element that requires intent. As a student of legal analysis, though, you need to stick to the elements of your legal rule.

Now that you know you need to think about the rule in terms of the elements and whether the elements apply to your factual situation, hopefully you can better recognize an applicable rule. Of course, some rules will have many more elements, such as a statute with multiple sub-parts and definitions. But the key is knowing that you need to focus in on the elements of the statute to see whether it applies to your fact pattern.

---

[2] William J. Sloan, The Development of Crimes Requiring No Criminal Intent, 26 Marquette L. Rev. 92 (1942) (explaining the evolution of crimes without intent, such as criminal nuisance, as an extension of police power to protect the public).

PART II. FINDING THE APPLICABLE LEGAL RULE: A MORE IN-DEPTH LOOK AT RESEARCH STRATEGIES

Research is a recursive process, which means there are multiple steps or layers to work through. As you learn new information about how the law might potentially apply to your facts, you can use the additional information to inform, and perhaps revise, your searches. You have already learned some fundamental concepts to keep in mind during the research process. In Chapter 2 you were introduced to the concepts of jurisdiction, subject matter, key word searches, and secondary sources; in Chapter 3 you were introduced to the concept of the inter-relationships among the various sources, and the importance of conducting multiple key word searches, searching multiple jurisdictions, and reading multiple secondary sources.

Here, we will put that foundation together with specific strategies for using databases. You will learn the role that the *legally relevant facts* play in your searches and how to integrate some of the earlier concepts you have learned with the functions of Lexis and Westlaw. You will also learn how to compare and contrast the multiple and inter-related legal sources that you may find, and how to rank their authority with respect to one another.

One of the most important additional concepts we will discuss here is the date of the source and the importance of the date in determining the validity, or correctness, of the source. You should ALWAYS be looking at the date of your legal source. A source can still be valid if it's 25 years old, but that validity must be tested against other sources and against the *updating* functions of your database. Both Lexis and Westlaw have great *updating* functions. On Lexis this function is called *Shepardizing*, a service that tells you whether the legal source is still valid (that is, whether it has been overruled, replaced, or preempted) as well as ALL the other legal sources that have cited to your source. On Westlaw this function is called *KeyCite*, and it provides basically the same information.

Paying attention to the date can also highlight any issues regarding the primacy, or priority, of sources. If there are multiple sources of law on an issue, with multiple different dates, make sure you take note of the source with the most recent date. In other words, consider the date of the source when considering the value of its authority. For example, if there is case law on a certain issue, but the legislature subsequently passed a statute <u>on that same issue</u> and there is a conflict between the two, then the statute probably takes priority—in other words, officially preempts—the prior case law.

Remember, too, that you have the roadmap from Chapter 2: the "Sorting out the Legal Mess" questions. So as you begin to incorporate some of these strategies into your research, remember that you always have a direction for figuring out the context—the three "Legal Mess" questions, which are: 1) Where Am I?, 2) Whose Law Governs?, and 3) Which Courthouse Will I Go to? Keeping focused on these questions, and using them as a guide, should help prevent you from getting lost on a tangent (although tangents, especially for beginning legal researchers, are probably inevitable.)

Finally, unlike other textbooks, we have not included screenshots of Lexis and Westlaw, since the formatting and even the name of the tools on those databases evolve quickly. Focus here on the concepts and the general vocabulary of certain functions (like filters, databases, fields, *Boolean* searches, and advanced searches) that exist in both databases and serve to make them so sophisticated. Other free legal databases may not have all those functions, but at the very least, you should know what they are and look for them.

A. More on Constructing Searches

Here is a more comprehensive discussion of various search strategies, including the fundamental awareness of whether your search is narrow or broad, and experimenting with both on any given research question.

Key Word Searching: You already know that key word searching is simply entering key words and concepts into the search bar of your database. You also know that one key word search cannot be your only search method. What you may not know is the importance of using facts in your searches.

As you are constructing various key word searches, you may not know what the *legally relevant facts* are because you have not yet found the applicable rule and identified the elements. Indeed, for us to KNOW that a fact is relevant, we not only have to identify the rule, but we also have to identify the elements of the rule. So it is a little bit of a chicken and egg dilemma. However, at the outset, you should explore using various combinations of the facts provided, all with the "Legal Mess" questions as your guide.

One of the key concepts to think about as you construct various word searches is the idea of broad versus narrow searches. You should be performing BOTH broad and narrow key word searches—although as a beginner researcher you might not know which of your searches is broad and which is narrow.

Here are some ways to tell the difference. Usually, a broad search will pull up lots of results, while a narrow search will put up fewer. A broad search might use a basic but large legal concept like negligence, while a narrower search might use a specific theory under negligence, like slip and fall. Similarly, a broad search may use a vague or general fact, like "fall" or "accident," while a more narrow search might use more specific characteristics about the event, such as "unshoveled walkway," "snow fall," or "slippery." A search that is too broad will give you too many results to review, while a search that is too narrow might not give you enough. You should play around with various searches so you can compare the different types of results that you get, and use the variety of results as a tool to hone in on which facts are most relevant, even legally relevant, as well as the key words for the legal theory.

Using *citations*/"The One Good Case" method: One easy technique: if you are lucky enough to have the *citation* to a relevant statute, regulation, or case, then search by *citation*. Simply type the *citation* in your search bar, and voila! You have the source. For many sources, you can also do this on your internet search engine, since so many legal sources are available online.

If you don't know the entire *citation*, or if you don't know how to put your source into *citation* format, both Lexis and Westlaw have a "Find" or "Locate" function which provides a template that you can fill in to get to your source.

Additionally, if you know you have one relevant case, use this as the start of your research trail. After you have used the *citation* to pull up the case itself, you should: 1) read all the relevant primary and secondary authority cited in that relevant case that is relevant to your issue; 2) check the history of that case to make sure it is still current (to be discussed in more depth below); and finally, 3) read the *citation* references, that is, each and every time that source has been cited.

Following the trail of "one good case," is a great approach to a thorough research job.

Paying attention to *filters* and *databases*: Searching on sophisticated *databases* like Westlaw and Lexis is much more than constructing a word search. At the outset, you are also selecting databases. You can select specific databases for your jurisdiction, or for the type of legal source you are looking for—cases, statutes, regulations, or secondary sources, as well as forms, briefs, trial court orders, and *key numbers*. The phrase *key numbers* refers to the West digest system, which is a topical index system for case law addressed below. It can only be searched in Westlaw (although Lexis has its own topical index system).

You can also select databases in order to choose your jurisdiction—a broad jurisdictional database, like all federal and state sources, or a narrower jurisdictional database, such as just your state, or something in-between, such as your state and the federal decisions from your state. You know the importance of geographic jurisdiction, as well as the importance of the court level when it comes to determining the mandatory versus persuasive nature of precedent, so you know how important it is to pay attention to jurisdiction.

Once you have results, you can use *filters* to make your search narrower. You can *filter* for jurisdiction (for example, searching specific appellate jurisdictions) or you can use the filters to do specific word searches within a list of results.

As you are learning Westlaw and Lexis, be sure to experiment with database selections and with filtering search results so that you are comfortable with these tools.

Advanced Searching: Mr. *Boolean* and His Friends:

Turns out there really was someone named Mr. *Boolean* (1815–1864). George Boole was a famous mathematician and logician. Today, we use the word "*Boolean*" to refer to a shorthand developed for specific types of logical searches. *Boolean* searches use an easy-to-understand "code" to tell a database how to search for terms. But you do not have to know the code. Both Westlaw and Lexis have made *Boolean* searching easy for you by setting up a function called "Advanced Search" which develops the proper code connectors and prompts for the type of search you want to do. All you have to do is put your search terms in the appropriate boxes on the screen, and the advanced search function is already programmed to perform the corresponding *Boolean* search.

Whether you use the Advanced Search function or develop your own search, you should at least know some of the basic prompts and connectors behind *Boolean* searching:

- " "—paired quotation marks around a word or phrase instruct the system to search for sources in the database you have selected that contain the exact word or phrase found between the marks;

- /s—when placed between words, it is an instruction to search for items "in the same sentence." So the search **Boolean /s code** tells the system to search for sources in the database you have selected in which *"Boolean"* appears in the same sentence as "code."

- /p—when placed between words, it is an instruction to search for items "in the same paragraph." So the search **Boolean /p code** tells the system to search for sources in the database you have selected in which *"Boolean"* appears in the same paragraph as "code."

- !—The exclamation point symbol, when added at the end of a group of letters (a root word), is an instruction to search for that root word with all of its endings. So the search **"talk!"** tells the system to search in the database you have selected for sources that include not only the word "talk," but also talks, talking, talked, etc.

- Additional prompts and connectors allow you to give the system additional search instructions, such as to exclude sources that contain a word or phrase or to search for words found within a certain number of words of another word.

Field or *segment searching* is also a type of advanced search strategy. The term *field* just refers to different sections (or segments) of the type of document (source) you are looking for, such as heading, title, date, or case synopsis. Designating a specific *field* to search is a way of narrowing your search.

Here is a visual summary of search strategies:

Diagram 11:
Search Strategies

CONSTRUCTING SEARCHES	
REMEMBER:	Key Word Searches
	One good case
	Filters for jurisdiction
	Mr. *Boolean* and *Advanced* Searches

B. Sifting Through the "Lists": A "Print" Research Method That Can Be Done Online or with Books—but Which Should Definitely Be Done

When researching, there are many ways you can take advantage of other people's work in a completely ethical way. This saves you time and effort, and prevents you from getting lost in the weeds. The "sifting" approach is simply an approach that involves looking at other people's "lists"—relevant information as compiled by legal research attorneys and editors. Who wouldn't want to look at information that experts have decided is closely related?

These lists can come in a variety of shapes and sizes, and depend largely on the source of law you are looking at. Your discerning review of lists for material related to or relevant to your source is what many attorneys think of as "real" legal research. (When word searches were not reliable or available, back in the age of the books, this is what many law students and new attorneys had to do to learn their area of law and find their relevant topic). There are three different kinds of lists for legal sources:

1) a general listing of the legal topics covered by the source, in alphabetical order;

2) a detailed *table of contents* for the source; and finally,

3) the list at the end of the source—the index.

The *index* is always used when doing book research, but should likewise be considered when using a legal database.

Diagram 12:
Lists to Look at When You Research

LISTS		
LOCATION	SOURCES FOUND IN	TYPE OF LIST
Beginning	Statutes Case digests	List of legal topics
Right after the beginning	Statutes Administrative regulations	Table of Contents
At the end	Case digests Statutes Administrative regulations	Index

List 1: At the Beginning—List of Legal Subjects Covered by the Source

The first and most simple type of list we see, for statutes and case law, is a straightforward list of the legal topics covered, in alphabetical order. Such lists can be found at the start of a set of books or a database. In addition, if you are looking at the books in alphabetical order on a shelf in the library, the book spines will tell you which topics are covered in each book in the set.

For example, in New York statutes, the list of substantive areas covered starts with "Abandoned Property Law" and ends with "Workers Compensation." In the federal statutes, there are 54 titles, with Title 1 (after the Constitution) being "General Provisions," followed by a list of 52 topics, mostly in alphabetical order, that ends with Title 52, "Voting and Elections," and the most recently added title, Title 54, the "National Park Service and Related Programs."[3] The lists found in statutes would be of limited help to new legal thinkers, as these students of the law may not have the necessary context to recognize the relevant topic.

There exist similar lists in case *digests*. Case *digests* are essentially a subject-matter *index* of the U.S. system of case law (discussed thoroughly below in Section D). The cases themselves are published in chronological order in each jurisdiction, so it would be impossible to find cases on a specific topic without a subject-matter index. The West case *digest* system is based on an alphabetical outline of over 400 legal topics that is used to organize all case *digests* published by West.

The case *digest* list is the same regardless of jurisdiction, beginning with Abandoned and Lost Property and ending with Zoning and Planning. Again, although perhaps this list will not always be helpful to new researchers, there will be some research problems that you have, like ones in negligence, and you will easily be able to find the matching legal topic—negligence. In addition, making sure you check the list—and checking it twice!—will help provide you with context, knowledge, and ideas for future research projects.

List 2: Right After the Beginning—the *Table of Contents*

At the beginning of most publications, there is a *table of contents*. Legal sources are no different. Statutes, regulations, and case *digests* all have *tables of contents*.

Typically, each statutory or regulatory scheme will start off with an outline of all the statutory or regulatory sections in that scheme, and that outline is the *table of contents*. In most legal databases, there is a "clickable" tab that will bring you to the *table of contents* for any statutory section you are looking at. Depending on the complexity of the administrative regulation or statute, the *table of contents* can be pages

---

[3]   Title 53 is being held in reserve for future use.

long, or simply a few lines long. Even if you think you need to look at only one particular statute or regulation, you should make a habit of checking the *table of contents* to see if there are equally applicable sections either before or after the section you are looking at. Again— perseverance and gathering information for context is critical when you are researching. By looking at the *table of contents*, you get a sense of the entire statute and may discover other sections that might relate to the section you are working on.

If the statute is annotated, there will be a collection of explanatory notes, including cross-references to other legal sources, after each statutory section or after the entire statute. Then you will have lots more lists to look at. And make sure you do. You can look at lists of secondary sources, but also at case "blurbs" (quick summary paragraphs) that editors have picked out as relevant to the statute's application and interpretation. This list of case blurbs is usually organized by topic, and could be called "*Notes of Decisions*" or "Cases" or "Decisions." It might have its own table of contents.

Because the Tables of Contents provide so much information about related topics, you should get into the habit of checking every table of contents you can.

List 3: At the End—Everything Has an *Index*

Finally, remember the *index*. Surely you have used an *index* before—in a cookbook? A textbook? Your grade school encyclopedia? Some *indices* (plural form of "*index*") are better than others. In legal research, the *index* for many of the sources is pretty good. If you are using books, for both cases and statutes, there is a traditional-looking multi-volume *index* placed at the end of the volumes on the library shelf, organized alphabetically by subject. Specifically, for statutes, whether federal or state, the *index* will consist in part of an alphabetized list of the general topics covered (such as Attorneys, Criminal Law and Procedure, Estates). In addition, under each general topic, you will see lists of sub-topics and issues (matched with statutory sections). So theoretically, a researcher with nothing but a statutory *index* can find the statute on point for a particular research problem.

For cases, we have the miracle of the *digests*, which are basically subject-matter *indices* published by West. When West publishes a case, it adds unique editorial features, designed specifically for researchers, at the front of the case, before the court's opinion starts. These features are called *headnotes*, and each one (most cases have multiple *headnotes*) summarizes a point of law found in the court's opinion. To create the *digests*, West organizes the *headnotes* from all the cases included in that *digest* by topic and sub-topic. In other words, *digests* (for both federal and state case law) organize the cases by subject, and *digests* provide a variety of lists for you to check. *Digests* are discussed fully below, in subheading D.

Think of an *index* as providing another way into your research topic—another trail to follow or resource to check to make sure you have exhausted all your options.

C. *Updating* the Legal Rule—Arguably the Most Important Research Task

This item is not last because it is the least important; it is last because there is at least one aspect of it that is simple and straightforward—checking for the red flag or red stop sign on your legal database.

After you have found the law that applies to your factual issue, this is one of the most important questions you can ask: "Is this still good law?" That means, if it's a case, you are asking whether it has been reversed or overruled, and if it's a statute or a regulation, you are asking whether it has been superseded (replaced by a subsequent statute), overruled as unconstitutional, or amended. If any of those things has happened to the law that you are looking at, then the answer to that question is "No, this is not good law."

Law changes, and the worst thing a lawyer or paralegal can do is to rely on law that is no longer valid. Relying on old law that is no longer valid has obvious repercussions—it can prejudice a client, cause the lawyer to get chewed out by a judge and lose a case, and generally foul things up pretty badly. A lawyer could even be sued for malpractice. The ABA Model Rules of Professional Conduct 3.3(a)(1) and (2) prohibit lawyers from making "a false statement of fact or law to a tribunal" and from failing "to disclose to the tribunal controlling legal authority." You (or the lawyer you are working for) risk doing one or both if you fail to check that a source is still good law.

Therefore, if you are using a legal *database*, one of your primary obligations when you are researching is to pay careful attention to that database's signal for overruled or superseded law for every source of law you find. In general, this means simply paying attention to whether there is a red flag (Westlaw) or a red STOP sign (Lexis) at the top of the page (regardless of whether it's case law, a statute, or a regulation). These red "stop" symbols in Lexis and Westlaw tell you when a law has been explicitly overruled, reversed, or superseded.

Case law, however, can also be implicitly overruled if it relied on law that is no longer good. So, in addition to checking the validity of every source that you use, in case law, you should also check the validity of the sources relied on. Because the system is not perfect, it is possible that a case you are looking at looks like good law, and had no yellow or red warning symbols, but <u>one of the cases, statutes, or regulations relied on has been overturned, reversed, superseded or repealed</u>. You see, when a law is no longer good, although it will be clear if you look at that particular law, no one goes back and checks for all the cases that relied on that law. So be careful and be thorough, and make sure you check the validity of any sources that your research results rely on. This is an especially important step in free online sources, but both Westlaw and Lexis have tools that help you easily identify whether the case you are looking at relies on law that is no longer good.[4]

---

[4]   In Lexis, there is a Table of Authorities included in each Shepard's report that provides a list of cases your case cites to and whether that case is still good law. The Shepard's report also includes a signal for each citing reference which indicates the status of the cases that cite to your

You should also take the additional step of specifically checking the subsequent (later) history of your source—case history, statutory history, or the history of regulations are all included on the *databases*. Even if your source is technically still "good law," subsequent events may have affected how persuasive it is (for a case) or may suggest that changes in the law may be coming. In particular, you may see a yellow symbol (yellow flag in Westlaw and a yellow Caution sign in Lexis) that indicates, predictably, that you should proceed with caution. With case law, the caution symbol means that your case has been either criticized or not followed by another case—even a case in another jurisdiction (which may not matter that much to your supervising attorney). With statutes and regulations, it could mean that there are proposed statutes and regulations pending that may affect your statute.

D. The Miracle of *Digests* for Case Law

Both Westlaw and Lexis use a subject matter *index* and organize case law with short summaries, called *headnotes*, of the legal rules relied on in each case. In the print world, this index is a multi-volume set of *digests*.

In the beginning, the print West *Digest* system was one of the first subject matter *indices* that provided you with case law arranged by subject. In other words, without the *digest*, in order to find a case, you would need to know the specific *citation*, or know when and where it was published, because cases were published only chronologically. Before the *digest* system, which was John West's brain child in the late 1800s,[5] there was no way to look up cases according to the legal issue you were interested in. Then, attorneys in some localities and states started to write their own *digests*,[6] which were eventually purchased and consolidated into West's *digests* for all the states and the federal system.

---

case. In Westlaw, there is a new orange "overruling risk" icon with an explanation point which indicates if the case you are relying on relies on a case that has been overruled.

[5] Elizabeth G. Adelman et al., New York Legal Research 84–85 (3d ed. 2015).

[6] *See, e.g.,* Richard H. Phillips, Phillips' Connecticut Digest (Enfield, CT: Commission on Official Legal Publication 1943).

Although the advent of key word searching and the amazing search algorithms Lexis and Westlaw (not to mention internet search engines) provide may make it seem like *digests* are not so important anymore, that is not the case. Key word searching can be deceptive, especially for beginner researchers. Without fully knowing the range of legal vocabulary and legal issues that matter to your search strategy, you must be sure to compensate for that by using the *digests* and all the editorial features that go along with them.

For example, West categorizes case law into more than 400 main topics—another list to review when you start your research in a new topic (mentioned above). West calls it an outline, and it serves as both an outline and a table of contents (see reference to West outline of subjects as a "list" above in B). You can use this list of topics as a checklist against your research question, and if you want to explore any of the topics, each general subject of the 400 can be expanded into a more detailed outline of subjects, also marked by numbers, specifically "*key numbers*." Both the general outline of 400 topics and the outline of subtopics marked by *key numbers* are hyperlinked to the West *headnotes* and case law.

The West *headnotes* are the backbone of their index system and are each essentially a "blurb"—a "digestion"—of each holding and/or legal rule relied on in a case. They are included in the *digest* so that a researcher can see the gist of the case. The *headnotes* are written by West editors and are a great research tool. But because they are not actually part of the opinion written by the court, the *headnotes* can never be quoted or relied on—you must quote and rely on the actual text of the case (the court's opinion) itself. The *headnotes* can include both the case's holding(s), and the various legal rules relied on in a case, but they do not always include the *legally relevant facts* of the case. So, you must always read the actual case, pick out the *legally relevant facts*, and discern the holding yourself.

Each *headnote* is labeled with a topic and a *key number*, both of which are hyperlinked to the digest system. For example, topic number 272 in the list of 400 topics is Negligence, which is then broken down into an organized outline of *key numbers*. One of those *key number* is 202, *Elements*. Therefore, if a court set out the elements of negligence as part of its opinion, the case would be given a *headnote* that would be labeled with 272 Negligence 202 (with a key symbol preceding the 202). Just as with searching in general, you can take a narrow look at specific topic numbers and *key numbers* and those corresponding cases (i.e., other cases whose headnotes also include the same topic and *key number*), or you can take a broader look and see how your topic and *key number* fit into the topical outline. Taking that broader look through different layers of the *digest table of contents* can be an easy step to help you make sure you are not missing any other relevant *headnotes* or broader topics.

On Westlaw, you can access the West *digest* by clicking on the prompt "*key numbers*" on any page, and you will be brought to the corresponding *headnotes*. West's topic number and *key numbers* are integrated as *annotations* or cross-references into other sources of law published by West; since this is a proprietary system, they do not appear in other commercial databases like Lexis or free databases like FindLaw.

As a practical matter, what a hyperlinked subject matter *index* with *headnotes* sorted by topic number and *key numbers* gives you is another research trail to follow. When reviewing case law for relevancy, as soon as you find a relevant *headnote* you can use that to find additional cases with the same *key number*. You can also use the relevant *headnote* to take you back to the portion of the topical outline where the topic number and *key number* reside.

Lexis also has a subject matter *index* that can be used in a similar way. Lexis has *headnotes* for points of law discussed in the case, which are likewise numbered and part of an outline. When clicking on a *headnote*, you have the option of retrieving additional relevant documents, creating an automatic alert (discussed below), or viewing the headnote in the context of a topical *index*. On Lexis, the headnotes use the direct language of the court so you can immediately see how the court phrased a particular issue or rule of law. When you look at a *headnote*, you have the option of finding documents that use similar language or selecting from the topic path to locate cases that cover a broader topic.

E. Making Sense of What You Find: Sorting the Weight of Primary Sources

So, what happens when you actually find a lot of great, relevant primary sources? You have to sort your primary sources according to their value, or weight. Keep in mind: you are looking for authority that will persuade a court to rule in your favor. Even if you are researching a transaction, the big picture is that you want solid, mandatory authority that will persuade a court that your approach is correct in the event you ever have to fight in a court.

When sorting sources, remember that when it comes to secondary sources, they are always, as the term suggests, second to primary sources. As you know, secondary sources are not actual law—law journals and practice guides do not fall into any one of our four categories of primary sources—statutes, regulations, constitutions, or case law. Since secondary sources are not law, they have no actual authority in legal problem solving. Rather, secondary sources provide the researcher with context, guidance, citations, and ideas.

When it comes to weighing or prioritizing primary sources, you will need to consider several factors: 1) date, especially current validity; 2) whether the precedent is mandatory or persuasive (for case law); and finally, 3) relevancy, which means considering both the precise legal question as well as identifying the *legally relevant facts*. Keep in mind that many times you will need to prioritize a mixture of primary sources, such as statutes, cases, and regulations, or statutes and cases, or lots of cases. Sorting and ranking your legal authority is a very real legal skill, and you will have an opportunity to practice it with the end-of-the-chapter exercises.

First, let's look at the importance of the date. You know that law can change, and that before you rely on a primary source you need to see whether it's still valid. On Lexis and Westlaw this is as simple as noticing whether there is a red STOP sign (Lexis) or a red flag (Westlaw); red always means "stop" and that the source has been changed by another law or reversed or overruled. Specifically, for cases, it can mean that the entire holding has been invalidated or it can mean that at just one of several holdings in the case is no longer good law. Not only is updating your primary sources straightforward, but checking for current validity is also probably one of the single most important research tasks. If all the relevant primary authority you found is valid, then you can shift to evaluating case law in terms of precedent value and relevancy value.

Second, let's look at how we rank case law, which necessarily includes a consideration of jurisdiction, as well as level of court—trial, mid-level appellate, or court of last resort. You reviewed mandatory versus persuasive precedent in Chapter 3, where you learned that the higher the court, the more persuasive the precedent. In general, the opinions of the courts of last resort in a state or in our federal judiciary (U.S. Supreme Court) are mandatory precedent for lower courts in their jurisdiction. Similarly, a mid-level appellate court is mandatory for trial courts in its jurisdiction, and persuasive for trial courts in differing jurisdictions. For other courts on their same level, courts are only persuasive.

Here is a chart, Diagram 13, providing a visual depiction for mandatory versus persuasive precedent in state courts:

Diagram 13:

Mandatory and Persuasive *Precedent* in State Courts

STATE	Mandatory *Precedent* for:	Persuasive *Precedent* for:
COURT OF LAST RESORT	• All mid-level courts of appeal in that state • All trial courts and other lower courts in that state	• Courts of last resort in **other states**
MID-LEVEL COURT OF APPEALS	• All trial courts in **the same jurisdiction**	• Other mid-level courts in that state but **different jurisdiction**s • *Trial court*s in that state but in **different jurisdiction**s
TRIAL COURT	• none	• other *trial court*s

And here is Diagram 14, a chart providing a visual depiction for mandatory versus persuasive precedent in federal courts, which also shows the role of the U.S. Supreme Court in states:

Diagram 14:

Mandatory and Persuasive *Precedent* in Federal Courts

FEDERAL	Mandatory *Precedent* for:	Persuasive *Precedent* for:
U.S. SUPREME COURT	• All federal circuits • All federal district courts • All state courts for decisions about federal law	• Itself—the Supremes can change their mind
COURTS OF APPEAL (CIRCUIT COURTS)	• District courts in their own circuit	• Other Circuit Courts in different circuits • District courts in different circuits
DISTRICT COURTS	• none	• Other district courts in their own circuit • District courts in other circuits • When applying state law: state courts

Finally, let's look at *relevancy*. As with assessing dates and the value of case precedent, *relevancy* can be evaluated on a scale. The *relevancy* scale must consider two factors: the legal issue and the *legally relevant facts*. Considering both factors will help you stay on track, improve your analysis, and save time.

It makes sense that in assessing *relevancy* of a source, you are looking for a legal rule that precisely fits your legal issue. This means you are not only identifying the applicable overall rule, but you are also identifying the particular element that is at issue. For example, if you were presented with a legal question about potential liability regarding a slip and fall in a grocery store because of potentially negligent floor cleaning, specifically, failure to sweep up broken baby food jars and baby food, you might first find the rule for negligence in your state's case law. Negligence is the general over-arching rule, with the elements of duty, breach of duty, causation and damages. This rule, and the cases that rely on this rule, make a good start on your research. But if you had to rank the *relevancy* of a case that concerned a totally different type of negligence—such as rear-ending a car stopped in front of you—you would rank the *relevancy* of that case low because of the vastly different facts.

However, if you did further research to figure out which negligence element would be at issue in a slip and fall case, you would learn that in slip and fall cases dealing with spills, the issue of whether someone (like the landowner grocery store) has breached their duty of cleaning up—such as sweeping up broken baby jar glass and baby food—is an issue about the element of duty. Specifically, determining whether a landowner has a duty depends on how much notice (time) the landowner had about the spill before someone took a fall.

So the general legal rule—negligence—is *relevant*, but primary sources, like cases, that discuss the specific issue of duty and notice, are *highly relevant*. Cases that just discuss and apply the rule of negligence without the slip and fall scenario are of *low relevance*, while cases that deal with the same element and types of facts are of *high relevance*. Of course, sometimes you will not find case law on your specific element at issue, but you should always be checking to see whether it exists.

It should also make sense that you can't just consider the legal rule when you are considering *relevancy*—you must also consider facts. Facts only come into play when you are reading case law, as case law is the only primary source that involves a set of facts and applies a legal rule to those facts. Remember, the other primary sources are all just law— statutes, regulations, and constitutions.

Judging the *relevancy* of facts in case law depends on their similarity to the facts in your legal question. The facts do not have to be identical, and multiple cases with similar facts may require synthesis (see Chapter 7) in order to come up with guidelines. But remember: you must make sure BOTH that the facts are similar AND that the same element is at issue. If the facts are similar but a different element of the legal rule is discussed and resolved by the court, then the court's holding is not really a decision about how the legal rule applies to your specific facts and element.

For example, in the above slip and fall example with the baby food jar and baby food, if you find a case with similar facts, but the court discusses a different rule, or a different element of negligence, that case is not so relevant. Let's say you found a case with a fall in a grocery store caused by grapes that fell in the produce aisle. But the legal issue discussed is either another legal rule altogether—like the statute of limitations or an evidentiary ruling on what can be admitted at trial— OR the same rule, negligence, but instead of the duty element the court discusses the causation element (such as whether the plaintiff's fall was the cause of the plaintiff's back injuries). In either situation, that case is not so *relevant*. *Relevancy* is a continuum that requires you to look at rule, element, and similarity of facts.

Here is Diagram 15, a chart that provides a visual depiction of the *relevancy* scale:

Diagram 15:
Relevancy Scale

LOW *RELEVANCE*	MEDIUM *RELEVANCE*	HIGH *RELEVANCE*
Different rule Different facts	Same rule Different element Different facts Or Same rule Same element Different facts Or Same rule Different element Similar facts	Same rule Same element Similar facts

F. Good Research Habits

It's easy to get carried away in a clickable frenzy for hours without noticing either the specific research trails you have taken or the specific research trails you have not taken. There are some things you can do to avoid that:

a. Have a Plan;

b. Keep track of what you do by taking notes or creating folders, or both;

c. Create alerts on your fundamental cases so you can stay updated.

First, a research plan is more than just a research question. Remember, in Chapter 2 you learned how to investigate and find out the context for your legal issue. So the first step in your research plan should be finding out the answers to the "Sorting through the Legal Mess" questions so that you know the jurisdiction and subject matter for your legal question. This means using secondary sources—and reading them. You also have to pay attention to the jurisdiction of the databases you are using. After you have taken the initial step of working through the "Legal Mess," you should be able to construct your research question.

Second, a thorough research plan should include not only the principal research question but also a variety of searches that include natural language and the relevant facts, and that use the advanced search feature. Remember, the overarching research question, as discussed in Section A of this chapter, includes *relevant* facts and the legal concepts that you are investigating. Since you may not know the *relevant* facts at the beginning of your search, the research plan should include time for you to try a variety of searches AND for you to read the results of your searches.

Third, a research plan should include various search strategies so that you don't overlook applicable law or secondary sources. For example, a thorough research plan is not just answering the "Legal Mess" questions, and then doing some key word searches. To be thorough, you must take measures to double-check yourself, which means using different methods of searching. Principally, in addition to key word searches, you should be sure to check, for each of the sources you consult, all three of the lists explained in section B of this chapter, such as the list of subjects covered, the *table of contents*, and the *index*. An intrinsic part of checking lists is checking the *digest* topic and *key numbers* for relevant cases you find, as well as the outline for that topic and its *key numbers* on West (or the comparable system on Lexis).

Fourth, if you haven't already, you must check to be sure you have investigated all sources of law—not just *primary* and *secondary* sources, but ALL *primary* sources—*statutes, administrative regulations, constitutions, and case law.* This can be accomplished by taking care to check cross-references and *annotations* when available.

Finally, you must carefully and consciously include the task of updating not only each *primary* source you plan to use, but also, the sources that your *primary* sources rely on.

In addition to having a research plan, you need to organize what you find. In "E. Making Sense of What You Find," above, you learned about the analytical tools you need to rank and synthesize what you find. You also need a way to remember what you have done as you move through your research plan. You can always take notes manually. What may be easier and quicker is to create folders (a function available on Westlaw and Lexis) for different research questions, with sub-folders (in outline form) for different parts of the same research question. Additionally, both Lexis and Westlaw allow you to highlight portions of the text as well as take notes so you can annotate each of your sources with notes on their usefulness, their priority, how up to date they are, and whether you have updated the source and the authority the source is relying on.

Finally, on both Lexis and Westlaw you can set up an alert system to keep you apprised of any changes in your sources. An alert is a search that runs automatically and informs you of the results. Alerts are set up per *citation*. You can set up an alert by entering or finding the *citation* and clicking on the alert icon.

G. When Do I Stop Searching?

Yes, there is an end in sight. You do not have to research forever, and students often ask how they know when to stop. There are a couple of techniques to help you answer this question. First, if possible, you should always ask your professor or your assigning attorney for his or her estimate on the amount of time the research task should take you, keeping in mind that their estimate could be wildly wrong. But it's a start.

Second, you should keep track of the time you spend researching and reading for each problem. Especially for beginners, often the work feels like it is taking longer than it actually is. So shut off your email, your social media, and your phone; set a timer; and focus on just the research task on hand. Remember, too, from the Chapter 3 discussion of reading strategies, that legal research often takes more reading than you are used to. You need to read to find the holding, read to find the *legally relevant facts*, and read to discern the elements of a rule. So effective research does take time.

Third, you should have a plan and keep track of what you do. You don't want to randomly follow interesting leads that might not be applicable or repeat steps you have already done. Focus your initial research, at least, on answering the "Sorting through the Legal Mess" questions. After you have used primary and secondary sources to answer these questions, you should begin to have a sense of how broad or narrow the legal question is. Make a list of areas you want and need to look into and how you are going to do so. Then, keep track of your progress as you follow your plan. As you keep track of your work, and check off items on your plan, you will make progress.

Finally, a good rule of thumb is that you have found all there is to find when you start running across the same statutes, regulations, or cases over and over. If you are not learning anything new, and you have mandatory precedent that helps you apply the rule, you are done. If you do not have mandatory precedent because it does not exist, but have highly persuasive precedent, and you are not learning anything new, your stare decisis research is done. In Chapters 3 and 9 you learn about the different persuasive and precedential value that cases have depending not only on their jurisdiction, but also on the *legally relevant facts* and how they can be analogized or distinguished to aid in your legal analysis.

Of course, you can't forget to update all your legal sources. You should be able to answer in the affirmative when asked—"Is this still good law?" It's only after you know that all your legal authority is valid that you can truly be done with your research.

CHAPTER 4 LEGAL SKILLS

- **Find and identify the applicable legal rule**
- **Identify the *elements* of a legal rule**
- **Identify the *legally relevant facts***
- **Employ a variety of search strategies**
- **Ensure that the applicable legal rule is still good law**

CHAPTER 4 VOCABULARY

- Annotations
- "Bluebook" (Uniform System of Citation)
- Boolean/advanced searching
- Databases
- Digests
- Elements
- Field/segment searching
- Filters
- Headnotes
- Index/indices
- Key number
- KeyCite, Shepardizing (updating law)
- Legally relevant facts
- Notes of Decisions
- Official versus unofficial reporters
- Regional vs. state reporters
- Relevancy
- Table of contents (statute, digest topic)
- Topic number

CHAPTER 4 RESEARCH AND ANALYSIS EXERCISES

I.   Identifying elements in legal rules:

To give you practice in identifying elements, to remind you that legal rules come in four forms, to give you practice in identifying elements in different forms of legal rules, and finally, to give you practice in citation, please work on the following:

1.   Find your state statute(s) on burglary in the first degree.

a.   Write the complete citation including the year.

b.   List the elements.

2.   Locate the exact text of the First Amendment on a free legal database such as FindLaw.

a.   Write the complete citation (no year necessary).

b.   It is often said that there are five basic and fundamental freedoms provided by the First Amendment. Can you list all five?

c.   As you can see when you read the First Amendment, there are several clauses which identify different freedoms. Looking at the entire clause about prohibiting speech, identify the elements of that clause.

3.   Find a case from your state's court of last resort about common law negligence.

a.   Write the complete citation including the year.

b.   List the elements.

4.   Look up the federal regulation dealing with sale of tobacco to minors, specifically, 21 C.F.R. § 1104.14 (a)(1). What are the elements of this regulation?

a.   Write the complete citation including the year.

b.   List the elements.

II.   Finding the applicable legal rule, the elements of the rule, and the legally relevant facts:

To give you practice in finding rules, identifying elements, and identifying relevant facts, please work on the following as directed. You do not have to do any further research or provide any preliminary conclusions or analyses.

1.   Social Host Liability:

Reyna Allerton is 17 and has never drunk alcohol because the legal drinking age is 21. Her friend Judas Priest is also 17 and decided to have a party when his parents were away in Italy celebrating their 25th wedding anniversary. He got his friend Tamar Soule, who is 21, to purchase bottles of grain alcohol so he could make a punch by mixing it with HiC juice cocktail. The night that Judas held the party, about 100 people came over, including Reyna, all under 21. Most of the partiers drank the HiC punch, and Reyna's best friends have stated that Reyna drank 5 large red cups of punch. Reyna subsequently passed out while driving home, causing a head-on collision that killed the other driver, Constance Hopkins, and that severely injured Reyna.

Your supervising attorney represents Reyna, and she wants to know:

a.   What are the applicable legal rules in your state (whether statutes, case law, or regulations), and the elements of **each** applicable legal rule?

b.   For each element of each rule, what are the relevant facts? Create a simple chart. Facts for some elements may be "unknown."

2.   Statute of limitations/Medical Malpractice:

Aki Chilton was having severe pain in her abdomen and was diagnosed by her doctor, Dr. Samuel Fuller, as having appendicitis. Dr. Fuller operated on Aki on September 1, 2016. Aki initially felt better, but then began experiencing severe abdominal pain again, along with persistent diarrhea. When Aki sought follow-up care from Dr. Fuller six months later, in March of 2017, Dr. Fuller initially diagnosed various digestive disorders, and advised Aki to follow special diets. Aki followed the diet and continued to suffer pain and cramping for the following two years. Eventually, she sought a second opinion from Dr. Russell in January of 2019, who ultimately did exploratory surgery and found that a surgical clamp had been left in Aki's abdominal cavity.

Your supervising attorney represents Aki, and he wants to know:

a.   What are the applicable legal rules in your state (whether statutes, case law, or regulations), and the elements of **each** applicable legal rule?

b.   For each element of each rule, what are the relevant facts? Create a simple chart. Facts for some elements may be "unknown."

3.   Continuous snow storm (or other weather event)/Duty to clear:

Emily Standish was desperately in need of a chocolate fix, and so ventured out to her grocery store, Shoprite, driving her VW bug in a raging snowstorm that had been going on for 6 hours. As she exited her car, she slipped on ice that had accumulated during the storm and simultaneously fell over a one foot snow drift, landing on her elbow and breaking it. The broken elbow caused Emily a lot of pain, requiring surgery and causing lost wages in her job as a teacher.

Your supervising attorney represents Emily, and would like to know:

a.   What are the applicable legal rules in your state (whether statutes, case law or regulations), and the elements of **each** applicable legal rule?

b.   For each element of each rule, what are the relevant facts? Create a simple chart. Facts for some elements may be "unknown."

III. Making sense of what you find—rank your legal authority:

To give you practice in prioritizing what you find in your research, work on the following. Remember to consider date, court level and jurisdiction, and relevancy. These problems involve different elements in a valid contract being at issue. A valid contract is usually thought to have six elements: 1) offer; 2) acceptance; 3) consideration; 4) mutuality of obligation ("meeting of the minds"); 5) competency and capacity of the parties; and, in certain cases, 6) a writing requirement.

1.   In a contract dispute where the element at issue is whether there was the "meeting of the minds" (mutuality of obligation) required to form

a legal contract, Mr. Lucy has sued Mr. Zehmer because Mr. Lucy wants to enforce what he thought was their agreement that Mr. Zehmer sell him his farm for $50,000.[7] Mr. Zehmer argued that he was drunk and did not intend to sell his farm, while Mr. Lucy argued that both men had agreed on the sale and the price. The jurisdiction is state trial level, and the mid-level appellate jurisdiction is the First District.

Answer the following relevancy questions. Then, rank the authority that follows, starting with 1 as the most persuasive and descending to 6 as the least persuasive.

- Relevancy: What is the element at issue? What are the legally relevant facts?

- A case from that state's Court of Last Resort reciting the elements necessary to form a contract where the issue was whether there was capacity of the parties to consent

- A state encyclopedia entry presenting a synthesis of state cases about the "meeting of the minds" requirement

- A federal district court case applying law from another state on the meaning of "meeting of the minds"

- A federal district court case applying law from your state on "meeting of the minds"

- A mid-level appeals court case from the Second District of your state providing an example and a holding on the meaning of "meeting of the minds"

- A mid-level appeals court case from the First District of your state providing an example and a holding on the meaning of "meeting of the minds"

2.   This is a contract dispute where the element at issue is whether the plaintiff, Sally Post, had "competency and capacity" to form a contract

---

[7]   This fact pattern is based on *Lucy v. Zehmer*, 196 Va. 493, 84 S.E.2d 516 (1954).

when she had been diagnosed with Alzheimer's by a neurologist but still appeared capable of managing her affairs. She signed a contract to allow her paperboy to mow her lawn for $100 per week. Sally's representative, Nan Hunt, has sued the paperboy, Joel Rapid. The jurisdiction is state trial level, and there is only one mid-level appellate court.

Answer the following relevancy questions. Then, rank the authority that follows, starting with 1 as the most persuasive and descending to 6 as the least persuasive.

- Relevancy: What is the element at issue? What are the legally relevant facts?

- Jury instructions on the definition of competency for wills and estates

- Decision from the Court of Last Resort in your state on the issue of competency for forming contracts where the question concerned a minor's competency

- Decision from the mid-level appellate court on the issue of "meeting of the minds" or mutuality of obligation where the plaintiff was diagnosed with a brain tumor

- Decision from another state's Court of Last Resort on the element of competency for the formation of a contract where the plaintiff had been diagnosed with Alzheimer's

- Decision from a trial court in your jurisdiction which recited the six elements of a contract, which dealt with a plaintiff with a neurological disease, and which did not discuss which element was at issue

- A magazine article from your state's bar association discussing do's and don'ts of representing someone with Alzheimer's

3.   The Carbolic Smoke Ball Company published an advertisement in the newspaper in 1995 during a flu epidemic stating that anyone who

used its carbolic smoke ball would not get the flu, and that if a buyer did become sick, the buyer would be awarded $100.[8] The plaintiff, Mrs. Carlill, bought the smoke ball and sued to collect the award money when she became sick despite using it. The Carbolic Smoke Ball Company argued that the advertisement was not a real "offer" but, rather, just a sales pitch. The jurisdiction is state trial level, and the mid-level appellate court is Second Circuit.

Answer the following relevancy questions. Then, rank the authority that follows, starting with 1 as the most persuasive and descending to 6 as the least persuasive.

- Relevancy: What is the element at issue? What are the relevant facts?

- An article from a paralegal magazine presenting a summary of your state's leading cases on recent court decisions about contracts

- A U.S. Supreme Court case on the constitutionality of the anti-discrimination statute on disability

- A case from 1997 from the Second Circuit in your state on the meaning of "offer" for a contract in the context of an advertisement

- A case from another state where the defendant was also the Carbolic Smoke Ball Company

- A case from your state's Court of Last Resort on the elements of a contract

- A statute enacted in 2000 that specifically prohibits companies from promoting their products with

---

[8]   This fact pattern is based on *Carlill v. Carbolic Smoke Ball Co.*, [1892] EWCA Civ, which is an English contract law decision by the Court of Appeal and often used to introduce law students to the elements of a contract.

advertisements that offer money to customers for trying their product

IV. Researching ethical issues:

1.   Your supervising attorney Pat took a personal injury case against a municipality and recently realized that the municipal thirty-day statute of limitations to file the notice of claim against the municipality was missed, which means the case cannot be brought. Pat is concerned about a possible legal malpractice claim.

Your supervising attorney Pat wants to know:

a.   The primary applicable legal malpractice rule. Find it and identify 1) the source of law (*statute, administrative regulation, constitution or case law*); and 2) the elements of the rule.

b.   What is the statute of limitations for a legal malpractice claim?

c.   For each element of each legal rule, what are the relevant facts? Create a simple chart. Facts for some elements may be unknown.

2.   Your supervising attorney Khala invites you to watch the appellate oral argument she will present in front of five judges on your state's mid-level appellate court. At the argument, after Khala says "May it please the court," the presiding judge tells her that she has misled the court by citing a case that has been overruled. The presiding judge also tells her that she has committed an ethical violation. Khala apologizes to the panel, tells them she will submit a corrected brief, and continues with her argument. Afterwards, she asks you to check your state's professional rules to figure out what rule she has broken.

a.   Which rule and specific subsection has Khala violated by submitting an appellate brief that contained an overruled case?

b.   Are there also specific rules and subsections which require attorneys to inform the court of legal authority that is adverse to their position?

c. Are there any other rules governing how an attorney should behave in front of a court? If so, identify them and summarize.

When Your Legal Issue Comes Along: IRAC

This section of the book will be organized around IRAC—Issue, Rule, Application, and Conclusion—which is the basic organization, or structure, of legal analysis. First, in Chapter 5, you will see for yourself what a simple IRAC analysis looks like. That explanation will be the springboard for the following chapters, in which you will explore the Issue (Chapter 6), the Rule (Chapter 7), and the Rule Application (Chapters 8 and 9). All that work supports the last two chapters (Chapters 10 and 11) in Section III, Conclusion: Putting It All Together, in which you put all the skills together for two typical legal writing products: a legal memo and a motion.

Issue, Rule, Application and Conclusion

Legal Skills:

- Understand and identify an *IRAC* analysis
- Draft a simple *IRAC* analysis
- Draft a simple *case brief*
- Use the *IRAC* method to do a *case brief*

PART I. THE BUILDING BLOCK OF LEGAL ANALYSIS—*IRAC*

What happens when a real live legal issue comes along? Indeed, what is a legal issue? A legal issue asks if and how a legal rule applies to a set of facts. Therefore, the issue has two components: facts and law. Facts, not just law, are part of the equation when it comes to legal analysis. Since a set of facts can present multiple legal issues, and since we like to conduct legal analysis one issue at a time, legal educators have developed a formula that is a reliable tool for working through the legal analysis of each issue you identify: IRAC, or *Issue, Rule, Application,* and *Conclusion.* In *IRAC* and in legal analysis generally, the facts—the legally relevant facts, that is—play a critical role. You saw this in Chapter 4 as well, when you learned the connection between the legal rule, its elements, and identifying the legally relevant facts. So, from now on, as we discuss the law and legal analysis, our discussion will also include the facts.

Here is a way to think about each part of the *IRAC* analysis, which we will then explore in greater depth in the remaining chapters of the book. Then we can use these tools in matters of increasing complexity when we compose legal memos and briefs. Notice that, except for the *Rule* section, each part of *IRAC* involves the legally relevant facts.

Diagram 16:

Understanding *IRAC*

IRAC	
ISSUE	The Issue is the question about how the legal rule intersects with a given set of facts. It includes both the legal rule and/or the element at issue, and the legally relevant facts.
RULE	This is the legal Rule, which as we know, can be from any one of the four primary sources—statutes, administrative regulations, constitutions, or case law. Think of the Rule section like an upside-down triangle with the wider part on top: every rule has elements, and you start out the Rule section by listing those elements. Your focus then shifts to the element at issue. Think of the element at issue as its own mini-rule. Once you set out the mini-rule, you use this Rule section to explain the mini-rule. (Rule explanation is further discussed in Chapter 7.)
APPLICATION	The Application is when you show how the rule applies to the facts, which means explaining in detail how the facts fit to the particular element. The facts you focus on in this section are the legally relevant facts.
CONCLUSION	This is not a mechanical restatement, but rather a supported and reasoned explanation of your recommendation on this point.

Perhaps the best way to understand the different parts of *IRAC* is to read some examples of *IRAC* analysis based on fact hypotheticals.

Think of each fact hypothetical that follows as a set of facts that provide fertile ground for a legal question. In each *IRAC* exercise that accompanies each hypothetical, the rule is supplied. (As noted in Diagram 16, we will discuss *Rule Explanation* in Chapter 7 as a necessary skill that is often part of the *Rule* section in *IRAC*. But for the quick examples that follow, we will look at simple *rules*.) For your work with *IRAC*, of course, instead of the legal rule being supplied, you will be the one to find the legal rule. Note that the rule in each *IRAC* that follows is a hypothetical one, with a realistic citation to improve familiarity with citations, simplified for the purpose of working through the exercise.

Also, a note about repetition in legal writing: although it will seem repetitive to read the supplied rule in the *IRAC* problem, and then read it again in the *IRAC* analysis, there is a certain amount of repetition that is welcome in legal writing. Because legal writing is relaying an analysis, usually to a "busy reader," such as a supervising attorney, a step by step approach, with repetition, helps the reader understand the analysis without having to look back at the rule multiple times.

As you read the samples, remember that no sample is perfect, and that these straightforward examples are presented to you so you can see for yourself the pattern and mode of this basic cornerstone of legal analysis. Also remember that *IRAC* is just a model that can be used and adapted in different ways in different settings. It is not something to get dogmatic about. For example, your professor may choose an alternate format, or the factual hypotheticals you work on in class may be more complicated, with multiple issues. But variations do not change the basic components and approach to the skill of legal analysis based on a simple rule: facts, application of legal rules to facts, and conclusion.

IRAC Examples #1 (Criminal): Third Degree Burglary

Fact Hypothetical 1 "Handyman Mike Needs a Place to Sleep": Mike earns a living by doing odd jobs for people in his neighborhood. He was recently thrown out of his apartment for failure to pay utilities.

Since it was winter in his northern Michigan city, it was snowing and temperatures ranged from 30 degrees to 15 degrees with the wind chill. Mike needed a warm place to spend the night so he broke into the home of Tom and Jerry Chilton, people in the neighborhood who had helped him. When Jerry Chilton saw someone sleeping in her basement, she screamed and called the police. When the police arrived, they arrested Mike and charged him with Third Degree Burglary.

Rule **(hypothetical, with realistic statutory cite from Michigan):** Mich. Comp. Laws § 10.10.10 (2018): A person is guilty of burglary in the third degree when he knowingly enters or remains unlawfully in a building with intent to commit a crime therein.

Elements: 1) person; 2) knowingly enters OR remains unlawfully; 3) building; 4) intent to commit crime therein.

IRAC Analysis for "Mike the Handyman"

Issue **(element at issue is #4):** Whether Mike had the "intent to commit a crime" necessary for conviction of Third Degree Burglary when he broke into the Chiltons' home so he could spend the night in a warm place?

Rule: Mich. Comp. Laws § 10.10.10 (2018): A person is guilty of burglary in the third degree when he knowingly enters or remains unlawfully in a building with intent to commit a crime therein.

Application: Although it seems Mike acted illegally when he broke into someone else's home, at the time he did so, he reports his intention was only to sleep in a warm place. Since sleeping in a warm place is not a crime, Mike did not have the "intent to commit a crime" inside the Chilton's home. Without satisfying that element, Mike cannot be guilty of Third Degree Burglary.

Conclusion: Mike did not have the requisite intent to commit a crime and cannot be guilty of Third Degree Burglary under the Michigan statute.

* * *

Fact Hypothetical 2 "Connie Loves Cookies": Connie Garden loves cookies, and as she was walking by the Janis Bake Shop in Miami, Florida, she saw a plate of warm chocolate chip chunk cookies on a counter next to an open and screenless window of the shop. Connie could not resist the smell of the cookies, and before she knew it she had reached through the window and grabbed a cookie. The owner, Janis, saw her, became furious, and while she yelled "Stop thief!" she called the police on her cell phone. At Janis's urging, when the police arrived they arrested Connie for Third Degree Burglary.

Rule **(hypothetical, with realistic statutory citation from Florida):** Fla. Stat. § 10.10.10 (2018): A person is guilty of burglary in the third degree when he knowingly enters or remains unlawfully in a building with intent to commit a crime therein.

Elements: 1) person 2) knowingly enters OR remains unlawfully 3) building 4) Intent to commit crime therein.

IRAC Analysis for "Connie Loves Cookies"

Issue **(element at issue is #2):** Whether Connie "entered" the bake shop when she reached through a shop window and grabbed a cookie, and was therefore guilty of third degree burglary?

Rule: Fla. Stat. § 10.10.10 (2018): A person is guilty of burglary in the third degree when he knowingly enters or remains unlawfully in a building with intent to commit a crime therein.

Application: The issue in this problem is the definition of "enter" for the purposes of the Third Degree Burglary statute. A prosecutor could argue that entry means crossing a property line or threshold, which would include an arm reaching through a window. On the other hand, Connie's defense counsel could argue that "enter" means that one's entire body has to cross the threshold into the "building." Because only Connie's arm reached over the property line, arguably she didn't enter the bake shop.

Conclusion: Reaching an arm through a window should qualify as an entry under Florida's Third Degree Burglary statute because this act still crosses the property boundary and is also sufficient to accomplish the crime. Therefore, Connie has violated the statute.

* * *

IRAC Examples #2 (Civil): Dog Bite

Fact Hypothetical for "Nan and Richard's Bassadors": Nan and Richard own two mixed Basset Hounds and Labradors, otherwise known as "Bassadors." One dog is named Gavin, and one is named Mahoney. Nan and Richard like to walk their dogs throughout the neighborhood. While being walked, on two separate occasions, both Gavin and Mahoney bit toddlers (approximately age 3) who were trying to pet them. After that, Nan and Richard decided they would only take the dogs to dog parks, where they can be let off the leash in an enclosed area. In the Pulvino Memorial Dog Park, dogs and their humans are allowed to walk around, and the dogs walk without leashes. Everyone is welcome at Pulvino Memorial Dog Park. The dog park is enclosed, is about 1 acre, and consists of open fields, woods, and walking paths. After about two months of taking their dogs to this park, while on another visit, Gavin bit a young child named Lilly on the face. Lilly was about 8 years old.

    Rule **(hypothetical, with realistic statutory citation from New Jersey):** N.J. Stat. Ann. § 10.10.10 (West 2018): The owner of any dog that has bitten a human being shall have the duty to take such reasonable steps as are necessary to remove any danger presented to other persons from bites by the animal.

    Note: The term "reasonable" above is a legal term that deserves attention, as it is a fundamental idea in negligence and also permeates other areas of the law. In general, when we say reasonable, we mean the degree of care that a reasonable person would use under the circumstances. In other words, what is reasonable always depends on the specific facts of the situation.

Elements: 1) owner; 2) dog that has bitten a human being; 3) duty to take reasonable steps as are necessary to remove any danger presented to other persons from bites by the animal.

IRAC Analysis for "Nan and Richard's Bassadors"

Issue (element at issue is #3): Whether Nan and Richard's steps to remove the danger posed by the biting Bassadors Gavin and Mahoney was "reasonable" under the State Civil Code when they took the Bassadors to the Pulvino Memorial Dog Park where the dogs would be off-leash and could encounter people?

Rule: N.J. Stat. Ann. § 10.10.10 (West 2018): The owner of any dog that has bitten a human being shall have the duty to take such reasonable steps as are necessary to remove any danger presented to other persons from bites by the animal.

Application: The issue is what constitutes reasonable in Nan and Richard's ownership and care of their Bassadors given the Bassadors' history of both biting three-year-olds. On one hand, you could argue that the steps they took to give up their walks around the neighborhood and take their dogs to a designated dog park showed concern and foresight because it got the dogs off the streets. It seems their action also got the dogs away from toddlers trying to pet them. After all, the Bassadors did not bite another toddler, but instead chose an older eight-year-old child, and Nan and Richard could not have anticipated this type of bite. On the other hand, because the Pulvino Memorial Dog Park was open to the public and allowed everyone in, this particular dog park was not the best choice for the Bassadors. Arguably, Nan and Richard should have kept them in a confined space such as an enclosed back yard.

Conclusion: Given the Bassadors' biting history, reasonable care required Nan and Richard to make sure their dogs were not around people, or at least children. Therefore, they violated the New Jersey statute.

* * *

Hopefully, these examples give you some exposure to the process of applying the rule to the facts. Note that the analytical formula of *IRAC* can be used across multiple topics, criminal or civil. Note also that if you look carefully at the *Application* section, the discussion includes both law and facts—and the facts focused on are the legally relevant facts. It's also important to realize that although the above examples use statutes, the legal rule for an *IRAC* can be from any source—statute, regulation, constitution or case law. Finally, note that sometimes, the *Application* requires the writer to evaluate the arguments on both sides (Bassador example, *IRAC* #2), while other times, the *Application* is more clear cut (Handyman Mike example, *IRAC* #1).

Now we will move on to another classic paradigm in legal education, the *case brief*.

PART II. IRAC AS A WAY TO UNDERSTAND THE *CASE BRIEF*

Just as *IRAC* is a fundamental tool to build legal analysis, the *case brief* is a tool to identify and articulate the legal analysis of a court, which in turn becomes another building block for legal analysis. A *case brief* is just an organized way of taking notes about a court's decision, and it helps the reader to develop their skills of identifying and articulating the analytical work of appellate judges. Understanding the *holding* and *reasoning* of the court is often a worthwhile exercise by itself, which then allows you to develop your own legal analysis.

Although not always taught side by side, both tools (*IRAC* and a *case brief*) require identification of many of the same things. Let's take a look at the different sections of each tool:

Diagram 17:

Comparison of *IRAC* and the *Case Brief*

IRAC AND THE CASE BRIEF	
IRAC	**CASE BRIEF**
Facts (from the client)	*Facts (as recited by the court)*
	Procedural History
Issue	*Issue*
Rule	*Rule*
Application	*Reasoning* (How the court applied the *rule* to the *facts* to come up with the analysis)
Conclusion (your prediction of how a court would rule on the *Issue*)	*Holding* (court's decision on the *Issue*)

Looking at these parallel methods of teaching or identifying legal analysis, you can learn several things. First, one of the hallmarks of presenting legal analysis (except if you are a court) is a specific type of organization that you might not find in other disciplines—organization by section. In law, we tend to use sections when we present our analysis, and each section is more or less separate and discrete from the other sections. Although this does NOT mean that we can't mention the relevant facts when we are applying the rule to the facts, it DOES mean that we don't insert a summary or recitation of all the facts in any other section other than *Facts* section.

Second, we love headings. Each section serves a specific purpose, and the heading for each section alerts the reader to the subject of that section. Headings provide a clear visual cue about the organization of a document and alert the reader to what's coming up.

Third, to reiterate the first point, the sections are separate and discrete—think of them as separated by a big brick wall. Other than the *Application* section, which, of course, requires you to apply the legal rule to the relevant facts (and mention those facts), each section is limited to content from that section only. This might be a challenge for certain creative types, but it assists both the reader and the writer in staying organized.

Finally, as you can see, both for developing legal analysis and for reporting legal analysis there are distinct components: the *Facts* (what happened); the legal *Rule* being relied on (for an *IRAC* exercise, you may have been provided with that; in a *case brief*, you have to identify the legal *Rule* that corresponds with the *Issue* the court is deciding); the *Issue*, which is basically the question of how the legal *Rule* should be applied to the relevant *Facts*; the *Application* or *Reasoning*, which is an explanation and summary of how you or the court actually applied the *Rule* to the *Facts*; and the *Conclusion* or *Holding*, which is the answer to the *Issue*. Think of identifying and developing these fundamental components as building the framework for your legal analysis abilities.

Here is a way to think about each part of the *case brief*. Notice that you are already familiar with the idea of identifying these different parts of legal analysis.

Diagram 18:
Parts of the *Case Brief* Explained

CASE BRIEF	
FACTS	Summarize the relevant facts here. This is not a time to cut and paste, but rather, to look at the story of what happened in this case and summarize it in your own words. Remember to include the legally relevant facts, that is, the facts that the court relies on in its *Reasoning*. Often, the court will summarize the facts at the beginning of its opinion. While this is helpful, make sure you take note of the facts the court discusses in its *Reasoning*. Those facts are more likely to be the legally relevant ones.
PROCEDURAL HISTORY	Try to answer these questions: First, what level court is the case in? And second, how did the case get there? Often, the court will summarize the *Procedural History* at the beginning of the opinion.
ISSUE	Identify the legal question the court is trying to resolve. Remember, the issue is how the legal *Rule* (or *mini-rule* about one element) applies to the *Facts*.
RULE	What is the legal rule/mini-rule that the court is applying in the *Issue*? Remember, the legal rule can be from any of the four primary sources: statutes, regulations, constitutions, or case law.
HOLDING	This is the answer to the *Issue*; it is the court's decision.
REASONING	What are ALL the reasons why the court decided what it did? The court will probably not list the reasons in bullet points, but rather, will seem like it's talking through its decision-making process. The court is, in fact, demonstrating how it weighed the arguments from both sides and then stating declaratively its view of the law.

All cases are not created equal. Although we will deal with some simple examples in this chapter, later on we will be reviewing more complex Supreme Court cases. So, in preparation for a variety of complexity levels in the cases that you read, here are some beginners' tips for reading and understanding cases and writing *case briefs*.

First, do a brief preview of the case by setting the stage and answering these questions: when was the case decided? What jurisdiction is the case from? How long is the case? What general topic is the case about? Is there a summary of the case (such as a syllabus) or headnotes that you can review to get a first glimpse into the issues? If you read just the *topic sentences*, what ideas do you get about what's important in the case?

Second, make sure you read the case all the way through before you begin to compose your *case brief*. After all, how can you truly understand which *Facts* are relevant before you know what the *Issue* is? And how can you figure out each *Issue* before you know the legal *Rule* and the elements of that *Rule*? So be cautious: don't rush to complete each section of the *case brief* in the specific order provided before you have read the entire case.

Third, after you have read the case all the way from beginning to end, read through it again. In order to identify each part of the *case brief,* it helps to figure out what the court is doing in each part of the case, so focus on the *topic sentences* (first sentence of each paragraph). You can even try reading JUST the *topic sentences* to see how the court organizes and works its way through the discussion.

Fourth, try to identify the legal *Rule(s)* at the heart of the *Issue*. (There may be just one *Issue* the court is resolving, or there may be multiple *Issues*.) Remember, each element of the broader *Rule* has its own *mini-rule*, so when you identify the legal rule, you should likewise identify the element at issue and the *mini-rule* for that particular element. This relevant legal *Rule*/*mini-rule* can often be identified easily when the court states the *Issue* or *Issues*. Often, courts start out their decision with a statement of each *Issue* and the factual story. Identifying the legal *Rule* for each *Issue* will help keep you focused. Remember, the source of a legal *Rule* can be a statute, regulation, constitution or a case. Also, the court may mention many different types of rules in its *Reasoning* process. Try to focus on the particular *Rule* that the court is applying to each *Issue* at hand.

Fifth, identify the *Issue(s)*—sometimes the court has done it for you quite succinctly. Remember, each *Issue* is about how the *Rule* (or a specific element of the *Rule*) applies to the *Facts*. Think of the *Issue* as a question. If there is more than one *Issue*, make sure you identify each of them.

Sixth, identify the *Holding(s)*, which is how the court has answered each *Issue*.

Finally, identify the reasons for the court's *Holding(s)*, which should also help you figure out the *Facts* that are relevant. Whatever *Facts* the court relies on or mentions in its *Reasoning* are the legally relevant facts from the story. There can be multiple reasons for the court's decision, or multiple steps in the court's *Reasoning* process. Try to be as inclusive and complete as you can.

SKILLS DEVELOPMENT

Steps for Assisting Reading Comprehension of a Case

Step 1: Preview the case by noting the date and jurisdiction, and by skimming any easy-to-read editorial enhancements such as headnotes.

Step 2: Read the case all the way through.

Step 3: Read the case again, focusing on the topic sentences to get a sense of the "outline" of the court's decision.

Step 4: Identify the legal Rule(s) the court is applying.

Step 5: Identify the question(s), or Issue(s), the court is resolving.

Step 6: Identify the court's Holding(s) or final decision on each issue; look for language clues that indicate a conclusion, like "We hold" or "In conclusion" or "Therefore."

Step 7: Identify ALL the reasons for the holding(s), which includes identifying the legally relevant facts—what did the court rely on or mention in the Reasoning process?

Don't get discouraged. Although this process may take a considerable amount of time the first time, it will get easier. All it takes is practice.

Now, let's look at some examples of simple cases so we can learn to identify the different sections. The following examples are based on real cases but have been modified and simplified for the purposes of illustration. Our first example is a state trial court applying a common law rule about lost property. Notice that the top of the case where the case name is, otherwise known as the "caption," not only includes the case name but two citations as well (to an official and an unofficial reporter). You can also see that the court decision was issued by a single judge. The paragraphs are numbered here for ease of discussion, and the *topic sentences* are bolded for easy reading (but these enhancements don't exist in the real decision).

77 Misc.2d 61,
353 N.Y.S.2d 288
(Queens Co. Ct. 1974)

Conti v. American Society for Prevention of Cruelty to Animals

DECISION.

Niam Meyer, Judge.

1.   Chester is a parrot. He is fourteen inches tall, with a green coat, yellow head and an orange streak on his wings. Red splashes cover his left shoulder. Chester is a show parrot, used by the defendant SPCA in various educational exhibitions presented to groups of children.

FACTS

2.   On June 28, 1973, during an exhibition, Chester flew the coop and found refuge in the tallest tree he could find. For seven hours the defendant sought to retrieve Chester. Ladders proved to be too short. Offers of food were steadfastly ignored. With the approach of darkness, search efforts were discontinued. A return to the area on the next morning revealed that Chester was gone.

FACTS

3.   Several days later, plaintiff, Mr. Edwin Conti, saw a green-hued parrot with a yellow head and red splashes seated in his backyard. Mr. Conti offered him food and the parrot eagerly accepted. Not knowing what to do with the parrot, Mr. Conti called the SPCA, and that organization then sent two representatives to Mr. Conti's house. When they saw the parrot, they realized that this

FACTS

parrot was none other than Chester. This was further confirmed by the identification tag on Chester's right leg. The SPCA representatives took Chester back home. At the trial the SPCA workers testified that Chester knew how to say several words, including "hello," and how to dangle by his legs, and that they used him for various educational exhibits for children.

4.   The plaintiff then initiated this action to get Chester back. Since the parties agree that this parrot is Chester, who is entitled to ownership—the plaintiff, who found Chester in his back yard, or the SPCA, who are the original owners of Chester?

> PROCEDURE
> AND ISSUE

5.   The plaintiff argued that the SPCA's ownership ended after Chester escaped and was captured and placed under the control of plaintiff.

> Plaintiff's
> Argument

6.   The law is well settled that the true owner of lost property is entitled to the return thereof as against any person finding same. (*In re Wright's Estate*, 15 Misc. 2d 225, 177 N.Y.S.2d 410) (36A C.J.S. Finding Lost Goods s 3). However, this general *rule* is not applicable when the property lost is an animal. When the lost property is an animal, the question is whether the animal was domesticated or wild, *ferae naturae*. If the animal is wild, the owner can only have a limited, or qualified, right to the property, and if the animal escapes, that ownership right is wholly lost.

> RULE

> APPLICATION

7.   Therefore, the *issue* is simply whether
Chester was domesticated or wild.

ISSUE

8.   In Amory v. Flyn, 10 Johns. (N.Y.) 102,
**plaintiff sought to recover geese of the wild
variety which had strayed from the owner.** In
granting judgment to the plaintiff, the court pointed
out that the geese had been tamed by the plaintiff
and therefore were unable to regain their natural
liberty.

EXAMPLE
OF RULE
APPLICATION
FROM
ANOTHER
CASE

9.   **This important distinction was also
demonstrated in Manning v. Mitcherson, 69
Ga. 447, 450—51, 52 A.L.R. 1063, where the
plaintiff sought the return of a pet canary.** In
holding for the plaintiff the court stated "To say that
if one has a canary bird, mocking bird, parrot, or
any other bird so kept, and it should accidentally
escape from its cage to the street, or to a
neighboring house, that the first person who caught
it would be its owner is wholly at variance with all
our views of right and justice."

EXAMPLE
OF RULE
APPLICATION
FROM
ANOTHER
CASE

10. **The Court finds that Chester was a
domesticated animal, subject to training and
discipline.** Thus the *rule* of *ferae naturae* does not
prevail and the defendant as true owner is entitled
to regain possession.

HOLDING

11. **Judgment for defendant dismissing the complaint
without costs.**

* * *

First, let's follow the seven steps in the Skills Development to see
how that can help us.

Step 1:   Since this is a simplified case, there are no publication enhancements like headnotes or a preliminary case summary. If you skimmed the *topic sentences*, you would know this case is about a lost parrot.

Steps 2 and 3: You have read the case all the way through. Now, here is the outline of the *topic sentences* (in bold above for easy recognition) with italics to help you make sense of it all and see what you still need to figure out:

- **Chester is a parrot.** *(You know the case is about a parrot!)*

- **On June 28, 1973, during an exhibition, Chester flew the coop and found refuge in the tallest tree he could find.** *(And you know the parrot has escaped.)*

- **Several days later, plaintiff, Mr. Edwin Conti, saw a green-hued parrot with a yellow head and red splashes seated in his backyard.** *(Someone—who is the plaintiff—has luckily found the parrot.)*

- **The plaintiff then initiated this action to get Chester back.** *(Plaintiff must have lost possession of the parrot, but wants him back.)*

- **The law is well settled that the true owner of lost property is entitled to the return thereof as against any person finding same.** *(Does not sound good for the plaintiff, who was the "finder" of Chester and not the original owner.)*

- **Therefore, the *issue* is simply whether Chester was domesticated or wild.** *(Note to ourselves—this distinction must be important but why? Be sure to figure this out when reading.)*

- **In Amory v. Flyn, 10 Johns. (N.Y.) 102, plaintiff sought to recover geese of the wild variety which had strayed from the owner.** *(The court is looking to other cases about lost animals—precedent—to decide the question.)*

- This important distinction was also demonstrated in Manning v. Mitcherson, 69 Ga. 447, 450–451, 52 A.L.R. 1063, where the plaintiff sought the return of a pet canary. *(Sounds like there is a very similar case out there about a lost canary that was about the plaintiff trying to get a pet back.)*

- The Court finds that Chester was a domesticated animal, subject to training and discipline. *(The court has resolved the earlier-noted question.)*

- Judgment for defendant dismissing the complaint without costs. *(The plaintiff does not get Chester back!)*

So, to summarize, we know that the case is about an escaped parrot, that plaintiff found the parrot and wants him back, and that there is a legal *rule* about returning lost property to the owner. Significantly, we also know the *issue*—"simply whether Chester was domesticated or wild" and the court's answer to that *issue*, the *holding* "[t]he court finds that Chester was a domesticated animal." Note that focusing on the *topic sentences* does not tell us the whole story, but it does tell us a lot of the story, and highlights some of the steps in the court's *reasoning*. This technique can be a good first step to really digesting all that is going on in your case.

Step 4 *(identify the legal rule the court is applying)* and Step 5 *(identify the legal issue the court is resolving)* go hand-in-hand, and require you to identify the main legal *rule* the court is applying, which will in turn help you identify the *issue*. We see from our *topic sentence* outline and from paragraphs 6 and 7 that the legal *rule* the court relies on is that in the case of animals, what determines whether the animal should be returned to its original owner is whether the animal has been tamed and is domesticated, or is still wild. Therefore, the court states the *issue* as being whether Chester the parrot was domesticated or wild.

Finally, for Steps 6 *(identify the court's holding)* and 7 *(identify ALL the court's reasons and the legally relevant facts)*, we see that the court holds that Chester is domesticated and does not go back to the plaintiff. We really only see one reason provided by the court in paragraph 10 for the finding that Chester was domesticated—"subject to training and discipline." The court does not tell us why it thinks that Chester was subject to training and discipline, but if we look at the *facts* in paragraph 3, we see that Chester has an identification tag on his leg, and that he has been trained to talk, how to dangle by his legs, and has been used for educational purposes. Those are the legally relevant *facts* that support the court's *conclusion.* Note that making this connection requires you to make an inference.

Now, let's look at one version of a brief for this case, with each section explained and discussed.

SAMPLE *CASE BRIEF*

FACTS: A parrot named Chester escaped from the SPCA and was found by the plaintiff, Edwin Conti. When he called the SPCA to find out what to do with him, the SPCA workers claimed that Chester belonged to them and took him back. *(Note how many of the details—like Chester's colors and how he escaped—were not included as they are not that relevant to the story.)*

PROCEDURAL HISTORY: This opinion is from a court at the trial level in Queens County, after a trial. *(The Procedural History here is simple because there really is none—only one level of court heard and decided the case.)*

RULE: The court is applying the common law *rule* that lost property, including domesticated animals, should be returned to the owner, while ownership of wild animals is qualified (or limited) and therefore wild animals belong to no one after escaping. *(By understanding that this is the rule the court is applying to figure out what to do with Chester, the lost parrot, you can better understand and articulate the issue. Note also that there is one citation for the legal rule, and then in the court's reasoning, there are additional citations to relevant precedent.)*

ISSUE:

(EXAMPLE 1): Whether Chester the parrot is domesticated and should therefore be returned to his owner, the SPCA, after flying away and becoming lost? *(Note how this is a question that begins with* *"whether" and which includes relevant facts—that Chester the parrot was lost and now is found.)*

(**EXAMPLE 2**):   Whether Chester the parrot is domesticated or wild and whether the common law *rule* of returning lost property to the original owner applies? *(Note how this issue is also phrased as a question, and in addition to including the relevant fact that Chester the parrot has been lost, also refers to the common law rule about returning lost property to its original owner.)*

HOLDING:

(**EXAMPLE 1**):   Yes, Chester is a domesticated animal and should therefore be returned to his original owner, the SPCA. *(Note how the holding simply answers the question posed in the Issue. The holding is simple and easy to understand—there is no doubt where the court stands.)*

(**EXAMPLE 2**):   Chester the Parrot is domesticated and the common law *rule* of returning lost property to the original owner does apply. Therefore, Chester should be returned to the SPCA, his original owner. *(This is the same as the above holding but answers the Example 2 Issue precisely.)*

REASONING: *(Notice that the court does not specifically state why it believes that Chester is a domesticated animal, yet if we look at the facts, the court does state at the beginning—in its recounting of the Chester story—that Chester knew how to do some tricks, including saying "hello" and dangling from his legs.)* The court finds that Chester is a domesticated animal "subject to training and discipline," and this finding seems consistent with the SPCA testimony that Chester was used for educational exhibits, could state "hello," and could dangle by his legs. Because the parrot is a domesticated animal, the common law *rule* that lost items get returned to their owners applies (the court relies on *In Re Wright's Estate*). The court notes the common law *rule* that if the lost animal is a wild animal, it does <u>not</u> get returned to the owner because an owner of a wild animal has only a limited right of ownership. The court also relies on two cases in which domesticated animals—geese and a canary—were returned to their original owners after being lost (*Armory v. Flynn* and *Manning v. Mitcherson*).

* * *

What do you notice about the case and the *case brief*? Note that each part of the *case brief* is written in the writer's own words, and there are no parts of the court's decision that are simply "cut and pasted" into the brief format. Remember, a *case brief* is a tool to help you think about and recognize what is happening in the case. Although it may appear to be just a form that needs to be filled out, that is not the case. Use it to help you think.

Note also that the *Reasoning* section required some intellectual work on the part of the reader, because it took a *conclusion* of the court (at the end of the decision) and connected it to some of the *facts* presented by one of the parties. Also, instead of simply stating that the court's decision relied on precedent—a statement that probably applies to many court decisions—the writer instead names and explains the cases and the common law *rules* that the court relies on. In other words, the reader of this *case brief* has explained the entire *reasoning* process, including the specific legal *rules* and how the court applied these legal *rules* to the *facts*. In order to help both you and any additional reader of your *case brief*—supervising attorney, professor—really understand the case and the court's *reasoning*, you want to spend as much time thinking about and summarizing the court's *reasoning* as possible.

Let's look at another simplified example based on a real case. This is a state court of last resort (in many states, and in this case, the Supreme Court), applying the First Amendment to a prospective Nazi march in a small town of Holocaust survivors. Again, in order to help us go through Steps 1–7 from the Skills Development, the paragraphs are numbered and the *topic sentences* are in bold.

69 Ill.2d 605

373 N.E.2d 21

(1978)

Supreme Court of Illinois.

The **VILLAGE OF SKOKIE**, Appellee,

v.

The **NATIONAL SOCIALIST PARTY OF AMERICA** et al., Appellants.

PER CURIAM.[1]

1. **The plaintiff, Village of Skokie, brought this lawsuit seeking injunctive relief in order to prevent the National Socialist Party ("Nazis") from holding a rally and march in the Village in which they would march in Nazi uniform, complete with swastika and arm band with signs stating "White Free Speech," "Free Speech for the White Man," and "Free Speech for White America."** At the hearing on plaintiff's motion, the trial court heard sworn testimony that the Village of Skokie has a population of about 70,000 people, roughly half or 40,500 of which are Jewish, and of that portion, between 5,000 to 7,000 are Holocaust survivors. Two residents also testified that as a survivor of the Holocaust, they perceived this march to be a clear threat that the Nazis "are not through with you", and that due to the planned counter-demonstration of 12,000 to 15,000 people, there would likely be violence.

PROCEDURAL HISTORY/ FACTS

PROCEDURAL HISTORY/ FACTS

---

[1]   *Per curiam* is Latin for "By the Court." This means that there is not one justice who single-handedly authored the opinion, but rather, the court as a whole authored the opinion.

2. The Circuit Court Trial Judge issued the injunction, and the Nazis appealed. The Court of Appeals modified this order, allowing the Nazis to march, but affirmed the injunction against the intentional display of the swastika during the march. The Nazis appealed again.

> PROCEDURAL
> HISTORY

3. The only *issue* before this court is whether the circuit court order enjoining the defendants from displaying the swastika violates the First Amendment rights of the defendants. We are of course bound by the United States Supreme Court in its interpretation of the United States Constitution, and those decisions, particularly *Cohen v. California*, 403 U.S. 15 (1971), compel us to permit the Nazis to wear the swastika during the planned march.

> ISSUE

> HOLDING

4. First, it is clear that the protection of the First Amendment extends to symbols such as the swastika, given that symbols can be a form of political speech. This premise was articulated in *Tinker v. Des Moines Independent Community School District*, 393 U.S. 503 (1969), which held that public school children had a first amendment right to wear black arm bands in protest of the Vietnam War.

> RULE/RULE
> APPLICATION
> FROM
> ANOTHER
> CASE

5.   Plaintiff seeks to extend the "fighting words" doctrine to compel the restraint of the march. The "fighting words" doctrine was first articulated in *Chaplinsky v. New Hampshire*, 315 U.S. 568 (1942), and was designed to permit punishment of extremely hostile personal communication likely to cause immediate physical response. In the *Cohen* case, the Supreme Court described fighting words as "those personally abusive epithets which, when addressed to the ordinary citizen, are, as a matter of common knowledge, inherently likely to provoke violent reaction." Although the "fighting words" *rule* affirmed a *statute* punishing abusive speech, plaintiff asks this Court to extend the *rule* to allow the prior restraint of the Nazi march. In our judgment, we are precluded from doing so.

> Plaintiff's Argument

> RULE APPLICATION FROM ANOTHER CASE

> RULE APPLICATION FROM ANOTHER CASE

> Plaintiff's Argument

> HOLDING

6.   In *Cohen*, the Supreme Court overturned a criminal conviction which stemmed from the defendant wearing a jacket stating "Fuck the Draft" in a Los Angeles courthouse. The Court reasoned that the freedom of expression is necessary for our diverse society, and serves to educate and unite people from all walks of life, stating "That the air may at times seem filled with verbal cacophony is in this sense not a sign of weakness but of strength .... while the particular four-letter word being litigated here is perhaps more distasteful than most others of its genre, it is nevertheless often true that one man's vulgarity is another's lyric."

> EXAMPLE OF RULE APPLICATION FROM ANOTHER CASE

7. Although the swastikas are equally repulsive, the offensiveness of the speech doesn't matter when it comes to the First Amendment. Plaintiffs are not a captive audience and have the opportunity to turn away or "avert their eyes," as stated in *Erzoznik v. City of Jacksonville*, 422 U.S. 205 (1975). According to *Erzoznik*, the "Constitution does not permit the government to decide which types of otherwise protected speech are sufficiently offensive to require protection for the unwilling listener or viewer." The swastika does not fall under the "fighting words" doctrine and we cannot use that *rule* to overcome the presumption against prior restraint.

EXAMPLE OF RULE APPLICATION FROM ANOTHER CASE

HOLDING

8. We accordingly reluctantly conclude the Nazi's use of the swastika is protected speech under the first amendment, and that the citizens of Skokie have the burden to avoid the offensive symbol. We are constrained to reverse the appellate court judgment enjoining the display of the swastika, and the judgment is affirmed in all other respects.

HOLDING

HOLDING

* * *

First, just as we did for the previous case, let's follow the seven steps in the Skills Development to see how that can help us.

Step 1:   You know that the case involves a possibly controversial political party, the National Socialist Party, that the case is being brought by a village, and that the case occurred in 1978.

Steps 2 and 3: You have read the case all the way through. Now, here is the outline of the *topic sentences* (in bold for easy recognition) with italics to help you make sense of it all and see what you still need to figure out:

- The plaintiff, Village of Skokie, brought this lawsuit seeking injunctive relief in order to prevent the National Socialist Party ("Nazis") from holding a rally and march in the Village in which they would march in Nazi uniform, complete with swastika and arm band with signs stating "White Free Speech," "Free Speech for the White Man," and "Free Speech for White America." *(As this is a long first sentence, we know what the plaintiffs are seeking—to stop the Nazi march in their community. Note that the word "injunction," according to Black's Law Dictionary, means "a court order commanding or preventing an action.")*

- The Circuit Court Trial Judge issued the injunction, and the Nazis appealed. *(This tells us that the plaintiff got what it wanted at the trial level.)*

- The only *issue* before this court is whether the circuit court order enjoining the defendants from displaying the swastika violates the First Amendment rights of the defendants. *(The court neatly summarizes the issue before it—very helpful.)*

- First, it is clear that the protection of the First Amendment extends to symbols such as the swastika, given that symbols can be a form of political speech. *(This is the first step in the court's reasoning, and makes the connection between the word "speech" in the First Amendment and the Nazi swastika symbol—the swastika is speech protected by the First Amendment.)*

- Plaintiff seeks to extend the "fighting words" doctrine to compel the restraint of the march. *(The Village of Skokie has identified a legal argument in support of its request for an injunction.)*

- In *Cohen,* the Supreme Court overturned a criminal conviction which stemmed from the defendant wearing a jacket stating "Fuck the Draft" in a Los Angeles courthouse. *(The court refers to this unique and dramatic Supreme Court case, which is an example of First Amendment application.)*

- Although the swastikas are equally repulsive, the offensiveness of the speech doesn't matter when it comes to the First Amendment. *(Here we see what seems to be a significant concept—that offensive and even repulsive speech is protected by the First Amendment.)*

- We accordingly reluctantly conclude the Nazi's use of the swastika is protected speech under the First Amendment, and that the citizens of Skokie have the burden to avoid the offensive symbol. *(We know the court's conclusion that the First Amendment protects the swastika, and that anyone offended has to simply avoid it.)*

So, to summarize, we know that the case is about the Village of Skokie's desire to prevent the Nazis from marching in the village while wearing swastikas. We might have questions on the court's *reasoning* on the "fighting words" doctrine, and why the offensiveness of the speech doesn't matter, but we do know that the swastikas were protected speech despite their offensiveness.

Step 4 *(identify the legal rule the court is applying)* and Step 5 *(identify the legal issue the court is resolving)* go hand-in-hand, and require you to identify the main legal *rule* the court is applying, which will in turn help you identify the *issue.* The court is applying the First Amendment as the legal *rule,* and we can easily identify the legal *issue,* based on paragraph 3, as whether the First Amendment protects the Nazi marchers' use of the swastika.

Finally, for Steps 6 *(identify the court's holding)* and 7 *(identify ALL the court's reasons and the legally relevant facts),* we see that the court holds that the swastika is protected speech under the First Amendment, that plaintiff made an argument that "fighting words" should be a theory used to restrain the use of the swastika, and that the swastika will be allowed despite its repulsiveness.

Now, let's look at one version of a brief for this case, with each section explained and discussed.

SAMPLE *CASE BRIEF*

FACTS: The plaintiff Village of Skokie wanted to stop the Nazi march, and when that failed, wanted to at least stop the use of the swastika during the march. Because the village was comprised of a majority of Jewish people, and a large percentage of those were Holocaust survivors, they argued that the march was extremely offensive and would cause violence. *(Note that this is not cut and pasted, but rather a synthesized summary in the writer's own words.)*

PROCEDURAL HISTORY: The trial court in Illinois, the Circuit Court, enjoined the march. On appeal, the Illinois Court of Appeals reversed all of the injunction except for the provision barring the wearing of swastikas. *(Notice that the Procedural History includes what happened at each level of court—meaning that the writer specified the specific relief that the court granted.)*

RULE: The First Amendment protects speech, which according to *Tinker* includes symbolic speech such as the wearing of political symbols. *(Note that this rule statement includes not only a reference to the First Amendment but also a reference to the relevant interpretation of the First Amendment under Tinker; in other words, this rule section includes the rule and a bit of rule explanation.)*

ISSUE: Whether the ban on swastikas violates the Nazis' First Amendment right to freedom of speech? *(Again, a question that references the specific relevant facts—the Nazis wearing the swastika—as well as the legal rule implicated—the freedom of speech clause under the First Amendment.)*

HOLDING: Yes, the Nazis cannot be prohibited from wearing the political symbol of the swastika. *(A very simple statement that answers the question posed in the issue with a "yes" and provides a full sentence while not going into the reasoning.)*

REASONING: The Illinois Supreme Court first referred to the First Amendment, and then relied principally on two U.S. Supreme Court cases about the freedom of speech—*Tinker* and *Cohen*. According to the *Tinker* holding, political symbols are protected by the First Amendment's protection of speech, which means that swastikas are protected. Then, the court relied on the holding of *Cohen*, which held that even highly offensive speech is protected. The court also referred to *Erzoznik*, in which the U.S. Supreme Court stated that the burden is on the viewer, the audience, to avert their eyes and avoid offensive speech. Thus, even though swastikas were offensive and upsetting for Skokie's Jewish population, the symbols are protected speech under the First Amendment and the Nazis are allowed to march with them. *(Note, again, that the reasoning explains the specific precedent relied on, the holding from those cases, and how that holding applies to these facts; also, the writer lays out the reasoning in a simple step-by-step structure that is easy to follow.)*

* * *

What do you notice about this *case brief?* One of the principal differences between the *Skokie* case and the *SPCA* case is that in *Skokie*, the *reasoning* is more involved. The court engaged in a *reasoning* process that is much more explicit, direct, and complex than the SPCA case. You could even say there were multiple steps in the *reasoning*: Step 1—political symbols are covered by the First Amendment; Step 2—offensive speech is protected by the First Amendment; Step 3—those who might be offended by speech have the burden of looking away or avoiding; and Step 4—the Nazi swastika is protected by the First Amendment even though it's offensive, and the Jewish citizens of Skokie have the burden of looking away or avoiding the protest.

Don't skimp when you are summarizing and reporting the *reasoning*. Rather, you should try to understand all aspects of the court's *reasoning*—this will help you develop your skills in legal *reasoning* and legal argument. You should also learn to identify the reason the court is relying on a specific case—it's never enough to say in the *reasoning* section that "the court relied on precedent." Instead, name the case and the principle the case stands for, and how this principle contributed to the court's *reasoning.*

CHAPTER 5 LEGAL SKILLS

- **Understand and identify an *IRAC* analysis**
- **Draft a simple *IRAC* analysis**
- **Draft a simple *case brief***
- **Use the *IRAC* method to do a *case brief***

CHAPTER 5 VOCABULARY

- Case brief
- Facts, Procedural History, Rule, Issue, Holding, Reasoning
- Ferae naturae
- Habeus corpus
- IRAC
- Issue, Rule, Application, Conclusion
- Mini-rule
- Per curiam

CHAPTER 5 RESEARCH AND ANALYSIS EXERCISES

I.   Drafting an IRAC analysis:

The following problems provide a fact scenario as well as an actual legal rule. For each problem, read the facts and the rule provided, and identify the element at issue in the rule. Try to phrase the issue as a question that includes both the element, the broader rule, and then proceed to draft a simple IRAC analysis, using the headings **ISSUE, RULE, APPLICATION, CONCLUSION.** Note that some of the IRAC exercises have a very simple application, with arguably little doubt, while for others the application may be a bit more difficult, and may require you to recognize and articulate the arguments on both sides.

1.   FACTS: In Los Angeles, Yashahiro Saito and his girlfriend Sara Tanaka met each other at UCLA, and after falling in love and dating for several years, decided to get married. Yashahiro proposed to Sara at the Griffith Observatory, and gave her a beautiful engagement ring made out of a very expensive cultured pearl. Soon after their engagement, Sara decided to become a professional acrobat and travel the world with a circus. She left L.A. and has never been heard from since. In the meantime, Yashahiro has decided to become a lawyer and asks you if he has any right to get the ring back. He needs it for tuition.

RULE (loosely based on Cal. Civ. Code § 1590 (West 2018)):

A person who gives a ring to another person (donee) in contemplation of marriage can recover the ring if the donee refuses to enter into marriage, or a portion of the ring's value, considering all the circumstances and as found by a court or jury to be just.

2.   FACTS: Jonathan was in the NoBucks coffee store working on a research and writing memo for his paralegal class on his laptop computer. He had forgotten his charging cord but thought he had enough power to finish his memo and send it to his professor. After he used spell check and proofread the memo three or four times, he was ready to email it to his professor. Right at that moment, his laptop ran out of power and died. Jonathan looked around and noticed that a young couple, Said and Katherine, had just left their laptops unattended to go outside. He looked around the whole coffee shop to see if anyone was looking, and then grabbed one of the power chargers from the unattended laptop to power up his own laptop. He muttered to himself: "I could really use a spare charger." After he emailed his memo, he got a text from his neighbor that his dog Einstein had escaped from the backyard and was running free on the street. Jonathan rushed out with his laptop and the borrowed cord so he could find Einstein as soon as possible.

RULE:

Larceny is the taking and carrying away the personal property of another with the intent to permanently deprive the person of their property.

3.   FACTS: Vince the veteran has a prosthetic lower leg and foot, from the knee down, due to an IED (improvised explosive device) that blew up in front of him when he was serving in Iraq. He also had a scarred face from the explosion. While he was standing sitting at the bar of Ends of the Earth Tavern, a group of men came in and started mocking him and calling him "scarface." One of them, Tommy, got really riled up and kicked Vince in his prosthetic shin.

RULE:

Battery is the intentional touching or physical contact of another person without consent in a way that is unwanted or offensive.

4.   FACTS: Minnie lived in a very snowy city that received over 100 inches of snow a year. One day, immediately after it had snowed about a foot, Minnie shoveled the sidewalk in front of her house and made sure it was free of snow and ice. After the sidewalk was clear, Stefan was walking down the sidewalk in front of Minnie's house and tripped because one of the heels on his dress shoes suddenly came flying off. He broke his leg.

RULE:

To prove negligence, the plaintiff must establish by the preponderance of evidence that the defendant had a duty, defendant breached the duty, and that breach caused damages.

5.   FACTS: Minnie's town was undergoing a second huge snowstorm that deposited approximately two feet of snow. Immediately after it stopped snowing, Minnie shoveled the sidewalk and made sure it was free of snow and ice, except for one icy spot that Minnie just forgot about. Brooke was walking down the sidewalk and in front of Minnie's house she slipped and fell on the patch of ice that Minnie had forgotten about. Brooke is very athletic and flexible, and was wearing a padded clown suit. She suffered no injuries.

RULE:

To prove negligence, the plaintiff must establish by the preponderance of evidence that the defendant had a duty, defendant breached the duty, and that breach caused damages.

II. Drafting case briefs:

1.   **Discussion/Group exercise:** Look up sample case briefs with your search engine, and compare the actual text of the case with the case brief. There are a lot of sample case briefs that can readily be found with simple searches; you can also search by name based on cases that interest you. To get you started, here are the citations to some famous Supreme Court cases: *Brown v. Board of Education*, 347 U.S. 483 (1954); *Miranda v. Arizona*, 384 U.S. 436 (1966); *Brandenburg v. Ohio*, 395 U.S. 444 (1969); *Dred Scott v. Sandford*, 60 U.S. 393 (1857).

If there is another content area that you are interested in, you can find famous cases is that area too by doing simple searches on your search engine ("famous supreme court contract cases" or "famous supreme court discrimination cases"), getting the help of your professor, doing a little bit of in-depth research on your topic, or simply reviewing a list of landmark Supreme Court cases and choosing one that interests you.

After you have read both the case and the case brief, answer the following questions about the case brief:

a.   How were the facts of the case summarized in the case brief? Were the facts too detailed, not detailed, or just right? Do the facts contain all the legally relevant facts?

b.   Is the issue statement a question? Does it indicate the legal rule and the legally relevant facts?

c.   What are the legally relevant facts?

d.   Does the reasoning include ALL the court's reasoning laid out in a clear way? What changes would you make?

III. Drafting IRAC exercises on ethics:

1.   FACTS: A paralegal working as a solo independent paralegal was approached by prisoner who wanted to know his chances of success on a habeus corpus petition challenging his conviction on constitutional grounds. The prisoner and the paralegal entered into a contract for

"paralegal services" that required the paralegal to review the prisoner's case and render an opinion on the potential success of the petition.[2]

> RULE (based on state statutes that prohibit the unauthorized practice of law): No person without a license to practice law shall practice law in this state.

2.   FACTS: An attorney had his own firm in a major metropolitan area. The firm represented banks in foreclosure actions and grew quickly, especially in the paralegal department. The firm was called "Castellani LLP," had one attorney and about 20 paralegals. Florine Lagos was one of the paralegals and her business card states: "Castellani Law Firm LLP" with her name below it—simply "Florine Lagos."[3]

> RULE: A lawyer is responsible for taking reasonable measures to ensure that clients, courts, and other lawyers are aware that a paralegal, whose services are utilized by the lawyer in performing legal services, is not licensed to practice law.[4]

---

[2]   Based on *Carter v. Flaherty*, 37 Misc. 3d 46, 953 N.Y.S.2d 814 (App. Term. N.Y. 2012).

[3]   Based on *In Re Castelli*, 131 A.D.3d 29, 11 N.Y.S.3d 268 (2d Dep't 2015).

[4]   American Bar Association Model Guidelines for the Utilization of Paralegal Services, Standing Committee on Paralegals (ABA 2018). Note that these guidelines are NOT the same as the ABA Model Rules on Professional Conduct, which are the model ethics rules.

Determining the Legal Issue and the Legally Relevant Facts

Legal Skills:

- Identify the *legal issue*
- Identify which element(s) of the legal rule are at issue
- Identify the legally relevant facts
- Articulate the legal issue using the "whether" "under" "when" format or a variation of that format

PART I. ISSUES

A. What Is a *Legal Issue?*

We often talk about issues—issues in politics, issues in families, or money issues, for example. In law, "issue" has a very specific meaning, as you learned in Chapter 5, where we defined it as if and how a legal rule applies to facts. Perhaps in many fields an "issue" is something vaguely problematic that involves some sort of conflict and invites discussion. Although that may be true for *legal issues*, too, the precise meaning of a *legal issue* is the intersection of facts and the legal rule. That's because legal analysis is simply the application of a legal rule to a set of facts. That is, an issue is a question: do these facts violate, or fulfill, the legal rule? In order to spot a *legal issue* or articulate a *legal issue*, you must know the rule. In other words, it's not a *legal issue* unless there is a legal rule involved. And there are always facts.

On a basic level, thinking about *legal issues*—the intersection of facts and the law—also includes thinking about the elements of the rule and the legally relevant facts. When it comes to legal rules, we know from Chapter 1 that there will be elements (separate parts) of the rule. Therefore, a *legal issue* will likewise center on a specific element (or more) of the rule. Likewise, we learned in Chapter 4 that legally relevant facts are those facts that make a difference in the meeting or fulfilling of one element. So, the *legal issue* will similarly include reference to the legally relevant facts.

In this chapter, we will be looking at how to **articulate** a *legal issue*, complete with an element and legally relevant facts; how to **spot** a *legal issue* in a client/factual hypothetical scenario; and how to **identify** a *legal issue* in a court opinion. **Articulating** a *legal issue* clearly requires that you include both the element and the legally relevant facts, so we will start there. We typically **spot** *legal issues* when a client presents us with facts and a legal question, and then we need to find the legal rule to answer it. Finally, when we read case law, we need to **identify** the *legal issue* the court is resolving. This helps us to understand the court's reasoning. All three skills are important and will give you the tools to do legal analysis.

B. How Do We Articulate the *Legal Issue?*

In order to convey the most information, and to refer to the legal rule, the specific element, and the legally relevant facts, it can be helpful to use prompts to articulate the *legal issue*. Think of prompts as cues to remember the three components to articulating the *legal issue*. There are many prompts that you can use, and what will work may vary from situation to situation. But here is a good start:

Diagram 19:

Articulating a *Legal Issue*

Prompts	Components of *Legal Issue*
Whether	The question
Under	The legal rule and/or the specific element at issue
When	The legally relevant facts

For example, assume Barbara the baker is accused of running a red light in her Buick and hitting Antoine the architect while he was in his Audi, and both Philip the photographer and Yolanda the yurt-builder witnessed the accident. If Philip and Yolanda disagree about what color car Barbara the baker was driving, we could say we have an issue. Is that a *legal issue*? Probably not, because based on these facts, the color of the car has nothing to do with the fault of the driver in running the red light.

But we would have to know the legal rule to be sure. If the legal rule is **negligence**, with the elements of **duty, breach of duty, causation, and damages**, and the specific legal rule about one element, **duty**, states: "Disobedience of any traffic signal, including traffic lights and traffic signs, is a violation of the driver's **duty** of care"—then we know running the red light is a legal problem for Barbara, but the color of her car is not relevant to that legal rule. Rather, the *legal issue* here is whether Barbara the baker breached her duty of care when she ran the red light.

After spotting a *legal issue*, our next task is to precisely articulate that *legal issue* including both the **element at issue and the legally relevant facts**. We will use this precise articulation later on, when we construct our legal memo, and the specific identification of the element at issue together with the legally relevant facts will help the reader understand your subsequent analyses. Precise articulation is also very helpful to the researcher, as it keeps you focused on the element at issue, and therefore the relevant legal rules.

Here is how you could articulate the *legal issue* within the framework above:

Diagram 20:
Using a Chart to Articulate the *Legal Issue*

Prompts	Components of *Legal Issue*	*Legal Issue*
Whether	question	Whether Barbara was negligent
Under	Legal rule/element at issue	And breached her duty of care under the legal rule
When	Legally relevant facts	When she ran a red light and hit Antoine the architect

As you can see, all the components are included, and although the prompts were not exactly followed, as we see a reference to the legal rule in the first component, the specific element is mentioned in the second component, and the relevant facts are mentioned in the third component. However, the chart provides a nice visual summary of the different parts of a precise *legal issue* statement.

SKILLS DEVELOPMENT

Steps for Spotting, Identifying, and Articulating the Legal Issue

To Spot or Identify a Legal Issue:

Step 1: Find and examine the legal rule, whether it's a common law rule, a statute, a regulation, or a Constitutional clause.

Step 2: Separate the legal rule into its elements (depending on the rule, it may also be necessary to figure out the definitions of those elements).

Step 3: See which facts fall under which elements to determine relevant facts.

Step 4: Determine which elements are at issue (which element does not match with any facts, enough facts, or conflicting facts? Or, which element needs to be defined or better defined?).

To Articulate the Legal Issue:

Step 5: For each element at issue, create a precise statement of the legal issue that includes three parts in a formula something like this: whether—(question)—under—(element of legal rule at issue)—when (legally relevant facts).

The "whether—under—when" formula provides helpful prompts so that you can remember all three items necessary in a precise *legal issue* question—the question, the element of the legal rule at issue, and the legally relevant facts. Of course, it is not the ONLY formula that works, and there are a variety of correct ways to put a *legal issue* question together, including "Under—does—when," or "Is—when—because," "Whether—when" or "Can—if—when." As with any formula, its purpose is to supply helpful prompts for beginners.

Now that you know the definition and components of a *legal issue*, and how to articulate a legal issue, let's turn to spotting a *legal issue*. You will have two basic situations when you will need to spot or define a *legal issue*: 1) when YOU are doing the analysis, and you have a set of facts and a rule (either you have found the rule or you are supplied with the rule); and 2) when the COURT has done the analysis, and you have to read (and try to understand) a court opinion. In both cases, the legal rule is paramount.

C. Importance of the Rule in Spotting a Legal Issue

Issue spotting is a valued legal skill that we will practice here. Lawyers typically use the term *"issue spotting"* to refer to when they are presented with a factual situation and have to figure out what the *legal issues* are. We know that spotting a *legal issue* requires knowledge of the legal rule. Sometimes, you will have the legal background to know the legal rules, and that may make spotting the *legal issue* easier. As a beginner, however, you will often have to find the legal rule with research. Here, you can practice looking at a factual situation alone, and then with a legal rule, so you can see the steps to spot a *legal issue*.

Let's take a look at this hypothetical fact situation about the issue of common-law marriage:

> Sally and Stu have lived together as a couple for 30 years in the same state, have had joint checking accounts, and have held themselves out to the public as man and wife. They never officially married and they have no children. They consider themselves to have a common-law marriage, although they have never looked up whether that is legal in their state. When Stu died at the age of 66, his doctor believed it was due to complications arising from Gulf War Syndrome. The documents for Stu's military pension specify that the proceeds can go to his spouse. Stu never got around to specifically naming Sally as the beneficiary to his pension.

First, let's think about the *factual issues* Sally wants resolved. Remember, you are not expected to know any legal rules off the top of your head. Nor should you assume that you do know legal rules that you don't, in fact, know. If you are not afraid to ask questions, and you do not assume you know a legal rule without actually reviewing it, then you will avoid a major mistake: making assumptions about the law such as what spouse means, what common-law marriage means, or whether your state recognizes it. For example, it's easy to have familiarity with the term "common-law marriage" yet not know the precise legal definition in your state.

So, after reviewing our hypothetical, we can begin to identify the initial *factual* and *legal issues*.

These are some questions that might come to mind:

- Of course, the first obvious issue or "threshold" issue that Sally would be asking us as our client is does Sally have any right to Stu's pension?

- Anything special about a military pension that we need to know?

- In Sally's state, what is common-law marriage and what are the legal rights of people in a common-law marriage? In other words, what is the legal rule?

- Anything special about Gulf War Syndrome that we need to know?

- Does Stu have other relevant documents that would help Sally?

Again, these are some preliminary questions that you can start with. Note that these preliminary issues are not the same as a well-framed *legal issue* that includes both facts and the law, simply because there is no reference to a specific legal rule. Indeed, we don't yet have a legal rule. If you can specifically frame the preliminary issues BEFORE you go hunting for the legal rule, this step can be a tool for helping you understand the legal rule(s) you have to find.

For example, articulating the issue in the following way gives us specific information about the legal rule we need to find:

ISSUE: Whether Sally's relationship qualifies as a common-law marriage and whether the common-law marriage qualifies her as his spouse for the purposes of Stu's military pension?

Notice that the issue is really asking about a definition—what are the definitions of common law marriage and spouse for the purposes of the military pension law? To help you identify *factual* and *legal issues*, you often want to think about the facts in terms of definitions—what terms need to be defined or need to be better defined? What terms or facts need legal definitions? Often, the first instinct of a lawyer is to ask "What does _____ mean?" In the case of Sally and Stu, the definition of spouse under military pension law is especially relevant for determining whether Sally gets the pension. The first instinct of a lawyer would be to ask that question and find out if there is an answer in the statute. The lawyer would find that the Veterans Administration allows benefits for common-law marriage and looks to the law of the state jurisdiction in question to determine whether common-law marriage is legally recognized.

For the purpose of this exercise, let's assume for now that the jurisdiction is New York. The legal research question will then be the definition of "common-law marriage" in New York. In looking up "common-law marriage" in New York, we discover the legal rule according to *Mott v. Duncan Petroleum Trans.*, 51 N.Y.2d 289, 434 N.Y.S.2d 155 (1980):

> It has long been settled law that although New York does not itself recognize common-law marriages (citations omitted) a common-law marriage contracted in a sister State will be recognized as valid here if it is valid where contracted.

So, according to the highest court in New York, there is no common-law marriage in New York. When we combine the question of Sally's need for Stu's pension with the New York rule that there is no common-law marriage in New York, the *legal issue* might look like this:

ISSUE: **Whether** Sally, the 30 year companion of Stu, counts as his spouse in terms of his veteran pension benefits **when** New York does not recognize common-law marriage and Sally and Stu were never "officially" married?

Under New York law, the answer is **NO**, given the New York rule that New York does not recognize common-law marriages.

Now let's try the same facts, and a different rule. Remember, the legal rule is fundamental to the *legal issue*. In order to demonstrate the importance of the legal rule, and how it can change the statement of the *legal issue*, while also demonstrating the basic federalism concept that different states can have vastly different rules, let's look at the same case of Sally and Stu in another jurisdiction with a much different rule. So, if we pick a new state that has a much different rule, like Rhode Island, what happens?

Here is Rhode Island law on common-law marriage in a quote from the reasoning of the Rhode Island Supreme Court (Rhode Island's court of last resort) in the case *Smith v. Smith*, 966 A.2d 109, 111 (R.I. 2009) (note: to make this long quote easier to read, the sentences are set out in separate paragraphs):

This state recognizes common-law marriage. *Souza v. O'Hara,* 121 R.I. 88, 91, 395 A.2d 1060, 1062 (1978).

"Although marriage is of the nature of a civil contract, it is a contract which is subject to the regulation of the state, in which in its inception or its dissolution the state has a vital interest." *Silva v. Merritt Chapman & Scott Corp.,* 52 R.I. 30, 32, 156 A. 512, 513 (1931).

Therefore, to establish a common-law marriage, we have adopted the clear and convincing standard of proof. *See id.*

A common-law marriage requires "evidence that the parties seriously intended to enter into the husband-wife relationship." *Sardonis v. Sardonis,* 106 R.I. 469, 472, 261 A.2d 22, 24 (1970) (citing *Ibello v. Sweet,* 47 R.I. 480, 482, 133 A. 801, 801–02 (1926)).

In addition, the conduct of the parties must be "of such a character as to lead to a belief in the community that they were married." *Id.* (citing *Williams v. Herrick,* 21 R.I. 401, 402, 43 A. 1036, 1037 (1899)). The elements of intent and belief are demonstrated by "inference from cohabitation, declarations, reputation among kindred and friends, and other competent circumstantial evidence." *Id.*

We purposefully left in the court's citations to other cases so you can be exposed to the density of legal text and how often courts need to cite to legal authority. Try not to be overwhelmed by the case citations. This is simply how courts write—every proposition is supported by a case, especially because the court is laying out the legal rule about common-law marriage. Remember, there has to be a legal source for the legal rule.

How would you digest that paragraph? Try to make a list that represents each sentence:

- Rhode Island recognizes common-law marriage as legal;

- The state has an interest in how legal marriage is defined;

- Marriage must be established by clear and convincing evidence:

  o Serious intent to enter into husband-wife relationship **(intent)**

  o Behavior that leads the community to believe they are married **(community belief)**

  o Proof of the two elements **intent** and **community belief** through cohabitation, declarations, reputation, and other *circumstantial evidence.*

Note that the last bullet point provides that the two elements of intent and community belief can be established by *circumstantial evidence. Circumstantial evidence* means what it sounds like—indirect evidence or "circumstances." *Circumstantial evidence* can be every bit as reliable, or unreliable, as direct evidence. One way to explain the difference is that direct evidence goes directly to establishing a fact, no guesswork, while indirect or *circumstantial evidence* requires you to make an inference before you get to that fact. To explain the difference, an example often used is that direct evidence would be a witness stating that she saw it raining outside, while indirect evidence of rain would be a witness coming inside with a wet coat and umbrella.[1]

For Sally and Stu, an example of direct evidence of community belief that Sally and Stu are married would be a statement by the town mayor referencing their marriage. An example of indirect evidence of their marriage would be a picture of both of them in white, holding hands.

So if the above list is the Rhode Island rule on common-law marriage, how would you articulate the *issue*?

> *ISSUE:* **Whether** Sally and Stu's relationship qualifies as a common-law marriage under Rhode Island law **when** they lived together for 30 years, had joint checking accounts, and "held themselves out to the public" as man and wife?

We have seen that there are many ways to articulate a *legal issue*. In the above example, it is implied that Rhode Island law recognizes common-law marriage, and the elements of the legal rule (remember, **intent** and **community belief**) are not specifically mentioned. Rather, the relevant facts regarding the marriage are mentioned. Specifically, the relevant facts about the marriage are: living together for 30 years, having joint checking accounts, and holding themselves out to the public as man and wife. Why are those facts relevant? Because they could satisfy the specific elements (**intent** and **community belief**) in the Rhode Island rule.

Another way to articulate the *legal issue* could be to include more information (e.g., the elements) about the specific legal rule:

---

[1] *See* Eugenee M. Heeter, Chance of Rain: Rethinking Circumstantial Evidence Jury Instructions, 64 Hastings L.J. 527, 528–529 (2013).

ISSUE: Whether under Rhode Island law, which recognizes common-law marriage, Sally and Stu can show **serious intent** to enter into a husband and wife relationship and that they led the **community to believe** that they were married?

So here, you can see that Rhode Island's rule—recognition of common-law marriage—and the specific elements—**serious intent** and **community belief**—are explicitly mentioned in the articulation of the *legal issue*. You do not see the specific facts from the hypothetical about Sally and Stu's marriage—their cohabitation, the length of their cohabitation, their joint checking account, etc.

Yet a third and final way to articulate the *legal issue* would be to include both the rule and the elements as well as a few of the most relevant facts. For example:

ISSUE: **Whether** Sally and Stu have a common-law marriage **under** Rhode Island law, which requires clear and convincing proof of serious intent to marry and couples' behavior that leads to community belief that they are married, **when** they lived together for 30 years, had a joint checking account, and "held themselves out" as husband and wife?

As you can see, this is by far the longest articulation of the *legal issue*, and it provides the most information—both the legal rule and the relevant facts—about the *legal issue*. Discuss with your professor which statement of the *legal issue* works best for your class for the legal problem that you are working on.

PART II. *FACTUAL ISSUES:* SPOTTING A *FACTUAL ISSUE* REGARDING ONE ELEMENT

Now that you know the basic anatomy of a *legal issue*, we will see what a *factual issue* looks like. We will look at the same Rhode Island rule about common-law marriage and a similar hypothetical to see how there can be a *factual issue* about one element. This is slightly different than what we did in Part I, where we asked whether, considering all the circumstances of Sally and Stu's marriage, the elements for common-law marriage were met. Here, as you will see, the question is how the facts would be resolved regarding one specific piece of proof.

Here is the factual hypothetical:

> Neva and Neal have been in a committed relationship for the past 15 years, and are seeking to have their marriage declared a valid common-law marriage in Rhode Island. Fifteen years ago, when they decided to be in a committed relationship, they chose not to buy a house together because Neva works in Boston, Massachusetts during the week and returns to Providence, Rhode Island on Fridays to spend the weekend with Neal. Neal owns his own home in Providence. Boston and Providence are about 45–50 miles apart. (No additional facts about their relationship are known at this time.)

Here is the Rhode Island rule for common law marriage (same as above but repeated here for your convenience):

> Rhode Island will recognize a marriage as a valid and legal common law marriage if the couple can demonstrate 1) serious intent to enter into a common law marriage and 2) that they behaved in a way to make the community believe they were man and wife. Elements 1 and 2 can be proven by cohabitation, declarations, reputation, and other circumstantial evidence.

Unlike the hypothetical situation with Sally and Stu, where we had a lot of information about behavior as a couple, the only information we have about Neva and Neal is their living situation. As you know from working with the rule, one of the facts to look at is cohabitation— and information about cohabitation is the only information provided. As tempting as it is to want to elaborate on the facts, add facts, or guess at additional facts to embellish the hypothetical, you have to accept (or pretend) that these are the only facts we have. Since you know that cohabitation is only one of the pieces of evidence that can establish common-law marriage, it is only natural that you would ask your client about whether any of the additional *factors* exist (which you can't do in this situation). However, you would still need to know whether the parties' living arrangements could qualify as cohabitation.[2]

So if we look at the rule, and we look at the facts, we see that because "cohabitation" is not defined, it may not be clear whether Neva and Neal have met the definition of cohabitation. As you know, cohabitation is one of the facts that can prove the elements **intent** and **community behavior.** Here is how the *factual issue* could be articulated:

> *ISSUE:* **Whether** Neva and Neal have a common-law marriage and can satisfy the definition of cohabitation **under** Rhode Island law **when**, although they report being a committed couple for 15 years, they have lived in separate cities and spend only the weekends together at Neal's house?

In other words, here, the facts are conflicting—on the one hand, they seem to have the **intent** to be a long-term couple because they identify themselves as a committed couple. On the other hand, they chose not to buy a house together and not to live in the same city. Therefore, the facts—and the facts alone—could be argued in opposing ways. Neva and Neal have the **intent** to establish a common law marriage and have demonstrated their commitment to each other by remaining in a committed relationship over a 15-year time period, despite the fact that they see each other only on the weekends. Or, Neva and Neal don't have the **intent** for a common law marriage because they did not co-habitate or buy a house together during that time. Therefore, there is a *factual issue* over one of the elements.

---

[2]   To clarify, according to *Smith v. Smith*, 966 A.2d 109 (R.I. 2009), although **intent** can be inferred from cohabitation, cohabitation alone is not conclusive of intent to be husband and wife.

PART III. *LEGAL ISSUES:* IDENTIFYING A *LEGAL ISSUE* IN A SUPREME COURT CASE

Now you will take a look at an edited U.S. Supreme Court case and follow the steps to identify and articulate the *legal issue* you see in the case. Sometimes, the court will start its opinion by clearly stating the *legal issue* for the reader. Sometimes, the court will start its opinion with the factual story of the case. Finally, sometimes the court will start its opinion with the procedural history of the case. It is your job to figure out which way the court starts the opinion. In general, in reading a complex case, students find it helpful to note on each paragraph what action the court is engaging in: **articulating** the *legal issue*, **telling** the factual story, **explaining** what happened in the courts below, **setting** out the rule, **explaining** the meaning and application of the rule, or **applying** the rule to the factual situation. Note that these key words have been inserted for you.

Remember the Skills Development tips from Chapter 5 to help with reading comprehension: 1) preview; 2) read; 3) read again but focus on topic sentences to understand outline of case; 4) identify the legal rule(s) being applied; 5) identify the issue(s) the court is resolving; 6) identify the court's holding(s); and 7) identify all the reasons for the court's holding.

Here, to preview the case, you can look at the shading labels of the case parts and perhaps skim or read the topic sentences for those paragraphs. Previewing can also include taking a look at a few sections of the case. For example, look at the first paragraph of the opinion below. Does the Court articulate the *legal issue* clearly? Since there is not an explicit reference to a rule, there likewise does not appear to be a clear statement of the *legal issue*, especially to a beginning legal reader. However, you can see roughly what the case is about: liberty and same-sex marriage. (Hint: can you get a sense—or guess—from the tone of the paragraph and the way it is set up whether the Court thinks liberty includes same-sex marriage? Don't worry if you cannot answer this question, but start to pay attention to the arrangement of text and the nature of a court's descriptions and definitions. Try to determine whether the Court is defining liberty broadly, i.e., inclusively, or narrowly.)[3]

* * *

Supreme Court of the United States
James OBERGEFELL, et al., Petitioners

v.

Richard Hodges, Director, Ohio Department of Health, et al.;
Valeria Tanco, et al., Petitioners

v.

Bill Haslam, Governor of Tennessee, et al.;
April DeBoer, et al., Petitioners

v.

Rick Snyder, Governor of Michigan, et al.; and
Gregory Bourke, et al., Petitioners

v.

Steve Beshear, Governor of Kentucky.

Decided June 26, 2015.

. . .

Opinion

Justice KENNEDY delivered the opinion of the Court.

The Constitution promises liberty to all within its reach, a liberty that includes certain specific rights that allow persons, within a lawful realm, to define and express their identity. The petitioners in these cases seek to find that liberty by marrying someone of the same sex and having their

> Articulating the Legal Issue

---

[3] By defining "liberty" broadly—as the right to define and express one's identity—the Court is signaling a broad or expansive definition of this word, which would indeed include same-sex marriage.

marriages deemed lawful on the same terms and conditions as marriages between persons of the opposite sex.

I.

[Facts omitted]

. . .

II.

. . .

III.

Under the Due Process Clause of the Fourteenth Amendment, no State shall "deprive any person of life, liberty, or property, without due process of law." The fundamental liberties protected by this Clause include most of the rights enumerated in the Bill of Rights. See *Duncan v. Louisiana,* 391 U.S. 145, 147–149, 88 S.Ct. 1444, 20 L.Ed.2d 491 (1968). In addition these liberties extend to certain personal choices central to individual dignity and autonomy, including intimate choices that define personal identity and beliefs. *See, e.g., Eisenstadt v. Baird,* 405 U.S. 438, 453, 92 S.Ct. 1029, 31 L.Ed.2d 349 (1972); *Griswold v. Connecticut,* 381 U.S. 479, 484–486, 85 S.Ct. 1678, 14 L.Ed.2d 510 (1965). The identification and protection of fundamental rights is an enduring part of the judicial duty to interpret the Constitution. That responsibility, however, "has not been reduced to any formula." *Poe v. Ullman,* 367 U.S. 497, 542, 81 S.Ct. 1752, 6 L.Ed.2d 989 (1961) (Harlan, J., dissenting). Rather, it requires courts to exercise reasoned judgment in identifying interests

> Setting out the Rule

> Explaining the Meaning and Application of the Rule

of the person so fundamental that the State must accord them its respect. *See ibid.* . . .

The nature of injustice is that we may not always see it in our own times. The generations that wrote and ratified the Bill of Rights and the Fourteenth amendment did not presume to know the extent of freedom in all of its dimensions, and so they entrusted to future generations a charter protecting the right of all persons to enjoy liberty as we learn its meaning. When new insight reveals discord between the Constitution's central protections and a received legal stricture, a claim to liberty must be addressed.

Applying these established tenets, the Court has long held the right to marry is protected by the Constitution. In *Loving v. Virginia*, 388 U.S. 1, 12, 87 S.Ct. 1817, 18 L.Ed.2d 1010 (1967), which invalidated bans on interracial unions, a unanimous Court held marriage is "one of the vital personal rights essential to the orderly pursuit of happiness by free men." The Court reaffirmed that holding in *Zablocki v. Redhail*, 434 U.S. 374, 384, 98 S.Ct. 673, 54 L.Ed.2d 618 (1978), which held the right to marry was burdened by a law prohibiting fathers who were behind on child support from marrying. The Court again applied this principle in *Turner v. Safley*, 482 U.S. 78, 95, 107 S.Ct. 2254, 96 L.Ed.2d 64 (1987), which held the right to marry was abridged by regulations limiting the privilege of prison inmates to marry. Over time and in other contexts, the Court has reiterated that the right to marry is fundamental under the Due Process Clause. *See, e.g., M.L.B. v. S.L.J.*, 519 U.S. 102, 116,

> Explaining the Meaning and Application of the Rule

117 S.Ct. 555, 136 L.Ed.2d 473 (1996); *Cleveland Bd. of Ed. v. LaFleur,* 414 U.S. 632, 639–640, 94 S.Ct. 791, 39 L.Ed.2d 52 (1974); *Griswold, supra,* at 486, 85 S.Ct. 1678; *Skinner v. Oklahoma ex rel. Williamson,* 316 U.S. 535, 541, 62 S.Ct. 1110, 86 L.Ed. 1655 (1942); *Meyer v. Nebraska,* 262 U.S. 390, 399, 43 S.Ct. 625, 67 L.Ed. 1042 (1923).

It cannot be denied that this Court's cases describing the right to marry presumed a relationship involving opposite-sex partners. The Court, like many institutions, has made assumptions defined by the world and time of which it is a part. This was evident in *Baker v. Nelson,* 409 U.S. 810, 93 S.Ct. 37, 34 L.Ed.2d 65, a one-line summary decision issued in 1972, holding the exclusion of same-sex couples from marriage did not present a substantial federal question.

Still, there are other, more instructive precedents. This Court's cases have expressed constitutional principles of broader reach. In defining the right to marry these cases have identified essential attributes of that right based in history, tradition, and other constitutional liberties inherent in this intimate bond. *See, e.g., Lawrence,* 539 U.S., at 574, 123 S.Ct. 2472; *Turner, supra,* at 95, 107 S.Ct. 2254; *Zablocki, supra,* at 384, 98 S.Ct. 673; *Loving, supra,* at 12, 87 S.Ct. 1817; *Griswold, supra,* at 486, 85 S.Ct. 1678. And in assessing whether the force and rationale of its cases apply to same-sex couples, the Court must respect the basic reasons why the right to marry has been long protected. *See, e.g., Eisenstadt, supra,* at 453–454, 92 S.Ct. 1029; *Poe,*

> Explaining the
> Meaning and
> Application
> of the Rule

supra, at 542–553, 81 S.Ct. 1752 (Harlan, J., dissenting).

This analysis compels the conclusion that same-sex couples may exercise the right to marry. The four principles and traditions to be discussed demonstrate that the reasons marriage is fundamental under the Constitution apply with equal force to same-sex couples. . . .

Holding

. . . [Four principles applying right to same-sex marriage omitted]

The right to marry is fundamental as a matter of history and tradition, but rights come not from ancient sources alone. They rise, too, from a better informed understanding of how constitutional imperatives define a liberty that remains urgent in our own era. Many who deem same-sex marriage to be wrong reach that conclusion based on decent and honorable religious or philosophical premises, and neither they nor their beliefs are disparaged here. But when that sincere, personal opposition becomes enacted law and public policy, the necessary consequence is to put the imprimatur of the State itself on an exclusion that soon demeans or stigmatizes those whose own liberty is then denied. Under the Constitution, same-sex couples seek in marriage the same legal treatment as opposite-sex couples, and it would disparage their choices and diminish their personhood to deny them this right.

Applying the Rule

The right of same-sex couples to marry that is part of the liberty promised by the Fourteenth amendment is derived, too, from that Amendment's guarantee of the equal protection of the laws. The Due Process Clause and the Equal Protection Clause are connected in a profound way, though they set forth independent principles. Rights implicit in liberty and rights secured by equal protection may rest on different precepts and are not always co-extensive, yet in some instances each may be instructive as to the meaning and reach of the other. In any particular case one Clause may be thought to capture the essence of the right in a more accurate and comprehensive way, even as the two Clauses may converge in the identification and definition of the right. *See M.L.B.,* 519 U.S., at 120–121, 117 S.Ct. 555; *id.,* at 128–129, 117 S.Ct. 555 (KENNEDY, J., concurring in judgment); *Bearden v. Georgia,* 461 U.S. 660, 665, 103 S.Ct. 2064, 76 L.Ed.2d 221 (1983). This interrelation of the two principles furthers our understanding of what freedom is and must become.

> Holding
> and
> Applying
> the Rule

. . .

These considerations lead to the conclusion that the right to marry is a fundamental right inherent in the liberty of the person, and under the Due Process and Equal Protection Clauses [*note that the reasoning concerning the Equal Protection Clause was edited from this version of the case*] of the Fourteenth amendment couples of the same-sex may not be deprived of that right and that liberty. The Court now holds

> Applying
> the Rule

that same-sex couples may exercise the fundamental right to marry. No longer may this liberty be denied to them. *Baker v. Nelson* must be and now is overruled, and the State laws challenged by Petitioners in these cases are now held invalid to the extent they exclude same-sex couples from civil marriage on the same terms and conditions as opposite-sex couples.

IV. . . .

* * *

No union is more profound than marriage, for it embodies the highest ideals of love, fidelity, devotion, sacrifice, and family. In forming a marital union, two people become something greater than once they were. As some of the petitioners in these cases demonstrate, marriage embodies a love that may endure even past death. It would misunderstand these men and women to say they disrespect the idea of marriage. Their plea is that they do respect it, respect it so deeply that they seek to find its fulfillment for themselves. Their hope is not to be condemned to live in loneliness, excluded from one of civilization's oldest institutions. They ask for equal dignity in the eyes of the law. The Constitution grants them that right.

The judgment of the Court of Appeals for the Sixth Circuit is reversed.

It is so ordered.

* * *

So after reading the first paragraph, you know what the case is about: liberty and same-sex marriage. You can also see that much of the case has been edited—this is what the ellipses (sets of three consecutive dots: . . .) mean. This case is edited because of its length—typically, U.S. Supreme Court opinions include complex reasoning or extensive legal history so the reader can put the opinion in context. Consequently, they are usually quite lengthy.

Remember the steps for spotting, identifying and articulating a *legal issue* from page 193:

SKILLS DEVELOPMENT

Steps for Spotting, Identifying, and Articulating the Legal Issue

To Spot or Identify a Legal Issue:

Step 1:　Find and examine the legal rule, whether it's a common law rule, a statute, a regulation, or a Constitutional clause.

Step 2:　Separate the legal rule into its elements (depending on the rule, it may also be necessary to figure out the definitions of those elements).

Step 3:　See which facts fall under which elements to determine relevant facts.

Step 4:　Determine which elements are at issue (which element does not match any facts, enough facts, or conflicting facts? Or, which element needs to be defined or better defined?).

To Articulate the Legal Issue:

Step 5:　For each element at issue, create a precise statement of the legal issue that includes three parts in a formula something like this: whether— (question)—under—(element of legal rule at issue)—when (legally relevant facts).

In other words, now, you have to follow the steps to identifying the *legal issue*:

1) Find the rule;

2) Separate the rule into elements; AND (when necessary) figure out how to define the elements.

3) Match the facts to the elements;

4) Create a question(s).

After learning what the case is about, look for the legal rule that the court relies on. Easy enough here, where Sections I and II have been omitted; the next section, Section III, begins with a quote and explanation of the Due Process Clause of the *Fourteenth Amendment* of the Constitution.[4] Could this be the rule? The answer is yes.

Courts will sometimes be quite explicit, and specifically state the rule governing the dispute or the case. But often, it is very obvious to the Court (and most of the time the readers) that they wouldn't be discussing a rule unless it applied. That is the case in *Obergefell*: when a legal rule such as a Constitutional clause—in this case the Due Process Clause of the *Fourteenth Amendment*—begins a paragraph, you can be sure it is very relevant to the dispute.

After identifying the rule, the next step is identifying and defining the elements. For the Due Process Clause, which is "no person shall be deprived of life, liberty, or property without due process" there are some very broad terms to be defined. Remember, "element" was defined in Chapter 3 as a "constituent part" of a legal rule. What are the parts of the rule for the Due Process Clause? The parts or elements are in bold below:

"No **person** shall be **deprived** of **life, liberty, or property** without **Due Process**."

Now you have to identify which element is at issue in the quoted parts of the case included here. One big hint would be the focus on "liberty" in the first paragraph—where the Court even tells us that the petitioners seek the "liberty" to marry someone of the same sex. That is certainly the element at issue. However, if you were not sure or wanted to double-check, you could carefully and methodically go through all the elements. If we consider the elements in order, there is never any discussion about whether the petitioners qualify as "person(s)"; nor do we see any discussion of "life," "property" or "due

---

[4]   The *Fourteenth Amendment* is as follows: "No state shall make or enforce any law which shall abridge the privileges or immunities of citizens of the United States; nor shall any state deprive any person of life, liberty, or property, without due process of law; nor deny to any person within its jurisdiction the equal protection of the laws." The Due Process clause is "No person shall be deprived of life, liberty, or property without Due Process."

process."[5] Again, it's safe to say that "liberty" is the element at issue which the court is defining in this case.

Indeed, you can see that the Court goes on to devote a great deal of time and space to defining "liberty." Much of the Court's discussion has been omitted here, but you should have enough of the discussion to figure out the *legal issue*. Can you create a question out of the request to allow same-sex marriage and the rule, "liberty," under the Due Process Clause? It could be any one of these questions:

- Does "liberty" in the Constitution's Due Process Clause include the right of same-sex couples to marry?

- Whether the Constitution's Due Process Clause protects the right of same-sex couples to marry?

Do you see how both statements of the *legal issue* include both the legal concept—the definition of "liberty"—and the specific facts relevant to the petitioners' request—the right to marry someone of the same sex? Do you likewise see how when the articulation of the *legal issue* has both the legal concept and the specific facts involved in the dispute, it is quite helpful? For example, which of the following articulations of the *legal issue* is more informative:

- What does "liberty" mean in the Constitution?

- Whether same-sex couples have the right to legally marry under the Due Process Clause "liberty" protection?

The answer is: the second one. Therefore, when you are summarizing the *legal issue* from a court case, remember to include both the legal rule AND the relevant facts. In fact, you can follow the same formula that you followed in the first two examples: **Whether— under—when**. Using those prompts will help you remember to include all the components of a thorough *legal issue*—after **whether**, the

---

[5] Remember, the decision has been heavily edited and the reasoning concerning the Equal Protection Clause has been taken out.

question; after **under**, the legal rule; and after **when**, additional relevant facts.

Here, using that formula, the *legal issue* could look like this:

ISSUE: **Whether** a same-sex couple have the right to legally marry **under** the Fourteenth Amendment's Due Process Clause **when** an opposite-sex couple has that legal right?

Unlike more involved factual situations, there are not really a lot of relevant facts in this case aside from the desire of a same-sex couple to marry legally. However, including the fact that opposite-sex couples could marry legally does help the reader understand that this is really a fairness issue about treating people equally.

Congratulations. You have identified and articulated a *legal issue* in a Supreme Court case. You are ready to be set loose on the great wide world of *legal issues*—you can articulate issues, you can spot issues, and you can identify issues.

CHAPTER 6 LEGAL SKILLS

- **Identify the *legal issue***
- **Identify which element(s) of the legal rule are at issue**
- **Identify the legally relevant facts**
- **Articulate a legal issue using the "whether" "under" "when" format or a variation of that format**

CHAPTER 6 VOCABULARY

- Circumstantial evidence
- Factual issue
- Fourteenth Amendment
- Legal issue

CHAPTER 6 RESEARCH AND ANALYSIS EXERCISES

I.   Articulating the issue:

To demonstrate how an issue can be articulated and to assist you in recognizing the different components of an issue, use the chart from this chapter, inserted here, to identify the facts, the law, and the issue in the following issue statements:

Diagram 21:
Using a Chart to Articulate the *Issue*

Prompts	Components of *Legal Issue*	*Issue*
Whether	question	
Under	Legal rule/element at *issue*	
When	*Legally relevant facts*	

1.   (Negligence) Whether the defendant driver breached his duty of care when he was driving the speed limit on Delaware Avenue on his way back from taking his neighbor and her child to the emergency room at 4 a.m. and he hit a pedestrian who was crossing against a red light?

2.   (First Amendment) Whether the public school administration is prohibited under the free speech clause of the First Amendment from forbidding grammar school students protesting gun violence to wear black armbands during the school day?

3.   (Negligence) Whether the defendant driver had a duty of care to be aware of his surroundings and see what was there to be seen when there was a pedestrian crossing the street in front of him whom he hit without braking?

4.   (First Amendment) Whether the public grammar school administration is prohibited under the First Amendment from enforcing a dress code which does not allow gang symbols or any other symbols to be worn by the students in order to maintain school safety?

II. Spotting an issue in a Supreme Court case:

Now, let's try out your issue-spotting skill with another Supreme Court case on marriage, albeit an older one that is a little shorter and—hopefully—a little easier to analyze than *Obergefell*.

Read the *Loving v. Virginia*, 388 U.S. 1 (1967), case below and see whether you can **identify** and **articulate** the legal issue. *Loving* is another famous case on marriage that was decided way before *Obergefell*, although also at a time when societal mores were changing. (Note that *Loving* is mentioned in the *Obergefell* decision.)

Remember to follow the **Skills Development: Steps for Spotting, Identifying and Articulating the Legal Issue** (Chapter 6) and the **Skills Development: Steps for Assisting Reading Comprehension** (Chapter 1) just as we did with the *Obergefell* case. (Note that footnotes and page number references have been omitted.)

Another exercise you can do is to label each paragraph of the case with what the Supreme Court is doing in that paragraph (explaining the rule, providing the holding, etc.) as was done above in the *Obergefell* case.

Supreme Court of the United States
Richard Perry LOVING et ux., Appellants,
v.
COMMONWEALTH OF VIRGINIA.

Opinion

Mr. Chief Justice WARREN delivered the opinion of the Court.

This case presents a constitutional question never addressed by this Court: whether a statutory scheme adopted by the State of Virginia to prevent marriages between persons solely on the basis of racial classifications violates the Equal Protection and Due Process Clauses of the Fourteenth Amendment. For reasons which seem to us to reflect the central meaning of those constitutional commands, we conclude that these statutes cannot stand consistently with the Fourteenth Amendment.

In June 1958, two residents of Virginia, Mildred Jeter, a Negro woman, and Richard Loving, a white man, were married in the District of Columbia pursuant to its laws. Shortly after their marriage, the Lovings returned to Virginia and established their marital abode in Caroline County. At the October Term, 1958, of the Circuit Court of Caroline County, a grand jury issued an indictment charging the Lovings with violating Virginia's ban on interracial marriages. On January 6, 1959, the Lovings pleaded guilty to the charge and were sentenced to one year in jail; however, the trial judge suspended the sentence for a period of 25 years on the condition that the Lovings leave the State and not return to Virginia together for 25 years. He stated in an opinion that:

'Almighty God created the races white, black, yellow, malay and red, and he placed them on separate continents. And but for the interference with his arrangement there would be no cause for such marriages. The fact that he separated the races shows that he did not intend for the races to mix.'

After their convictions, the Lovings took up residence in the District of Columbia. On November 6, 1963, they filed a motion in the state trial court to vacate the judgment and set aside the sentence on the ground that the statutes which they had violated were repugnant to the Fourteenth Amendment. The motion not having been decided by October 28, 1964, the Lovings instituted a class action in the United States District Court for the Eastern District of Virginia requesting that a three-judge court be convened to declare the Virginia antimiscegenation statutes unconstitutional and to enjoin state officials from enforcing their convictions. On January 22, 1965, the state trial judge denied the motion to vacate the sentences, and the Lovings perfected an appeal to the Supreme Court of Appeals of Virginia. On February 11, 1965, the three-judge District Court continued the case to allow the Lovings to present their constitutional claims to the highest state court.

The Supreme Court of Appeals upheld the constitutionality of the antimiscegenation statutes and, after modifying the sentence, affirmed the convictions. The Lovings appealed this decision, and we noted probable jurisdiction on December 12, 1966, 385 U.S. 986, 87 S.Ct. 595, 17 L.Ed.2d 448.

The two statutes under which appellants were convicted and sentenced are part of a comprehensive statutory scheme aimed at prohibiting and punishing interracial marriages. The Lovings were convicted of violating s 20–58 of the Virginia Code:

> 'Leaving State to evade law.—If any white person and colored person shall go out of this State, for the purpose of being married, and with the intention of returning, and be married out of it, and afterwards return to and reside in it, cohabiting as man and wife, they shall be punished as provided in s 20–59, and the marriage shall be governed by the same law as if it had been solemnized in this State. The fact of their cohabitation here as man and wife shall be evidence of their marriage.'

Section 20–59, which defines the penalty for miscegenation, provides:

> 'Punishment for marriage.—If any white person intermarry with a colored person, or any colored person intermarry with a white person, he shall be guilty of a felony and shall be punished by confinement in the penitentiary for not less than one nor more than five years.'

Other central provisions in the Virginia statutory scheme are s 20–57, which automatically voids all marriages between 'a white person and a colored person' without any judicial proceeding, and ss 20–54 and 1–14 which, respectively, define 'white persons' and 'colored persons and Indians' for purposes of the statutory prohibitions. The Lovings have never disputed in the course of this litigation that Mrs. Loving is a 'colored person' or that Mr. Loving is a 'white person' within the meanings given those terms by the Virginia statutes.

Virginia is now one of 16 States which prohibit and punish marriages on the basis of racial classifications. Penalties for miscegenation arose as an incident to slavery and have been common in Virginia since the colonial period.[6] The present statutory scheme dates from the adoption of the Racial Integrity Act of 1924, passed during the period of extreme nativism which followed the end of the First World War. The central features of this Act, and current Virginia law, are the absolute prohibition of a 'white person' marrying other than another 'white person,' a prohibition against issuing marriage licenses until the issuing official is satisfied that the applicants' statements as to their race are correct, certificates of 'racial composition' to be kept by both local and state registrars, and the carrying forward of earlier prohibitions against racial intermarriage.

I.

In upholding the constitutionality of these provisions in the decision below, the Supreme Court of Appeals of Virginia referred to its 1955 decision in Naim v. Naim, 197 Va. 80, 87 S.E.2d 749, as stating the reasons supporting the validity of these laws. In Naim, the state court concluded that the State's legitimate purposes were 'to preserve the racial integrity of its citizens,' and to prevent 'the corruption of blood,' 'a mongrel breed of citizens,' and 'the obliteration of racial pride,' obviously an endorsement of the doctrine of White Supremacy. Id., at 90, 87 S.E.2d, at 756. The court also reasoned that marriage has traditionally been subject to state regulation without federal intervention, and, consequently, the regulation of marriage should be left to exclusive state control by the Tenth Amendment.

While the state court is no doubt correct in asserting that marriage is a social relation subject to the State's police power, Maynard v. Hill, 125 U.S. 190, 8 S.Ct. 723, 31 L.Ed. 654 (1888), the State does not contend in its argument before this Court that its powers to regulate marriage are unlimited notwithstanding the commands of the Fourteenth Amendment. Nor could it do so in light of Meyer v. State of Nebraska, 262 U.S. 390, 43 S.Ct. 625, 67 L.Ed. 1042 (1923), and Skinner v. State of Oklahoma, 316 U.S. 535, 62 S.Ct. 1110, 86 L.Ed. 1655 (1942). Instead, the State argues that the meaning of the Equal

Protection Clause, as illuminated by the statements of the Framers, is only that state penal laws containing an interracial element as part of the definition of the offense must apply equally to whites and Negroes in the sense that members of each race are punished to the same degree. Thus, the State contends that, because its miscegenation statutes punish equally both the white and the Negro participants in an interracial marriage, these statutes, despite their reliance on racial classifications do not constitute an invidious discrimination based upon race. The second argument advanced by the State assumes the validity of its equal application theory. The argument is that, if the Equal Protection Clause does not outlaw miscegenation statutes because of their reliance on racial classifications, the question of constitutionality would thus become whether there was any rational basis for a State to treat interracial marriages differently from other marriages. On this question, the State argues, the scientific evidence is substantially in doubt and, consequently, this Court should defer to the wisdom of the state legislature in adopting its policy of discouraging interracial marriages.

Because we reject the notion that the mere 'equal application' of a statute containing racial classifications is enough to remove the classifications from the Fourteenth Amendment's proscription of all invidious racial discriminations, we do not accept the State's contention that these statutes should be upheld if there is any possible basis for concluding that they serve a rational purpose. The mere fact of equal application does not mean that our analysis of these statutes should follow the approach we have taken in cases involving no racial discrimination where the Equal Protection Clause has been arrayed against a statute discriminating between the kinds of advertising which may be displayed on trucks in New York City, Railway Express Agency, Inc. v. People of State of New York, 336 U.S. 106, 69 S.Ct. 463, 93 L.Ed. 533 (1949), or an exemption in Ohio's ad valorem tax for merchandise owned by a non-resident in a storage warehouse, Allied Stores of Ohio, Inc. v. Bowers, 358 U.S. 522, 79 S.Ct. 437, 3 L.Ed.2d 480 (1959). In these cases, involving distinctions not drawn according to race, the Court has merely asked whether there is any rational foundation for the discriminations, and has deferred to the wisdom of the state legislatures. In the case at bar, however, we deal with statutes containing racial classifications, and the fact of equal application does not immunize the statute from the very heavy burden of justification which the Fourteenth Amendment has traditionally required of state statutes drawn according to race.

The State argues that statements in the Thirty-ninth Congress about the time of the passage of the Fourteenth Amendment indicate that the Framers did not intend the Amendment to make unconstitutional state miscegenation laws. Many of the statements alluded to by the State concern the debates over the Freedmen's Bureau Bill, which President Johnson vetoed, and the Civil Rights Act of 1866, 14 Stat. 27, enacted over his veto. While these statements have some relevance to the intention of Congress in submitting the Fourteenth Amendment, it must be understood that the pertained to the passage of specific statutes and not to the broader, organic purpose of a constitutional amendment. As for the various statements directly concerning the Fourteenth Amendment, we have said in connection with a related problem, that although these historical sources 'cast some light' they are not sufficient to resolve the problem; '(a)t best, they are inconclusive. The most avid proponents of the post-War Amendments undoubtedly intended them to remove all legal distinctions among 'all persons born or naturalized in the United States.' Their opponents, just as certainly, were antagonistic to both the letter and the spirit of the Amendments and wished them to have the most limited effect.' Brown v. Board of Education of Topeka, 347 U.S. 483, 489, 74 S.Ct. 686, 689, 98 L.Ed. 873 (1954). See also Strauder v. State of West Virginia, 100 U.S. 303, 310, 25 L.Ed. 664 (1880). We have rejected the proposition that the debates in the Thirty-ninth Congress or in the state legislatures which ratified the Fourteenth Amendment supported the theory advanced by the State, that the requirement of equal protection of the laws is satisfied by penal laws defining offenses based on racial classifications so long as white and Negro participants in the offense were similarly punished. McLaughlin v. State of Florida, 379 U.S. 184, 85 S.Ct. 283, 13 L.Ed.2d 222 (1964).

The State finds support for its 'equal application' theory in the decision of the Court in Pace v. State of Alabama, 106 U.S. 583, 1 S.Ct. 637, 27 L.Ed. 207 (1883). In that case, the Court upheld a conviction under an Alabama statute forbidding adultery or fornication between a white person and a Negro which imposed a greater penalty than that of a statute proscribing similar conduct by members of the same race. The Court reasoned that the statute could not be said to discriminate against Negroes because the punishment for each participant in the offense was the same. However, as recently as the 1964 Term, in rejecting the reasoning of that case, we stated 'Pace represents a limited view of the Equal Protection Clause which has not withstood analysis in the subsequent decisions of this Court.' McLaughlin v. Florida, supra, 379 U.S. at 188, 85 S.Ct. at 286. As we there demonstrated, the Equal Protection Clause requires the consideration of whether the classifications drawn by any statute constitute an arbitrary and invidious discrimination. The clear and central purpose of the Fourteenth Amendment was to eliminate all official state sources of invidious racial discrimination in the States. Slaughter-House Cases, 16 Wall. 36, 71, 21 L.Ed. 394 (1873); Strauder v. State of West Virginia, 100 U.S. 303, 307—308, 25 L.Ed. 664 (1880); Ex parte Virginia, 100 U.S. 339, 344—345, 26 L.Ed. 676 (1880); Shelley v. Kraemer, 334 U.S. 1, 68 S.Ct. 836, 92 L.Ed. 1161 (1948); Burton v. Wilmington Parking Authority, 365 U.S. 715, 81 S.Ct. 856, 6 L.Ed.2d 45 (1961).

There can be no question but that Virginia's miscegenation statutes rest solely upon distinctions drawn according to race. The statutes proscribe generally accepted conduct if engaged in by members of different races. Over the years, this Court has consistently repudiated '(d)istinctions between citizens solely because of their ancestry' as being 'odious to a free people whose institutions are founded upon the doctrine of equality.' Hirabayashi v. United States, 320 U.S. 81, 100, 63 S.Ct. 1375, 1385, 87 L.Ed. 1774 (1943). At the very least, the Equal Protection Clause demands that racial classifications, especially suspect in criminal statutes, be subjected to the 'most rigid scrutiny,' Korematsu v. United States, 323 U.S. 214, 216, 65 S.Ct. 193, 194, 89 L.Ed. 194 (1944), and, if they are ever to be upheld, they must be shown to be necessary to the accomplishment of some permissible state objective, independent of the racial discrimination which it was the object of the Fourteenth Amendment to eliminate. Indeed, two members of this Court have already stated that they 'cannot conceive of a valid legislative purpose * * * which makes the color of a person's skin the test of whether his conduct is a criminal offense.' McLaughlin v. Florida, supra, 379 U.S. at 198, 85 S.Ct. at 292, (Stewart, J., joined by Douglas, J., concurring).

There is patently no legitimate overriding purpose independent of invidious racial discrimination which justifies this classification. The fact that Virginia prohibits only interracial marriages involving white persons demonstrates that the racial classifications must stand on their own justification, as measures designed to maintain White Supremacy. We have consistently denied the constitutionality of measures which restrict the rights of citizens on account of race. There can be no doubt that restricting the freedom to marry solely because of racial classifications violates the central meaning of the Equal Protection Clause.

These statutes also deprive the Lovings of liberty without due process of law in violation of the Due Process Clause of the Fourteenth Amendment. The freedom to marry has long been recognized as one of the vital personal rights essential to the orderly pursuit of happiness by free men.

Marriage is one of the 'basic civil rights of man,' fundamental to our very existence and survival. Skinner v. State of Oklahoma, 316 U.S. 535, 541, 62 S.Ct. 1110, 1113, 86 L.Ed. 1655 (1942). See also Maynard v. Hill, 125 U.S. 190, 8 S.Ct. 723, 31 L.Ed. 654 (1888). To deny this fundamental freedom on so unsupportable a basis as the racial classifications embodied in these statutes, classifications so directly subversive of the principle of equality at the heart of the Fourteenth Amendment, is surely to deprive all the State's citizens of liberty without due process of law. The Fourteenth Amendment requires that the freedom of choice to marry not be restricted by invidious racial discriminations. Under our Constitution, the freedom to marry or not marry, a person of another race resides with the individual and cannot be infringed by the State.

These convictions must be reversed. It is so ordered.

Reversed.

Mr. Justice STEWART, concurring.

I have previously expressed the belief that 'it is simply not possible for a state law to be valid under our Constitution which makes the criminality of an act depend upon the race of the actor.' McLaughlin v. State of Florida, 379 U.S. 184, 198, 85 S.Ct. 283, 292, 13 L.Ed.2d 222 (concurring opinion). Because I adhere to that belief, I concur in the judgment of the Court.

III. More issue spotting:

To give you practice in identifying legal issues in fact patterns, and to demonstrate that knowing the legal rule is essential to issue spotting, spot the issues in the following scenarios:

1.   FACTS: Pat is a transgender male at the law firm of Black and Case who works as an associate (junior attorney). Although he enjoyed his first two years working 80 hours a week reviewing documents for discovery, Pat then started noticing that other, non-transgender female and male associates were being assigned more interesting work, such as taking depositions, while he did not get such assignments. Although he asked for the same type of work that others were getting, nothing changed. After two more years, Pat was fired after being told he was not a good "fit" at Black and Case because his work had not advanced and was "stuck at the level of a new associate."

> RULE (based on federal and state statutes prohibiting discrimination[6]): No employer can discriminate on the basis of sex, religion, ethnicity, or race in making hiring and firing decisions.

---

[6]   Based on 42 U.S.C. 2000(e), commonly known as Title VII.

2.   FACTS: College student Garnette Pedro was driving her 1978 baby blue Chrysler LeBaron on a two-lane highway to get to her paralegal studies class after work. She realized she had forgotten to let her dog Gavin outside before she left. As she was thinking about calling her teenage son to ask him to do so, she looked down at her phone, which she kept face up on the console between the seats. At the moment she was looking down, a red pick-up truck traveling in the opposite direction crossed over the middle double yellow line and crashed head-on into Garnette's car.

> RULE (based on state statutes prohibiting cell phone usage while driving): No driver shall use a cell phone or any other electronic device while driving.

3.   FACTS: Gabby Vasquez went grocery shopping at EatRite around 3 p.m. She slipped on a puddle of water in the frozen food aisle, fell, and became immobilized from the pain in her neck and back. Her attorney Mr. Finch found out through the discovery process and EatRite's incident report that the store manager had seen the puddle around 10 a.m., had ordered a clean-up, and had blocked off the frozen food aisle on each side with buckets to warn the customers.

> RULE (based on landowner liability and common law negligence): A landowner has the duty to keep the owned premises safe and free of dangerous conditions and shall not be liable for injuries unless there is notice and the landowner has enough time to fix the dangerous condition.

IV. Ethics issue spotting:

To give you further practice in identifying legal issues in fact patterns, and to demonstrate that knowing the legal rule is essential to issue spotting, spot the issues in the following ethics-based scenarios:

1.   FACTS: Savannah had agreed to meet her mother for lunch at a popular local coffee spot, Café Du Monde. She was relieved to have time for lunch on Saturday, her day off, since her new job as a paralegal for a busy personal injury firm was so busy that sometimes she had to eat her lunch quickly at her desk. Savannah's mother wanted to hear all about the new job, even details about the cases, and explained to Savannah, "Since I

am a psychologist I know how to keep a confidence." She promised to be discreet about anything she learned about Savannah's new firm. Savannah then told her about a really big case she had begun working on. Her firm represents McDumbo's Burgers, and McDumbo's had just been sued by an elderly woman who had gotten scalded by coffee, suffered first degree burns, and had to be hospitalized. Savannah explained to her mother that McDumbo's had received numerous complaints about their hot coffee, but had not made any changes to its coffee-making process and could face some liability.

> RULE (based on the ABA Model Rule of Professional Conduct Rule 1.6, "Confidentiality of Information"): A lawyer shall not knowingly reveal confidential information, as defined in this Rule, or use such information to the disadvantage of a client or for the advantage of the lawyer or a third person.

2.   FACTS: Paul Coot became acquainted with Mark Zoot, the founder of Jawbook, when they worked together on two of Coot's projects, StreetFax and PageBook. Coot later brought a lawsuit against Zoot alleging that he owned a portion of Jawbook. In order to file the lawsuit, he hired a lawyer named Amy Ogden. Before filing the lawsuit, Amy told Coot that there had to be some proof to back up his allegations. Coot showed her the contract between him and Zoot, so Amy was satisfied. During the discovery process, after Zoot's experts examined the contract, they issued a report finding it to be fraudulent based on testing of the printer toner. Coot then started to act in a strange manner, would not return Amy's calls, and started claiming publicly that he was also friends with Warren Buffet, which Amy found hard to believe because the two men were from different parts of the country and Coot was not able to supply any additional details about their friendship.[7]

> RULE (based on ABA Model Rules of Professional Conduct 3.3, "Candor Toward the Tribunal"): A lawyer shall not knowingly make a false statement of law or fact to a tribunal or offer evidence that the lawyer knows to be false.

---

[7]   Loosely based on *Ceglia v. Zuckerberg*, 772 F. Supp. 2d 453 (W.D.N.Y. 2011).

The Rule, Synthesizing the Rule, and Explaining the Rule

Legal Skills:

- Remember that legal rules come in many shapes and sizes
- Synthesize the legal rule from case law
- Synthesize the legal rule from two statutes
- Draft a *topic sentence* that summarizes *synthesis*

PART I. A QUICK REVIEW OF RULES

As we look at rules again, please remember that legal rules come in many shapes and sizes—in other words, remember that legal rules come from statutes, administrative regulations, constitutions, and case law. And, as we have seen throughout this text, rules from those sources include both civil and criminal rules. In general, rules from all four sources can be both synthesized with one another, and synthesized together. We will read some examples below.

As a reminder, here are a few samples of rules from different sources, all of which have to do with a negligence claim in a state court:

A state statute of limitations on a negligence claim could be statutory, and it could read like this:

> State Civil Practice Law & Rules, Rule 123 (2018): The following actions must be commenced within three years: (1) an action to recover damages to property; (2) an action to

recover damages for person injury; (3) an action to annul a marriage based on fraud.

There could be a municipal administrative code that requires the city to receive notice of any defects on its property before a plaintiff can initiate a lawsuit:

> City Administrative Code, § 5–301(a) provides: Actions against the city. No action can be maintained for personal injury or injury to property against the city based on the conditions of its sidewalks, roads, or highways, unless there was written notice of the condition provided to the City at least thirty (30) days before the accident.

The top court in a state might start out its discussion of negligence with a recitation of the four elements:

> The elements of a cause of action for negligence are duty, breach of duty, causation, and damages. *Friedman v. Merck & Co.*, 107 Cal. App. 4th 454, 463 (2003).

You can see from these examples that for one concept, like negligence, you may have to synthesize various sources of law.

For our last example of legal rules, there are no U.S. Constitutional provisions on negligence. But here is a simple provision on the creation of inferior courts—a negligence suit could be filed in one type of inferior court, such as a federal trial court, assuming jurisdictional requirements are met:

> U.S. Constitution, Article III. The judicial Power of the United States, shall be vested in one supreme Court, and in such inferior Courts as the Congress may from time to time ordain and establish.

Now let's look at *synthesis*, which is an analytical and writing skill you may already be familiar with.

PART II. *SYNTHESIZING* THE RULE

A. What Is *Synthesis?*

What is *synthesis* and why is it necessary? *Synthesis* is simply the combination of multiple parts to form a whole. We have included *synthesis* in the chapter about the "Rule" section of IRAC because knowing how to *synthesize* the rule is so important, but you will also have to use the skill of *synthesis* in other areas of legal writing.

For example, you may need to *synthesize* the facts of your case. Let's say the story of your case comes from multiple sources—the client interview, a witness statement, and a police report. You would have to combine all those sources into one story that is coherent, not repetitive, and easy for your busy supervising attorney to read. Not only should you *synthesize* those sources, but you should also make your *synthesis* easy to read by drafting topic sentences relaying the *synthesis*. We will review *synthesis* of facts in Chapter 10 when we review writing a legal memo and summarizing facts. For now, we will focus on *synthesizing* primary sources of law in order to form a legal rule.

So let's say you are working in the *common law* area, and there are multiple cases with similar facts on the issue of a landowner's duty to people on the property. You would have to *synthesize* the common law cases in order to come up with one coherent rule that accurately reflects the courts' over-arching approach. Similarly, you may need to *synthesize* two statutes, or multiple cases interpreting one statute, so that you really understand the law and can communicate it clearly.

Although *synthesis* might sound academic, it is not a purely legal skill. Rather, it is a fundamental skill that you have probably already used in everyday situations. It is, though, also an academic skill that you can use in any discipline, especially when it comes to doing a research paper. Here are some real life and non-academic examples.

B. Everyday Examples of *Synthesis*

You have probably been in situations where you were looking at and evaluating facts from a variety of sources, when you realized that you would need to combine the sources into one coherent whole. Perhaps without knowing the word *synthesis*, you then performed *synthesis*. To demonstrate, let's try an everyday example that is similar to *synthesizing* a rule from a variety of cases. In our fact scenario, you have to advise Tammy the Teenager, who lives with her grandparents, Arturo and Elizabeth, on the grandparents' curfew rule for Tammy. Tammy is only 17, and therefore is not allowed to drink alcohol legally. Arturo and Elizabeth have said they want Tammy to "act responsibly," but haven't given her a firm or clear rule, and Tammy has incurred their wrath several times and gotten herself grounded. Tammy wants to keep socializing with her friends but does NOT want to keep getting grounded by her grandparents.

Scenario #1: One night, Tammy decided to go out dancing with her friend Mary. She picked Mary up from her house, and they drove to Dave's Disco, where they proceeded to drink alcoholic cocktails called sloe gin fizzes and dance the night away. They danced the hustle, the twist, and the boogie woogie. At about 2 a.m., after the effects of the alcohol had worn off, Tammy and Mary decided to head home. So Tammy drove home, dropped off Mary, and proceeded to her grandparent's home. Tammy arrived home at 2:30 a.m., and Arturo was waiting up for her. He was furious, accused her of drinking based on the alcohol he smelled on her breath, and told Tammy that she acted "dangerously" and "irresponsibly." He grounded her for one week.

Scenario #2: Another night when Tammy felt like socializing with a bunch of her high school friends, she decided to go to a high school party she had heard about. Around 10 p.m. at night, she walked by herself about half a mile through the suburb she lives in until she arrived at the home of Theo, who was hosting a keg party at his parents' house while his parents were away. Tammy drank beer, got to visit with many different groups of her high school friends, and was home by 1 a.m. Both Arturo and Elizabeth heard her come in because it woke them up. They told her they had heard about the party and that she was grounded for the following night.

Scenario #3: Tammy loves spending time outdoors with her orchestra friends, so she was happy to be invited to a dinner picnic at a nearby waterfall and lake called Lake Minnewaska. She loved this group of friends, and the lake environment was peaceful and beautiful. Since there would be park rangers working in the evening, Tammy and her friends decided not to bring any alcohol to their picnic. Instead, they grilled food, roasted marshmallows, and sang camp songs. Tammy lost track of the time and came home late, around 1 a.m. When Elizabeth and Arturo heard her come home and asked her if she had been drinking, she said no. Tammy did not get in trouble and did not get grounded.

* * *

In order to organize your thoughts and try to advise Tammy, you decide to do a *synthesis* chart. You realize that there are several elements that all of Tammy's adventures have in common: the events are with people; some of the events involve alcohol; all of the events are at night; and each event is at a different type of location. Therefore, you list the separate elements and what occurred in each of Tammy's stories for each of those elements.

Diagram 22:
Synthesis Chart of Everyday Scenario

Scenarios	Arrival at Home Time	Punishment	People Present	Drinking Alcohol	Location
#1 (Dancing at Dave's disco)	2:30 a.m.	Grounded for one week	One friend, Mary	**Yes** Two alcoholic cocktails	Dave's Disco
#2 (High school keg party)	1 a.m.	Grounded for one night	Many high school friends	**Yes** Drank beer	Home of friend
#3 (Lake Minnewaska outing)	1 a.m.	None	Small group of friends	**No** No alcohol	Lake

The chart helps you realize that it is not just Tammy's arrival time at home that is incurring the grandparents' anger and leading to the groundings. Although Tammy's punishment was the longest when she came home at 2:30 a.m., that was also the night that she drank the most. Although according to Scenario 1, she didn't actually tell her grandparents how much she drank that night, it was the one night when Arturo was "furious" because he smelled alcohol on her breath.

How would you fashion a rule for Tammy that would accurately predict whether she would get grounded? In addition to creating and reviewing the chart, you have to group the commonalities and differences together. In this example, this means that you group together when Tammy DID get in trouble, and when she DIDN'T get in trouble. For example, the scenarios have the following in common: Tammy got grounded by her grandparents both times she was out drinking; on the other hand, Tammy did NOT get in trouble when she was not drinking. Also, Tammy got in the MOST trouble the night she drank the most, at Dave's Disco, which was also the night she came home the latest.

Based on these patterns, what rules could you give Tammy? Here are some ideas:

- Tammy can stay out until 1 a.m. in the morning as long as she doesn't drink.

- Tammy should not drink hard alcohol while at a bar or disco.

- Tammy should not drink at all if she wants to go out with her friends.

SKILLS DEVELOPMENT

Steps for Synthesis

Step 1: Read the material that needs synthesis.

Step 2: Note the general categories of information—for rules, it will be elements, and for facts, there may be general categories of commonalities.

Step 3: Construct a chart to help you with the synthesis. The left column will be cases if you are synthesizing case law, or the fact scenarios if you are synthesizing facts. The top row will be the different categories of information, which will be elements if you are synthesizing a rule, or other categories if you are synthesizing information.

Step 4: Fill in the chart. As you fill it in, you may find you alter or refine the categories or elements on top.

Step 5: Almost done! Now that you have a visual and organized depiction of the subject matter, you can draw conclusions. Ask yourself: where are there commonalities? Where are there differences?

But keep in mind that your *synthesis* work does not stop once you have figured out your *synthesized* rule(s) based on your conclusion(s). An additional thing to know about *synthesis* is how to communicate it—and the way to do so in many types of writing, including legal writing, is starting your paragraphs with *topic sentences* that reflect your *synthesis*.

A topic sentence alerts the reader to what will come next, and to the topic of the paragraph. It's often helpful in predictive writing, like legal writing, to compose the topic sentence last, as many times it's only after you finish writing the paragraph that you truly know what it's about. Although you may compose the sentence last, it should not be the last sentence in the paragraph, It needs to start the paragraph because the reader needs a head's up, or an actual statement of the *synthesis*, in order to easily understand what follows.

SKILLS DEVELOPMENT

Steps for Drafting Topic Sentences to Show Synthesis

A topic sentence is a sentence that begins a paragraph and that prepares the reader for what's to come through synthesis, summary, or a simple statement describing the main subject or argument of the paragraph.

Step 1: The **WHY**—To prepare the reader for the content of the paragraph.

Step 2: The **WHEN**—You can write it anytime.

Step 3: The **WHERE**—First sentence in the paragraph.

Step 4: The **HOW**—Develop your synthesis: group the commonalities and/or the differences together, and find a general but accurate way to describe the group(s). Then, draft short, accurate sentences to start your paragraphs that reflect those groupings or general descriptive categories. Note the topic sentence examples in the next section.

C. *Synthesizing* the Rule from Case Law

As you can see, *synthesis* is the skill of combining and blending information, and could be necessary in any field or setting.

Case law probably provides one of the most natural forums for *synthesis*, for several reasons. First, as we know, case law demonstrates the application of rules to fact situations, and each rule application has the value of precedent. Since we need precedent to help us predict how a court will rule, we will always need to look at case law when possible. Looking at case law often necessitates *synthesis*.

As you know from Chapter 3, there are different types of case law—in other words, courts apply rules to facts using different types of primary sources. For example, a court can apply statutes, regulations, or constitutional clauses; in a given case, a court might be developing the common law on a subject, and perhaps doing some *synthesis* itself to do so. The case holdings in all these different situations could need to be *synthesized*.

Let's return to the sleeping in the park hypothetical we used in Chapters 2 and 4. But this time the question will be how to *synthesize* the case holdings in order to define "sleep," one of the elements of the statute.

The statute provides:

Penal Law § 1.01: It is unlawful for any person to sleep in the picnic areas of a state-owned park.

The elements of the statute are:

Element #1: "person"

Element #2: "sleep"

Element #3: "picnic area"

Element #4: "state-owned park"

The second element, "sleep," is the element at issue in this legal problem: a criminal defendant has been charged with violating the statute. The case law in our fictional state addressing this issue is as follows. Assume these are all cases from the mid-level appellate court in our jurisdiction, so they are therefore mandatory precedent for the trial court where the case would be heard:

Case #1 (Reinbaur): Ron Reinbaur was arrested in a state-owned park called Beaver Island. The arrest occurred at 2:30 a.m., after a police officer saw Reinbaur in a sleeping bag under a picnic table. The officer observed that Reinbaur had his eyes closed and observed him snoring for about five minutes. The officer then arrested Reinbaur for violating Penal Law § 1.01 because Reinbaur was sleeping in the park. On appeal from his conviction, the mid-level appellate court held that there was sufficient evidence to support the guilty verdict because Reinbaur was observed in a sleeping bag, under a picnic table, with his eyes closed, and snoring for five minutes.

Case #2 (Wilson): Jason Wilson was arrested in a state-owned park called Allegheny State Park. The arrest occurred at 4:30 a.m. The officer observed Jason lying on a park bench in the picnic area, with his head on his knapsack and an old blanket over his body. The officer assumed that Jason was asleep, but as the officer got closer, he saw that Jason's eyes were open. The officer smelled alcohol on Wilson's breath, and Wilson admitted to being "hung over." Wilson testified at trial that he had insomnia and generally can't sleep, except for one or two hours per night. Wilson also testified that he might have slept for a while on that park bench on the night he was arrested. Wilson was convicted of violating Penal Law § 1.01.

On appeal, the mid-level appellate court held that there was sufficient evidence to uphold the *conviction* because the evidence was consistent with the finding that at some time that night the defendant had been asleep on the bench.

The court also held that the *conviction* could be upheld on other grounds, as well. For one, using the park as a place to sleep went against the purpose of the statute. The court held that in enacting the statute, the state had intended that the parks would be used only for their intended purpose of providing a place for people to picnic, play, and relax, not as a place to sleep. Therefore, even if Wilson was not actually asleep in the park at the time he was arrested, he was using the park as a place to sleep, which is contrary to the intent behind the statute.

Case #3 (Savage): Michael Savage was arrested for sleeping in the park when the officer observed him snoring, with his eyes closed, at 1 p.m. in the afternoon at a state-owned park called Evangola State Park. The officer observed Savage, who had a lunch bag next to him, for about five minutes. The officer then woke Savage up and arrested him for violating Penal Law § 1.01.

The mid-level appellate court held that convicting Savage for violating Penal Law § 1.01 was contrary to the intent of the statute. Although the proof established that Savage was sleeping, the sleeping occurred in the middle of the day instead of the middle of the night. Therefore, Savage was not using the park as a place to sleep. The court held that his *conviction* should be *vacated*—set aside.

* * *

If you were asked by your paralegal studies professor how the mid-level court had interpreted the element "sleep" in the Penal Law § 1.01 statute, you would have to synthesize the above three cases. You might choose to do the following chart in order to organize your thoughts and get a clear visual picture of the factors going into the court's decision.

Diagram 23:
Synthesis Chart of Case Law

CASES	RESULT: *Conviction* upheld?	ARREST: Time	BODY: Eyes closed and snoring?	BED-LIKE: Blanket, pillows, sleeping bags?	POLICY?
Case #1 Reinbaur	YES	2:20 a.m.	Yes, eyes closed, snoring	Sleeping bag	No mention of policy
Case #2 Wilson	YES	4:30 a.m.	No, eyes open BUT Insomnia and testified that he might have slept at some point during the night	Knapsack, old blanket	The purpose of the statute is to make sure the parks are used for recreation; defendant instead used the park as a place to sleep
Case #3 Savage	NO	1:00 p.m.	Yes, eyes closed, snoring	No	

First, try to see the commonalities. What do the *convictions* that were upheld have in common? In both the Reinbaur and the Wilson cases, the defendants were arrested in more or less the middle of the night, and were using bed-like props such as a knapsack as a pillow, a blanket, or a sleeping bag. You can complete the sentence: In each of the cases where there was a *conviction* for violating Penal Law § 1.01 prohibiting sleeping in the park . . . (for example) the defendant was found by a police officer in the middle of the night, in the park, using bed-like elements.

Then, try to see the differences. When was the *conviction* NOT upheld? We really just have one occasion, and that is when the sleeping occurred in the middle of the day in the Savage case, at 1 p.m. Since the Savage case is otherwise similar to the Reinbaur case, because both Savage and Reinbaur had their eyes closed and were snoring, the time of the sleeping seems to be an important distinction. You can complete the sentence: In the case(s) in which the court held that there should NOT be a *conviction* for sleeping in the park . . . (for example) the defendant was found sleeping in the middle of the day without any bed-like items.

Is there any other information, commonality or difference that helps us further understand why the Savage *conviction* was not upheld? If we look at the one time that the court mentioned policy, we see that the court reported that the purpose of the statute is to ensure that the parks are used for their intended purpose of recreation. The result in Savage—where the defendant was sleeping at 1 p.m. and his *conviction* was *vacated*—is therefore consistent with the purpose behind the statute. Sleeping in the park at 1 p.m., after eating lunch, seems more recreational in nature and is not the same as using the park as a place to sleep.

What else? What about the fact that in the Reinbaur case, the *conviction* was upheld because the defendant's eyes were closed and he was snoring, but in the Wilson case, the *conviction* was upheld EVEN THOUGH the defendant's eyes were NOT open and he was NOT snoring? Is there anything in the chart that can explain that or make those seemingly inconsistent results consistent? Yes, the policy or purpose behind the statute reported by the court (see the POLICY column). In both Reinbaur and Wilson, the defendants were using the park as a place to sleep, which is supported factually by the time of arrest (middle of the night) and the bed-like stuff they had with them.

Therefore, a *synthesis* of the above cases that explains how the element "sleep" has been defined by the courts could result in the following topic sentences:

- Courts have held that "sleep" under Penal Law § 1.01 requires the defendant to be using the park as a place to sleep, which is consistent with the policy behind the statute of protecting the recreational park areas for recreation.

• To be "sleep"[ing] under Penal Law § 1.01, one of the most important criteria is the time of arrest, as that is a strong indicator as to whether the defendant is using the park as a place to sleep.

• Helpful facts for sustaining a *conviction* under Penal Law § 1.01, which prohibits sleeping in the park, include the time of arrest, whether the defendant was using the park as a place to sleep, and whether the defendant was found with bed-like "stuff" like pillows, blankets, or sleeping bags.

You can see that there are many different ways to write a topic sentence that reflects *synthesis*. Note that *synthesis* is not a repetition or listing of the elements being synthesized, but rather, an expression of an over-arching commonality.

D. *Synthesizing* the Rule from Two Statutes

In answering a research question, you may find that one statute either references another, or that one statute has an undefined term or phrase that ultimately references another statute. The New York *Dram Shop law* provides a good example of when you might need to *synthesize* two statutes. According to <u>Black's Law Dictionary</u>, a *"Dram Shop act"* is a statute "allowing a plaintiff to recover damages from a commercial seller of alcoholic beverages for the plaintiff's injuries caused by a customer's intoxication."

The New York *Dram Shop statute* refers to the illegal sale of alcohol. According to N.Y. General Obligations Law § 11–101(1) (McKinney's 2018), an injured person has a cause of action against a person who unlawfully sold alcohol:

1. Any person who shall be injured in person, property, means of support, or otherwise by any intoxicated person, or by reason of the intoxication of any person, whether resulting

in his death or not, shall have a right of action against any
person who shall, by unlawful selling to or unlawfully
assisting in procuring liquor for such intoxicated person, have
caused or contributed to such intoxication; and in any such
action such person shall have a right to recover actual and
exemplary damages.

This statute appears long and dense, so let's break it up into
elements. Although some of the elements are long, that is just because
they are modified or described.

Element 1: "Any person—injured—personally or in
property"

Element 2: "by an intoxicated person" OR "by reason of
the intoxication of the person"

Element 3: "shall have a right of action"

Element 4: "against any person"

Element 5: "who shall, by unlawful selling or unlawfully
assisting in procuring liquor for such person"

Element 6: "have caused or contributed to such
intoxication"

Element 7: and . . . "in any such action the person has the
right to recover actual and exemplary damages."

We can get the general idea that the statute protects someone who
was injured. If we read carefully—meaning slowly and several times—
we see that the cause of action for the injured person is actually against
the person (defendant) who "contributed to such intoxication" by
"unlawful selling or unlawfully assisting in procuring liquor."

In other words, let's say Paul the Paralegal Studies student was hit
by a drunk driver. The drunk driver was Shawn the Shoemaker. He had
been drinking at the bar "We Never Close." Shawn started drinking at
5 p.m. when his shoemaking shop closed, and according to Bella the
Bartender, he continued drinking until he was falling off the barstool

and slurring his words. Bella, as a new Bartender, continued serving him alcohol when he ordered it, even though she admitted he looked quite drunk.

The question is whether, under the statute, Bella was "unlawfully selling or unlawfully assisting in procuring" the alcohol for Shawn. What does the statute mean by "unlawful"?

We can't assume. So we check the General Obligations Law for *definitions* of "unlawful selling or procuring." We are directed to N.Y. Alcoholic Beverage Control Law § 65 (McKinney's 2018), which provides in part:

> No person shall sell, deliver or give away or cause or permit or procure to be sold, delivered or given away any alcoholic beverages to
>
> . . .
>
> 2.   Any visibly intoxicated person . . .

(Remember, the group of three dots in the middle is an ellipsis, and an ellipsis signifies that text was extracted.)

Again, we can divide the second statute into elements as well.

Element 1: "No person"

Element 2: "shall sell, deliver or give away" OR "cause or permit or procure"

Element 3: "to be sold, delivered, or given away"

Element 4: "any alcoholic beverages"

Element 5: "to any visibly intoxicated person"

So, now we know that under New York law, it is unlawful to sell alcohol to a person who is visibly intoxicated. In other words, with Paul the Paralegal Studies student in mind, we can *define* **Element 5** from New York's *Dram Shop law*, the General Obligations Law § 11–101, as selling alcohol to a visibly intoxicated person. Our *synthesis* in this situation, with these two statutes, is simply to allow one statute, the

Alcoholic Beverage Control Law, to *define* one of the elements—"unlawfully selling"—of the General Obligations Law.

So who has a cause of action against whom? In order to figure out how the two *statutes* work together to give Paul the Paralegal Studies student a cause of action, we can use the same principles to *synthesize* the two statutes, and make a chart. Note that this chart is a little different, but provides the same benefit of a visual aide.

Diagram 24:
Synthesis Chart of Two Statutes

Statute	Element 1	Element 2	Element 3	Element 4	Element 5	Element 6
General Obligation Law §11–101	Injured person **(Paul the Paralegal Studies Student)**	Injured by intoxicated person **(Shawn the Shoemaker)**	Has cause of action	Against person **(Bella the Bartender)**	**Unlawfully sold liquor =**	And contributed to such intoxication
Alcoholic Beverage Control Act §65					**= selling liquor to someone —Shawn the Shoemaker —who is visibly intoxicated**	

By looking at this chart, we can see that according to the General Obligations Law and the Alcoholic Beverage Control Act, Paul the Paralegal Studies student has a cause of action against Bella the Bartender because she unlawfully served alcohol to Shawn the Shoemaker when he was visibly intoxicated.

So, synthesizing two *statutes* that are inter-related in this situation is really simply combining one statute with the necessary *definition* from another statute. Unlike a factual *synthesis* or a case law *synthesis*, there are not many different factors that have to be evaluated and categorized. Rather, it is more like the combination of two sentences into one sentence, or two things into one.

You will not only have different primary sources to *synthesize*, and different settings in which to *synthesize*, but you will also have different amounts of information to *synthesize*. All these differences may alter the formula a little bit, but will not alter the idea that *synthesis* is the combining of elements into a simple, easy-to-read whole.

PART III. *EXPLAINING THE RULE*

Explaining the rule is what it sounds like. Your *rule explanation* can be as simple as providing the *statutory definition* for one of the terms in the statute or using cases to illustrate how the rule has previously been applied by a court, or it can be as complex as *synthesizing* numerous cases. Much of the time, your *rule explanation* falls somewhere in the middle, and you simply provide examples of how the rule has been applied in prior case law.

Your *rule explanation* is an important part of your legal analysis, and it is part of the "R" of IRAC. Sometimes legal educators alter the IRAC acronym to specifically reflect the *Rule Explanation*: IREAC. By illustrating how the rule has been applied in the past, you are helping the reader be prepared for the application that follows. You are providing important context. The need for *rule explanation* also applies to any mini-rule about a specific element, as discussed in Chapter 5.

First, let's look at a *rule explanation* for a statute using the statutory definitions. Most statutes have a set of *definitions* for key statutory terms, so in setting out the statutory rule, you would also have to include the *definitions* of the statutory terms you are using. As we learned in Chapter 4, checking the *definition* sections of a statute is a critical part of reading, understanding, and applying it.

For example, according to 42 U.S.C. § 2000e–2(a)(1):

It shall be an unlawful employment practice for an employer—

(1)   to fail or refuse to hire or to discharge any individual, or otherwise to discriminate against any individual with respect to his compensation, terms, conditions, or privileges of employment, because of such individual's race, color, religion, sex, or national origin . . .

So we know from reading that provision of the statute that it is illegal to discriminate based on sex (among other things). To be clear on what is included in the meaning of "sex," we would have to go to the *definitions* section of the statute. Although "sex" may seem clear enough, you may have an issue about whether "sex" includes sexual orientation (does the statute prohibit discrimination based on sexual orientation), or transgender status, or even pregnancy. The Table of Contents for the statute indicates that the *definitions* are in § 2000e, and the definition of "sex" is in § 2000e(k):

(k)   The terms "because of sex" or "on the basis of sex" include, but are not limited to, because of or on the basis of pregnancy, childbirth, or related medical conditions; and women affected by pregnancy, childbirth, or related medical conditions shall be treated the same for all employment-related purposes, including receipt of benefits under fringe benefit programs, as other persons not so affected but similar in their ability or inability to work, and nothing in section 2000e–2(h) of this title shall be interpreted to permit otherwise. . . .

In order to explain this rule as it pertains to sex, the federal law against employment discrimination, also known as Title VII (because it was Title VII of the 1964 Civil Rights Act), we would *synthesize* the prohibition against sex discrimination with the *definition* of sex and state the following:

Title VII prohibits discrimination on the basis of sex, which includes pregnancy, childbirth, or related medical conditions.

That is the *rule explanation* based on just the statute. To be certain about how the rule would be interpreted and applied, you would also want to find mandatory precedent from the U.S. Supreme Court and your federal mid-level appellate court—otherwise known as your federal circuit. You will have an opportunity to do this in the end-of-chapter exercises.

Second, let's look at an excerpt of *rule explanation* from the U.S. Supreme Court case you read in the prior chapter, *Obergefell v. Hodges*, 135 S. Ct. 2584 (2015). In this excerpt, the Court begins to explain the Due Process Clause, and starts out with the clause itself from the Constitution, and then uses holdings and quotes from case law to explain the meaning of the Constitutional clause.

> *Under the Due Process Clause of the Fourteenth Amendment, no State shall "deprive any person of life, liberty, or property, without due process of law." The fundamental liberties protected by this Clause include most of the rights enumerated in the Bill of Rights. See Duncan v. Louisiana, 391 U.S. 145, 147–149, 88 S.Ct. 1444, 20 L.Ed.2d 491 (1968). In addition these liberties extend to certain personal choices central to individual dignity and autonomy, including intimate choices that define personal identity and beliefs. See, e.g., Eisenstadt v. Baird, 405 U.S. 438, 453, 92 S.Ct. 1029, 31 L.Ed.2d 349 (1972); Griswold v. Connecticut, 381 U.S. 479, 484–486, 85 S.Ct. 1678, 14 L.Ed.2d 510 (1965). The identification and protection of fundamental rights is an enduring part of the judicial duty to interpret the Constitution. That responsibility, however, "has not been reduced to any formula." Poe v. Ullman, 367 U.S. 497, 542, 81 S.Ct. 1752, 6 L.Ed.2d 989 (1961) (Harlan, J., dissenting). Rather, it requires courts to exercise reasoned judgment in identifying interests of the person so fundamental that the State must accord them its respect. See ibid. . . .*

The court focuses on the word "liberty" from the Due Process Clause statement that no State shall "deprive any person of life, liberty, or property, without due process of law." To define "liberty," the Court explains what is included in that concept—"most of the rights enumerated in the Bill of Rights." Note that the Court provides authority for that contention by supplying a specific citation to a case it relies on. The Court then goes on to explain that "these liberties" also "extend to certain personal choices"—again supplying citations to specific cases that support this contention.

Very simply, the Court is supplying examples from its own precedent that show how "liberty" has been *defined*. Notice that the Court does not include the specific holdings of the cases it cites, but rather, explains the overall idea of what those cases stand for: "most of the rights enumerated in the Bill of Rights" and "personal choices central to individual dignity and autonomy." The latter sentence is an example of *synthesis*—using one common idea to represent the holdings of the following two cases cited.

Although you may have to include the case holdings (since you are not the Supreme Court and you will not necessarily be citing to cases that are as well-known as the two examples the Court provides here) you should also remember to try to *synthesize* the cases in your *rule explanation*. Find the common themes or ideas and use that commonality to express the meaning of those cases.

CHAPTER 7 LEGAL SKILLS

- **Remember that legal rules come in many shapes and sizes**
- **Synthesize the legal rule from case law**
- **Synthesize the legal rule from two statutes**
- **Draft a *topic sentence* that summarizes *synthesis***

CHAPTER 7 VOCABULARY

- Conviction
- Define/definition (statutory and case law)
- Dram Shop law/statute
- Rule explanation
- Synthesis/synthesize/synthesizing
- Vacated

CHAPTER 7 RESEARCH AND ANALYSIS EXERCISES

I.   Drafting synthesis:

To help you understand that synthesis is an everyday tool that you can use in many ways, to help you understand common law, and to give you practice synthesizing with easy everyday examples, work on the following:

1.   Working with a team, have each team member use free internet sites, <u>Black's Law Dictionary</u>, other law dictionaries approved by your teacher, and any subscription databases that are available, look up the definition of "common law."

Then, make a chart, listing the sources of the definitions in the left column, and the definitions in the right column. Note the common "elements" of the definitions and list them in the top row, following the **Common Law** label. After you have completed the chart, write **one synthesized sentence** that defines common law.

Common Law:	
Source	Definition

2.   In a small group or in class, each participant should give an example of a time they had to learn a new skill—whether it was a cerebral activity such as learning a language or another new subject, or a physical activity such as painting a room, cooking a new meal, or learning a new exercise. Each participant should also describe the process of learning this new skill, including the amount of time it took to learn; personal qualities that were helpful in the process; and any other observations about the experience.

Then, make a chart, listing the new skill in the far left, and making different columns for length of time, personal qualities, and a third column for other observations. Note the common "elements" of all the observations and list them in the top row, following the **Learning a New Skill** label. After you have completed the chart, write **one or two synthesized sentences** that describe the process of learning a new skill.

Learning a New Skill:			
Skill	Time	Personal Quality	Other Observations

II. Using synthesis for the rule explanation:

Pretend you are interning at a Public Defender's Office. You have noticed that your supervising attorney often asks you to do research on what constitutes evidence of intent under the state larceny statute. You decide to take the initiative to synthesize the case law you have found, summarized below following the statute, so that you and your attorney have a better understanding of the intent requirement, and so you can use this intent synthesis in future motion memos and appellate briefs.

Based on the statute and case material below, complete the synthesis chart that follows the case summaries. Then complete the blanks for a topic sentence you would draft for a paragraph explaining the results of your synthesis, and for the explanation that will follow in the paragraph.

STATUTE:

Larceny is the taking and carrying away of the personal property of another with the intent to permanently deprive the person of their property.

CASE 1: In a memorandum opinion, the court in *People v. Morillo* held that Jason Morillo demonstrated intent to keep the Relax watch he was accused of stealing because he failed to uphold his duty as the apartment building supervisor, which was to keep all lost and found items in the office safe, and instead started wearing the Relax watch every day. He therefore was guilty of larceny.

CASE 2: In *People v. Phillips*, Dylan Phillips was convicted of stealing the briefcases of two young women after he sat behind their table in a restaurant, flirted with them, and bought them each a cold brew coffee. The defense attorney for Phillips argued that, although he went out the restaurant back door with both briefcases, he did not demonstrate intent under the larceny statute because, instead of keeping them, he threw them in the restaurant dumpster after finding they contained no cash or jewelry. The court held, "Phillips' intent was pure and simple—to take the victims' briefcases—which he demonstrated by taking them without permission, leaving the restaurant, and checking them for cash. It is of no moment that he did not steal something lucrative or that he ended up throwing it away."

CASE 3: The court in *People v. Oliver* found that Heather Oliver satisfied all elements of the larceny statute when she took three pounds of green tea from a package on Margaret's porch that had been delivered by the Nile company, brought it to her nearby yurt, and then hosted a large green tea party to which she invited fifty of her closest friends.

CASE	INTENT HOLDING	LEGALLY RELEVANT FACTS

TOPIC SENTENCE:

EXPLANATORY PARAGRAPH:

III. Research and rule explanation:

Using the citation found in this chapter, locate Title VII, the federal statute that, among other things, prohibits discrimination on the basis of sex. Research your federal circuit to find out how your U.S. Court of Appeals has interpreted the term sex as used in the statute. Using the statute, the statute's definition of sex, and the case law you have found in your circuit, write a rule explanation.

IV. Research, synthesis, and rule explanation for ethics:

You have been asked by your supervising attorney Geri to help her put together a presentation for the local paralegal association on ethics and the paralegal. She would like you to start by performing legal research on two of the ethical rules she views as critical for paralegals to learn and understand: to avoid the unauthorized practice of law, and to be supervised adequately by an attorney. Since Geri is an adjunct instructor for the local community college Paralegal Studies program, she has divided this process up into the following steps. (Note the additional directions in parentheses to help you do this exercise yourself.)

1. Research whether there is an unauthorized practice of law statute in your state. (If not, do the rest of this exercise in a jurisdiction that does.)

2. If your state's statute is annotated and includes case law, review the case law to find cases in your appellate jurisdiction that provide examples of when a paralegal has engaged in the unauthorized practice of law. (If the statute you are using is not annotated or its annotations do not include case law, do the rest of this exercise in a jurisdiction where the statute is annotated and includes case law.)

3. Choose 2–3 cases that illustrate the concept of unauthorized practice by a paralegal.

4. Use this chart to help you synthesize them:

Case name and citation	Unauthorized practice	Legally relevant facts

5.   Draft a topic sentence that synthesizes the legally relevant facts into one definition of the unauthorized practice of law. Geri will want to use this sentence on her power point to explain your jurisdiction's examples of unauthorized practice of law.

6.   Then, use the name of the cases, and one or two holding sentences, to draft a paragraph that explains the topic sentence. Geri will want to use this paragraph as talking points to explain the topic sentence she uses on the slide.

7.   Repeat this sequence for the rule requiring that attorneys supervise paralegals.

Rule Application

Legal Skills:

- Recognize rule application
- Recognize and articulate the *substantive holding*
- Recognize and articulate the *procedural holding*
- Understand *summary* judgment
- Draft a case holding sentence

PART I. WHAT WE MEAN WHEN WE SAY *RULE APPLICATION*

This chapter continues to emphasize: DON'T FORGET THE FACTS! Throughout this book the skills you have learned all require working with facts and identifying the legally relevant facts. In this chapter you will learn more about the role of the facts in the *rule application*.

When lawyers talk about *application*, we mean *rule application* or *rule-based reasoning*. The important skill of *rule application* means applying the legal rule to the facts. We talk so much about the law, how to understand it, and the different shapes and sizes that legal rules come in, that we often forget an equally important part of legal analysis: the facts. Facts are critical to how the law will be applied; facts are critical to the "when, how and why" of *rule application*. Without the facts, there is no *rule application*, and without *rule application*, there is no legal analysis.

A. The Process of *Legal Reasoning:* Examples of Applying Law to Facts

First, let's focus on the actual process of *application*—the *legal reasoning* process of applying the law to the facts.

Although you may be reading a case in order to find a legal rule, and although you have learned in this book how to recognize different types of legal rules that may be cited in a case, the most important thing about any case you are reading is not the rule (which undoubtedly has been applied numerous times in numerous contexts), but the unique, once-in-a-lifetime set of facts in the case, and how the legal rule was applied to those facts. In other words, the most important thing about the case you are reading is its *rule application*.

So, when you are reading a court opinion, read the initial recitation of facts, and then, as you read more of the opinion, focus on how the court applied the law to the facts and, in particular, which facts the court mentions. The court will not necessarily explicitly tell you: "We think the most important fact is . . . ." But in its discussion and when applying the law, the court will mention some facts. Once you have read the opinion, go back and review the facts again, this time through the lens of which facts are most important to the story. After reading a case, you should be able to explain HOW the court got from the set of facts to its decision—in other words, how and why it APPLIED the rule as it did. This explanation is legal analysis, and this explanation should include facts.

1. *Example of Implicit Reasoning—the Parrot Case*

Sometimes the court does not explicitly spell out its *reasoning* process. We have a good example of this from the *Conti* case about Chester the parrot that you read in Chapter 5. Notice that the court lays out the facts, then states the rule, explains the rule using case law, and finally, reaches a conclusion. Review the case to see whether there is any explicit *rule application* or *reasoning* by the court:

77 Misc.2d 61,
353 N.Y.S.2d 288
(Queens Co. Ct. 1974)

Conti v. ASPCA

DECISION.

Niam Meyer, Judge.

[This paragraph recites facts].

1.   *Chester is a parrot.* *He is fourteen inches tall, with a green coat, yellow head and an orange streak on his wings. Red splashes cover his left shoulder. Chester is a show parrot, used by the defendant SPCA in various educational exhibitions presented to groups of children.*

[This paragraph recites facts].

2.   *On June 28, 1973, during an exhibition, Chester flew the coop and found refuge in the tallest tree he could find.* *For seven hours the defendant sought to retrieve Chester. Ladders proved to be too short. Offers of food were steadfastly ignored. With the approach of darkness, search efforts were discontinued. A return to the area on the next morning revealed that Chester was gone.*

[This paragraph recites facts].

3.   *Several days later, plaintiff, Mr. Edwin Conti, saw a green-hued parrot with a yellow head and red splashes seated in his backyard.* *Mr. Conti offered him food and the parrot eagerly accepted. Not knowing what to do with the parrot, Mr. Conti called the SPCA, and that organization then sent two representatives to Mr. Conti's house. When they saw the parrot, they realized that this parrot was none other than Chester. This was further confirmed by the identification tag on Chester's right leg. The SPCA representatives took Chester back home. At the trial the SPCA workers testified that Chester knew how to say several words, including "hello," and how to dangle by his legs, and that they used him for various educational exhibits for children.*

[This paragraph explains a bit of the procedural history—who is suing whom?]

4.   The plaintiff then initiated this action to get Chester back.
Since the parties agree that this parrot is Chester, who is entitled to ownership—the plaintiff, who found Chester in his back yard, or the SPCA, who are the original owners of Chester?

5.   The plaintiff argued that the SPCA's ownership ended after Chester escaped and was captured and placed under the control of plaintiff.

[This paragraph recites the rule].

6.   The law is well settled that the true owner of lost property is entitled to the return thereof as against any person finding same. *(In re Wright's Estate, 15 Misc.2d 225, 177 N.Y.S.2d 410) (36A C.J.S. Finding Lost Goods s 3). However, this general rule is not applicable when the property lost is an animal. When the lost property is an animal, the question is whether the animal was domesticated or wild, ferae naturae. If the animal is wild, the owner can only have a limited, or qualified, right to the property, and if the animal escapes, that ownership right is wholly lost.*

[Here, we have the issue].

*7.   **Therefore, the issue is simply whether Chester was domesticated or wild.***

[The court describes the *holdings* of two cases dealing with the ownership of animals—wild geese and a pet canary].

8.   In Amory v. Flyn, 10 Johns.(N.Y.) 102, plaintiff sought to recover geese of the wild variety which had strayed from the owner.

[In granting judgment to the plaintiff, the *Amory* court pointed out that the geese had been tamed by the plaintiff and therefore were unable to regain their natural liberty].

9.   This important distinction was also demonstrated in Manning v. Mitcherson, 69 Ga. 447, 450–451, 52 A.L.R. 1063,

where the plaintiff sought the return of a pet canary. In holding for the plaintiff the court stated 'To say that if one has a canary bird, mocking bird, parrot, or any other bird so kept, and it should accidentally escape from its cage to the street, or to a neighboring house, that the first person who caught it would be its owner is wholly at variance with all our views of right and justice."

[Here is the court's conclusion.]

10. The Court finds that Chester was a domesticated animal, subject to training and discipline. Thus the rule of ferae naturae does not prevail and the defendant as true owner is entitled to regain possession.

11. Judgment for defendant dismissing the complaint without costs

As you can see, the court in *Conti* doesn't really connect the dots for the reader—rather, you have to make the connection between the facts, the rule, and the rule explanation. Making that connection is the *reasoning* process: Chester is domesticated because there was evidence that the SPCA had trained him. In the paragraph reciting the facts, we learned that the SPCA trained him to speak, that they disciplined him, and that they used him for educational purposes. So, even if the court doesn't explicitly provide the "because" for its holding, you can do so—and that's the *application*, or *reasoning*, process.

2. Example of Explicit Reasoning—the Nazi March Case

Let's look at an excerpt from our other case law example, the *Skokie* case, where the court more explicitly connects the rule with the facts for us. Unlike with the *Conti* case, you can see the *legal reasoning* process more clearly here, where the court discusses the rule and the meaning of the rule, and then explains how that rule applies to the facts of the case. It's that back and forth that really illustrates the *reasoning* process.

For a visual depiction of how the *reasoning* process works, note that in the excerpt below, *the law is in italics.* Can you identify the other parts of the case as 1) plaintiff's argument; 2) procedural information; or 3) the court engaging in the reasoning process and applying the law to the facts of the case?

4.   First, it is clear that the protection of the First Amendment extends to symbols such as the swastika, given that symbols can be a form of political speech. *This premise was articulated in* Tinker v. Des Moines Independent Community School District, *393 U.S. 503 (1969), which held that public school children had a first amendment right to wear black arm bands in protest of the Vietnam War.*

5.   Plaintiff seeks to extend the *"fighting words" doctrine* to compel the restraint of the march. *The "fighting words" doctrine was first articulated in* Chaplinsky v. New Hampshire, *315 U.S. 568 (1942), and was designed to permit punishment of extremely hostile personal communication likely to cause immediate physical response. In the* Cohen *case, the Supreme Court described fighting words as "those personally abusive epithets which, when addressed to the ordinary citizen, are, as a matter of common knowledge, inherently likely to provoke violent reaction."* Although the "fighting words" rule affirmed a statute punishing abusive speech, plaintiff asks this Court to extend the rule to allow the prior restraint of the Nazi march. In our judgment, we are precluded from doing so.

6.   *In* Cohen, *the Supreme Court overturned a criminal conviction which stemmed from the defendant wearing a jacket stating "Fuck the Draft" in a Los Angeles courthouse. The Court reasoned that the freedom of expression is necessary for our diverse society, and serves to educate and unite people from all walks of life, stating "That the air may at times seem filled with verbal cacophony is in this sense not a sign of weakness but of strength . . . . while the particular four-letter word being litigated here is perhaps more distasteful than most others of its genre, it is nevertheless often true that one man's vulgarity is another's lyric."*

7.   Although the swastikas are equally repulsive, the offensiveness of the speech doesn't matter when it comes to the First Amendment. *Plaintiffs are not a captive audience and have the opportunity to turn away or "avert their eyes," as stated in* Erznoznik v. City of Jacksonville, *422 U.S. 205 (1975). According to* Erznoznik, *the "Constitution does not permit the government to decide*

which types of otherwise protected speech are sufficiently offensive to require protection for the unwilling listener or viewer." The swastika does not fall under the "fighting words" doctrine and we cannot use that rule to overcome the presumption against prior restraint.

8.   We accordingly reluctantly conclude the Nazi's use of the swastika is protected speech under the First Amendment, and that the citizens of Skokie have the burden to avoid the offensive symbol. We are constrained to *reverse* the appellate court judgment enjoining the display of the swastika, and the judgment is *affirmed* in all other respects.

You can see that the *legal reasoning* process is shown in topic sentences, which clearly signal to the reader the direction of the analysis. You can also see that when the case law is relayed, it includes the relevant facts and holding of each case. Sometimes short quotes are used. For example, paragraph 6 is entirely devoted to the explanation of the law, including *Cohen*'s holding, its relevant facts, and a quote from the opinion. Then, the following sentence offers a conclusion about how that law *applies* to the facts of the *Skokie* case. The sentences that follow after that are again about case law, followed by another conclusion that indicates how the law *applies* to the facts.

3.   Example of Explicit Reasoning from IRAC Exercises

In actual work product of lawyers and paralegals who are attempting to fully explain the law, you should see more of the *legal reasoning* process than you do in the above decisions. For example, let's look at the examples from the beginning of Section II: the *application* section of the different IRAC analyses. These examples of legal analysis are done with the explicit purpose of explaining the *application* of the law to the facts. Looking at just the *application* section of each exercise, what do you notice?

Handyman Mike Needs a Place to Sleep

Application: Although it seems Mike acted illegally when he broke into someone else's home, at the time he did so, he reports his intention was only to sleep in a warm place. Since sleeping in a warm place is not a crime, Mike did not have the "intent to commit a crime" inside the Chilton's home. Without satisfying that element, Mike cannot be guilty of Third Degree Burglary.

Connie Loves Cookies

Application: The issue in this problem is the definition of "enter" for the purposes of the Third Degree Burglary statute. A prosecutor could argue that entry means crossing a property line or threshold, which would include an arm reaching through a window. On the other hand, Connie's defense counsel could argue that "enter" means that one's entire body has to cross the threshold into the "building." Because only Connie's arm reached over the property line, arguably she didn't enter the bake shop.

Nan and Richard's Bassadors

Application: The issue is what constitutes reasonable in Nan and Richard's ownership and care of their Bassadors, given the Bassadors' history of biting 3 year olds. On one hand, you could argue that the steps they took to give up their walks around the neighborhood and take their dogs to a designated dog park showed concern and foresight because it got the dogs off the streets. It seems their action also got the dogs away from toddlers trying to pet them. After all, the Bassadors did not bite another toddler, but instead chose an older 9 year old child, and Nan and Richard could not have anticipated this type of bite. On the other hand, because the Pulvino Memorial Dog Park was open to the public and allowed everyone in, this particular dog park was not the best choice for the Bassadors. Arguably, Nan and Richard should have kept them in a confined space such as an enclosed back yard.

What are some characteristics of the *application* process you can observe in the above three examples? These examples show the same process of *application*—the *legal reasoning* process of applying the legal rule to facts—that we could see in a court opinion. We can see the reference to a specific element or legal term such as "reasonable"; a reference to the issue; and the writer drawing connections between the element or legal term. We also see in some cases that an opposing argument is entertained. Significantly, the *reasoning* process of applying the legal rule to the facts is NOT repeating the rule and repeating the facts, but rather, conducting a back and forth about how and why the rule *applies* or doesn't *apply* to the facts. You are identifying specific parts of the rule—like the element—and quite literally explaining how that part of the rule or element is satisfied or not satisfied in light of the relevant facts.

To summarize, it is the explicit back and forth among the rule, the rule explanation, and the facts that is necessary to demonstrate the *application*, or *legal reasoning*, process. The more explicit you are, the better your reader can understand your analysis.

In the next section, we will look at the idea of *case holdings* and *case holding* sentences. They also demonstrate the *application* process, and sometimes you can work backwards from the holdings to figure out the reasoning when the court is not that clear about its process.

PART II. *HOLDING* SENTENCES AND LEGALLY RELEVANT FACTS

You have been introduced to the importance of legally relevant facts many times in this book. You now know that a fact is legally relevant if it can have an effect on the *application* of a legal rule—a specific legal element—and on how to resolve the issue raised by that element. The concept of relevance regarding the admission of evidence in state and federal court proceedings states basically the same concept in a different way. The Federal Rules of Evidence, Rule 401, defines "relevance" as follows:

> "Relevant evidence" means evidence having any tendency to make the existence of any fact that is of consequence to the determination of the action more probable or less probable than it would be without the evidence.

But you also know that determining the legally relevant facts is critical at all stages of the research and analysis process. In Chapter 4, you learned both that you can and should use the legally relevant facts to help you find the applicable legal rule, and that the legal rules help you understand what the legally relevant facts are. In Chapter 5, you were introduced to one of the building blocks of legal analysis, IRAC, and learned that this is a method of explaining how the law *applies* to the facts and the importance of the legally relevant facts. Then in Chapter 6 you learned about defining the legal issue based on the legally relevant facts.

Likewise, when you are summarizing the holding and reasoning of a case, that *summary*, or "*holding sentence*," should include the relevant facts. Usually, including the relevant facts forces you to explain how the legal rule is being *applied* to the facts.

A. Examples of *Holding Sentences* from the Parrot Case

Let's focus on how to draft the *holding sentence* first. For example, using the same case examples, let's compare a *holding sentence* that includes the legally relevant facts with one that does not include the legally relevant facts.

To review, here are the summaries of the issue, holding, and reasoning sections from the sample brief for the case about the plaintiff who wanted to keep the escaped parrot, *Conti v. ASPCA*, which hinged on whether the parrot was domesticated or wild:

ISSUE (EXAMPLE 1): Whether Chester the parrot is domesticated and should therefore be returned to his owner, the SPCA, after flying away and becoming lost? (*Note that this is a question that begins with "whether" and that includes relevant facts—that Chester the parrot was lost and now is found*).

ISSUE (EXAMPLE 2): Whether Chester the parrot is domesticated or wild and whether the common law rule of returning lost property to the original owner applies? (*Note* *that this issue is also phrased as a question, and in addition to including the relevant fact that Chester the parrot has been lost, also refers to the common law rule about returning lost property to its original owner).*

HOLDING: Yes, Chester is a domesticated animal and should therefore be returned to his original owner, the SPCA. *(Note how the holding simply answers the question posed in the Issue. The holding is simple and easy to understand—there is no doubt where the court stands.)*

REASONING: The court finds that Chester is a domesticated animal "subject to training and discipline," and this finding seems consistent with the SPCA testimony that Chester was used for educational exhibits, could state "hello," and could dangle by his legs. Because the parrot is a domesticated animal, the common law rule that lost items get returned to their owners applies (the court relies on *In Re Wright's Estate*). The court notes the common law rule that if the lost animal is a wild animal, it does <u>not</u> get returned to the owner because an owner of a wild animal has only a limited right of ownership. The court also relies on two cases in which domesticated animals—geese and a canary—were returned to their original owners after being lost (*Armory vs. Flynn* and *Manning v. Mitcherson*). *(Notice that the court does not specifically state why it believes that Chester is a domesticated animal, yet if we look at the facts, the court does state at the beginning—in its recounting of the Chester story—that Chester knew how to do some tricks—including say "hello" and dangle from his legs.)*

Now, in order to discuss the *Conti* case, perhaps in a piece of legal analysis like a memo, you would need to start out by providing the most relevant information, which means explaining the court's decision and how the court applied the legal rule to the facts. A great vehicle for this is the *holding sentence*. As you will see, because it has to reflect the court's decision, the *holding sentence* cannot just recite the legal rule, nor can it just include the factual result of the court's decision. Rather, in order to really convey the full meaning of the court's holding, the reader needs to know both the facts and the law. For example, read the following attempts, and see if you can recognize the most helpful *holding sentence* below:

> a.   In *Conti v. ASPCA*, 77 Misc. 2d 61, 353 N.Y.S.2d 288 (Queens Co. Ct. 1974), the court held that Chester belonged to the SPCA.

> b.   In *Conti v. ASPCA*, 77 Misc. 2d 61, 353 N.Y.S.2d 288 (Queens Co. Ct. 1974), the court held that if an animal is domesticated, and it becomes lost, it should go back to its original owner.

> c.   In *Conti v. ASPCA*, 77 Misc. 2d 61, 353 N.Y.S.2d 288 (Queens Co. Ct. 1974), the court found that Chester the parrot was a domesticated animal, and, therefore, under the common law rule that lost items get returned to their original owner, held that Chester should be returned to the SPCA.

If you see "c." as the most helpful *holding sentence*, you are correct. Why is it the most helpful? That sentence provides the factual result (finding) that Chester is domesticated; it provides the factual consequence—Chester gets returned to the SPCA; and it provides the legal basis for the court's decision—the common law rule that lost items get returned to their owner.

Note that the *holding sentence* does not contain ALL of the court's reasoning. For example, the *holding sentence* does not include any reference to the other common law rule the court discussed, that owners of wild animals obtain only a limited right of ownership in the animal. The *holding sentence* you write need only include the most important legal rule (in other words, the rule that is applied in order to resolve the issue) and the most important factual results and consequences. You can prioritize.

Here is a diagram of the components of a *holding sentence:*

Diagram 25:
Components of a *Holding Sentence*

Court's finding (the result of *application* of legal rule to facts)	Legal Rule	Factual consequence
The court found that Chester was a domesticated animal	and therefore under the common law rule that lost items get returned to their original owner	Chester should be returned to the SPCA

B. Examples of *Holding Sentences* from the Nazi March Case

Let's look at another example of *holding sentences* from the other sample case brief, for *Skokie v. National Socialist Party*, where the Illinois Supreme Court had to decide if the Nazis could wear their swastikas when they marched in the mainly Jewish village of Skokie. To refresh your memory, here are the issue, holding, and reasoning from the sample brief:

ISSUE: Whether the ban on swastikas violates the Nazi's First Amendment right to freedom of speech? *(Again, a question that references the specific relevant facts—the Nazis wearing the swastika—as well as the legal rule implicated—the freedom of speech clause under the First Amendment.)*

HOLDING: Yes, the Nazis cannot be prohibited from wearing the political symbol of the swastika. *(A very simple statement that answers the question posed in the issue with a "yes," and provides a full sentence while not going into the reasoning.)*

REASONING: The Illinois Supreme Court first referred to the First Amendment, and then relied principally on two U.S.

Supreme Court cases about the freedom of speech—*Tinker* and *Cohen*. According to *Tinker*, political symbols are protected by the First Amendment's protection of speech, which means that swastikas are protected. Then, the court relied on the holding of *Cohen*, which held that even highly offensive speech is protected. The court also referred to *Erzoznik*, in which the U.S. Supreme Court stated that the burden is on the viewer, the audience, to avert their eyes and avoid offensive speech. Thus, even though swastikas were offensive and upsetting for Skokie's Jewish population, they are protected speech under the First Amendment and the Nazis are allowed to march with them. *(Note, again, that the reasoning explains the specific precedent relied on, the holding from those cases, and how that holding applies to these facts; also, the writer lays out the reasoning in a simple step-by-step structure that is easy to follow.)*

Keeping the necessary components of a *holding sentence* in mind, let's look again at three samples: one that refers to the facts only, one that refers to the law only, and one that refers to both:

a.   In *Skokie v. National Socialist Party*, 69 Ill. 2d 605, 373 N.E.2d 21 (1978), the Court held that the Nazis could wear their swastikas during a planned march.

b.   In *Skokie v. National Socialist Party*, 69 Ill. 2d 605, 373 N.E.2d 21 (1978), the court held that the First Amendment must be honored.

c.   In *Skokie v. National Socialist Party*, 69 Ill.2d 605, 373 N.E.2d 21 (1978), the Court held that the Nazi swastika was protected speech under the First Amendment, and that the Nazis were allowed to wear the swastika during their planned march in the Jewish village of Skokie.

Again, we see that "c." contains both the relevant part of the legal rule—the First Amendment's protection of "speech"—and the factual consequence—the Nazis can wear their swastikas. This is what the sentence looks like when we diagram it in our *holding sentence* chart:

Diagram 26:
Components of a *Holding Sentence*

Court's finding (the result of *application* of legal rule to facts)	Legal Rule	Factual consequence
The court held that the Nazi swastika was protected speech	under the First Amendment	Nazis allowed to wear the swastika during their march in Skokie

We started this chapter on *rule application* with the skill of drafting a case *holding sentence* because it provides a good example of what *rule application* looks like—facts, law, and a factual result. Also, of course, the skill of writing a case *holding sentence* will be necessary as you draft legal documents such as legal memos and motions, or even briefing cases. It will also help you understand the cases you read and the holding of the case if you make sure you can summarize the holding in a case *holding sentence.*

SKILLS DEVELOPMENT

Steps for Writing a Holding Sentence

A holding sentence is a one-sentence summary of the court's holding that includes the applicable legal rule, the facts that the rule was applied to, and the factual consequence of the holding.

Step 1:   Ask yourself—What is the main legal rule the court is applying?

Step 2:   Ask yourself—When the court applied that legal rule, what was the factual result, or finding?

Step 3:   Ask yourself—What are the key legally relevant facts that the court is applying the rule to?

Step 4:   Ask yourself—What happens as a result of the court's decision?

Step 5:   Use a chart to make sure you have all three components of a holding sentence.

Understanding the true holding of a case can be a good spot to work backwards from in order to understand the *rule application* or *legal reasoning* process. In the next sections, we will look at *procedural* versus *substantive holdings* so that you can have a clear understanding of the full scope of a court's decision—which in turn leads to a clear understanding of the *application* or *legal reasoning* process.

PART III. DISTINGUISHING BETWEEN THE *SUBSTANTIVE HOLDING* AND THE *PROCEDURAL HOLDING* IN CASES

There are two aspects of a court's *holding*: a *substantive* aspect (how the law applies to the facts in that case) and the resulting *procedural* aspect (what will happen to the attorney's *motion* or the lower court's decision). Knowing the difference helps you understand the court's *legal reasoning—application—*process AND clearly and accurately state both aspects of the holding in your legal writing. Knowing the difference between the *procedural* and the *substantive holding* also helps you better understand the *substantive holding* and the court's reasons supporting it. It's easy to latch onto whatever the court states more clearly—which might be only the *procedural holding*—but then you risk not really understanding what happened in the case. The goal of this section is to help you identify and understand the *substantive holding* of the case, as well as the supporting reasons.

First, let's review the meaning of "holding" in general. You were introduced to the concept of a case holding in Chapter 1, when you learned that a holding is a court's decision in a case. We also examined a holding in both Chapters 1 and 3 as another form of a legal rule that includes elements. Indeed, if you think about it in the physical and literal sense, a holding is a stopping of something in motion. To the extent that our law, rule-based though it is, can be fluid, then the court's holding is the court's momentary interpretation and "stopping" of that fluid law based on a certain set of facts. In other words, it's the court decision about how the law in question applies to the facts and, in light of that, whether the "stopping" is only temporary (the case can continue) or permanent (the case is dismissed or a dismissal is affirmed). Therefore, a full statement of the court's holding includes both law and facts, and for our purposes, includes both the *procedural* aspect and the *substantive* aspect.

A. Background on Procedural Versus Substantive Holdings

Now, let's review the idea of *procedure* in general. Both state court systems and the federal court system have a full set of their own *procedural* rules. In general, the *procedural* rules provide directions for how to conduct *litigation*. *Litigation* is simply "the process of carrying on a lawsuit." Black's Law Dictionary. In other words, the *procedural* rules tell the lawyers and the courts how to go about moving a case through the court system, from the beginning to the end. In both federal and state courts, there are *procedural* rules for civil cases, and separate *procedural* rules for criminal cases. There are also special *procedural* rules for courts of limited jurisdiction, such as the federal Bankruptcy court, or in a state Surrogate's court or Family court.

Procedural rules cover all phases of *litigation*, which in the civil world begins when you initiate an action with a summons and complaint and ends when you file a final judgment. For example, the Federal Rules of Civil *Procedure* range from Rule 1 to Rule 86, and they cover all stages of trial—the initial pleadings, *discovery*, various *motions*, *dispositive motions* like *motions to dismiss* and *summary judgment motions*, trials, and judgments. In the criminal arena, an action can be initiated with a complaint, or a warrant, or an arrest, and the criminal *procedural* rules also take us through all stages of a criminal trial.

The final step before learning to distinguish between the two types of holdings is to discuss the types of cases you will typically encounter and what happens in those cases. Most of the decisions you will read will not be trial court decisions; most of the decisions you read will be appellate court decisions. This is because at the trial level, the court does not always have to write an opinion—sometimes all the trial court has to do is make a decision. Even when the trial court *does* write an opinion, it doesn't necessarily have to publish that opinion.

When you do read a trial court's decision, there will be two things going on in terms of the court's decision-making. First, typically the court has decided whether to grant or deny a specific request made by one of the parties, called a *motion*.[1] This request could be for a myriad of things. Much of the time when there is a *motion*, it is based on the defendant, the party being sued, asking the court simply to get rid of the case by dismissing the plaintiff's (the party suing) complaint or by granting *summary judgment* (see Part IV, below). The part of the court's decision that grants or denies that request, or that announces where the

---

[1] Cases, or aspects of cases, are resolved at the trial level in a variety of ways, including by jury verdict at the end of a trial. But such resolutions do not typically result in the judge writing an opinion. If a judge writes an opinion at all, it is most often when the judge has resolved a *motion* and has chosen to write an opinion to justify the resolution (holding) reached.

case is in the *litigation* process (see below), is the *procedural holding*—
certainly important, but not the whole story.

Second, in making such a decision, the trial court is also deciding
how the legal issue should be resolved (how the law *applies* to the facts
in that case). Even if the trial court only states a *procedural holding*—
"*Motion denied*" or "*Motion granted*"—that result necessarily required the
court to make a decision about how the law *applies* to the facts in the
case.

Similarly, when you are reading an appellate court's decision, there
are also two things going on. One, the appellate court is making a
decision about what should happen to the trial court's decision as a
matter of *procedure* (*affirmed*, *denied*, *affirmed* in part, *denied* in part, *modified*,
or *remanded*); and two, it is also making that decision as a result of having
made a decision about how the law *applies* to the particular facts of that
case. And, because appellate courts include both mid-level appellate
courts and the court of last resort (highest level), you could be reading
about multiple levels of *procedural relief.*

In an appellate court opinion, the appellate panel—usually 3–5
judges, depending on the jurisdictional rules, but definitely more than
1—is deciding whether the trial court's decision on the *motion* is correct.
If the appellate court agrees with the trial court, it will *affirm* the
decision. If the appellate court finds that the trial court is wrong, it will
reverse the trial court. One way or the other, the appellate court will
provide an opinion on what the trial court did. Sometimes the trial
court is *affirmed* in part and *reversed* in part.

The important thing to remember is that by itself, this *affirming* or
reversing does not tell the whole story. For example, if you are asked to
report on a court's holding and you simply say that the court *affirmed*
the trial court, what does that say? That statement does not relay much
information. Most notably, it is missing *the relevant facts*; with such an
answer we do not even know what the case is about, nor do we know
the issue. A statement that a lower court decision is *affirmed* or *reversed*
is just a *procedural* statement on whether the appellate court agreed or

disagreed. The statement doesn't tell us what the dispute is about, which side the court took in the dispute, or why the court decided what it decided.

So, because there are always *procedural* rules that apply to *litigation*, at both the trial court level and the appellate level, there is always a *procedural* result in addition to a *substantive* result. In order to learn the difference between the *procedural* and the *substantive holding*, we will be examining both types of *holdings*. As a practical matter, a court has to reach its *substantive holding* first, since that will largely or fully determine what the *procedural holding* will be. But since it is probably easier to identify the *procedural holding* because of the language cues, we will first examine *procedural holdings*.

B. Recognizing *Procedural Holdings*

The first step is recognition. If you can recognize the *procedural holding*, then you can focus on finding and identifying the *substantive holding*. The language cues for *procedural holdings* are different depending on the level of court the decision is from. Here are two diagrams to demonstrate some examples of key words and vocabulary in *procedural holdings* on the trial and mid-appellate level.

The first diagram, for the trial court level, has divided the principal *motions* made according to the phase of trial at which they occur: pleadings (summons, complaint, answer), *discovery* (primarily meaning after the close of *discovery*, and not including any *motions* to actually get the *discovery* items, like *motions* to compel), and then the trial itself (again, principally the *motions* that come at the end of the trial).

Diagram 27:
Recognizing *Procedural Holdings* in Trial Court

Stages of Trial	*Relief* Sought in *Motion*	Trial Court's Holding Language
Pleadings	Plaintiff and defendant can move for: • Dismissal of causes of action in complaint or defenses in answer	The court *"dismisses"*: • Plaintiff's complaint • Defendant's affirmative defense The court *"grants"* or *"denies"*: • Plaintiff's/Defendant's *motion to dismiss*
Discovery	Defendant (or plaintiff) can move for: • *Summary judgment* (after *discovery*) on all or some of plaintiff's causes of action If there are more complicated parties and pleadings, such as third-party actions, or cross-claims between parties, or counter-claims, any of those claims can also be the subject of a *motion* for *summary judgment*	The court *"grants"*: • *Summary judgment* on count(s) of the plaintiff's complaint • Defendant's *motion* for *summary judgment* • *Summary judgment* on defendant's/plaintiff's cross-claim or counter-claim • Partial *summary judgment* The court *"denies"*: • Defendant's/plaintiff's *summary judgment* (see Part IV for a full examination of *summary judgment*)
Trial Verdict/Judgment	Defendant can move: • To set aside jury verdict or judgment	The court *"grants"* or *"denies"*: • Defendant's/plaintiff's *motion* for a directed verdict • Defendant's/plaintiff's *motion* to set aside the verdict The court "sets aside": • the jury's verdict • counts (x and x) of the jury verdict The court "enters judgment": • on the jury's verdict

The second diagram shows mid-level and the highest level appellate court and both the language and types of procedural *relief* that can be *granted*.

Diagram 28:

Recognizing *Procedural Holdings* in Appellate Court

Decision	Appellate Court's Holding Language
Mid-level appellate court: • Can agree or disagree with the appellant—in whole or in part	Mid-level appellate court: • *Reverse/affirm* trial court's decision • *Remand* case to trial court for further proceedings Can include procedural relief like: • *Grant/deny summary judgment* • Vacate or reinstate pleadings, such as complaints and answers
Highest appellate court: • Can agree or disagree with the appellant in whole or in part • Can affect the mid-level court's decision and/or the trial court's decision	Highest appellate court: • *Affirm/deny* mid-level court • *Affirm/deny* trial level court • *Remand* case to trial court for further proceedings Can include procedural *relief* like the above

So you can see, the pattern is that a *procedural holding* involves the disposition of a *motion*, such as *summary judgment* or *dismissal*, or the appellate court's agreement or disagreement with the lower court's result, such as *affirming, reversing,* or *modifying* the trial court's decision.

Hopefully, this visual depiction of the types and names of *procedural relief* can help you identify this type of *relief* in a court opinion. In other words, when the court, whether trial or appellate, makes statements about *summary judgment* or *dismissal,* this statement is about the disposition of the case—what will happen to it. Be careful, though, about stating the *procedural holding,* such as that "*summary judgment* was granted",[2] without really understanding which party won and why. For that understanding, you need to also grasp the legal or *substantive holding*—the legal "rule" of the case. Notice that such *procedural* statements do not include any substantive legal rules, nor do they include any legally relevant facts. When you relay the *substantive holding,*

---

[2]   See Part IV to learn about this type of motion—in just a few pages!

there will be enough law and facts in the statement that the reader will know something about the specifics of the case.

C. Recognizing *Substantive Holdings*

In contrast with the last two diagrams, the following diagram focuses on *substantive holdings* rather than *procedural holdings*. When a court relays its *substantive holding* (its *non-procedural holding* that says more about the parties and how it *applied* the law), the court usually relays some specific information about the case and the law, as well as using some typical language.

Here are some examples of key words and vocabulary in *substantive holdings* with appellate courts:

Diagram 29:
Recognizing *Substantive Holdings*

Trial and Appellate Court *Substantive holdings*	Language Cues
In general	• We hold • We conclude • We agree with plaintiffs/ *defendants* • We disagree with plaintiffs/ defendants
About the law	• The statute means/includes/was intended to/should be applied • The *doctrine* of _____ means/ applies/doesn't apply • The case law means/includes/ was intended to/should be applied • The legal rule means/includes/ was intended to/should be applied
About the facts and law	• All of the above

Sometimes a court will start its opinion with its conclusion—the *substantive holding*—and then repeat it; other times the court will end its opinion with its conclusion. As a reader, you should read the first and last paragraph of the court decision first to see if you can determine the court's conclusion. Once you know the court's conclusion, it can be easier to follow the court's recounting of the facts and the court's *legal reasoning* (especially if, as you learned in Chapter 5, you go through the topic sentences before reading the whole opinion).

To summarize, remember that you can tell whether you are relaying the *substantive holding* by whether you have included specific facts and law from the case. If your sentence or phrase relaying the holding could easily be applied to another case (e.g., *summary judgment affirmed/denied*), then you have not identified the *substantive holding* and the specific nature of what happened in that case. Remember, the *substantive holding* tells you how the court *applied* the legal rule at issue to the particular facts of that case.

PART IV. UNDERSTANDING *SUMMARY JUDGMENT*

Now let's examine *summary judgment* in more detail. As you research, and as you read appellate court opinions, you will come across *summary judgment. Summary judgment* is a type of *dispositive motion*, meaning it can "dispose of" a case. You can also think about the meanings of the words themselves. The word *"summary"* has two common meanings that are non-legal: according to Merriam Webster, one is "covering the main points succinctly"; another meaning is "done without delay or formality." (Merriam Webster Incorporated, online 2018—https:// www.merriam-webster.com.) Merriam Webster even has a legal definition: "conducted without the customary legal formalities." So you get the idea of something that is short and abbreviated. That is accurate, because the *summary judgment motion* seeks to dispose of, or resolve, a case before a trial.

Then, let's look at the word *"judgment."* Go straight to the legal definition of *judgment* in <u>Black's Law Dictionary</u>, which states: "A court's final determination of the rights and obligations of the parties in a case." In other words, a final decision on a party's cause of action, or on a party's entire case.

Together, the words mean a method of ending a case without a trial. *Summary judgment* can be the name of the order—a *summary judgment order*—or what you call the motion when you are requesting that relief—a *summary judgment motion*. A *motion* is a request to the court for an order. Therefore, when you make a *summary judgment motion*, you are requesting that the court make a final decision (issue an order) on a case or cause of action without a trial. Both the federal court system and the state court systems have procedural rules on how to litigate cases in those courts; both sets of rules include rules about *summary judgment motions*.

The idea behind *summary judgment* is that there are some disputes that are purely legal—no facts are in dispute—that therefore can be decided on a legal basis alone, without need of a trial or a fact finder like a jury. For example, the Federal Rule of Civil *Procedure* Rule 56, on *summary judgment*, provides in part that:

> The court shall grant *summary judgment* if the movant shows that there is **no genuine dispute as to any material fact** and the movant is entitled to *judgment* as a matter of law. The court should state on the record the reasons for granting or denying the *motion*.

(emphasis added). State *procedural* rules are similar. The bolded language above is key: in order for the court to grant a *summary judgment motion*, there can be **no issue of material fact**. This doesn't mean that there are no factual issues (disputes), just that those issues can't be *material* (legally relevant to resolving the issue).

This state and federal *procedural* rule—that *summary judgment* may be granted when there is no *material* issue of fact—is known as a *"standard."* Notice how Federal Rule 56 applies to the court: "The court shall grant summary judgment when . . . ." A *standard* is a specific way to view the law and facts, which is similar to the idea of a burden of proof. Both provide a lens through which to view the facts and evidence. Remember in Chapter 2 you learned about the different burden of proof for civil cases (preponderance of the evidence or clear and convincing evidence) and criminal cases (beyond a reasonable doubt). A *standard* is similar, and *standards* often apply to motions made by parties when there will be no trial. The *summary judgment standard* is one example—granting judgment when there is no material issue of fact; the *motion to dismiss standard* is another example—under the Federal Rules of Civil Procedure 12(b)(6) (as well as the parallel state rule), a court can grant a defendant's motion to dismiss when plaintiff has "failed to state a claim upon which relief may be granted." Note that both the standards mentioned here are used in civil cases (hence the Federal Rules of **Civil** Procedure), but there are similar types of motions that can be made in criminal cases. Typically in both types of motions, since the result would be getting rid of the plaintiff's case, the court looks at the proof "in the light most favorable to the plaintiff."

As you do legal research, you will come across *summary judgment* in the text of the court opinions. Especially when you are researching and reading appellate cases, which will often be the case, many times the appeal will be from the loss of a *summary judgment motion*. When either the grant of *summary judgment* to a defendant is appealed by the plaintiff, or the defendant's loss of a *summary judgment motion* is appealed by the defendant, it can become hard to understand who is "winning" on appeal, and what exactly they are "winning."

A. Recognizing *Summary Judgment*

Now that we know the basic meaning of *summary judgment*—a resolution of an issue (or entire case) without a trial when there is no issue of fact—look at this visual depiction of what it means for a party to "win" or "lose" a *summary judgment motion*.

Diagram 30:

Understanding *Summary Judgment*

Who is moving for *summary judgment?*	What did the court decide?	Winner versus loser?	Is there a trial?	Who appeals?	Can there still be a trial?
Defendant	Court *grants* *summary judgment motion* (dismissing some or all of plaintiff's causes of action)	Defendant wins the *motion*—the case goes away Plaintiff loses— never gets a trial and whole case is lost	No trial (on cause(s) of action that are dismissed)	Plaintiff appeals	Yes, if plaintiff wins appeal, the case will be sent back to the trial court for trial
Defendant	Court *denies* *summary judgment motion*	Defendant loses the *motion*— defendant will have to defend itself against plaintiff's claim Plaintiff Wins— plaintiff's claim survives but is not yet resolved	Yes! (either side can win at trial) In some states, defendant can appeal the motion ruling directly and put trial on hold	Whoever loses at trial OR, In some states, defendant can appeal the motion ruling directly before trial	Yes, if defendant appeals *motion* ruling and loses If no appeal of motion ruling, trial proceeds (If trial proceeds, the losing party can appeal the result of the trial)

The above chart shows some of the most common situations for *summary judgment*. A plaintiff can, but does not often, bring a *motion* for *summary judgment* on a claim it has brought. Remember that since the plaintiff is bringing the cause of action, the plaintiff would have the burden of proof on **all** the elements of its claim, with no question of fact on **any** of them. The defendant only has to show that the plaintiff fails to meet this burden for **one** element to show that the plaintiff has no claim justifying a trial. (Although plaintiffs can and do bring *motions* to dismiss or *motions* for *summary judgment* on defenses that *defendants* raise and have to prove, such *motions* don't typically resolve the entire case. Rather, if plaintiff were successful on such a *motion*, defendant can't present the dismissed defense at trial.)

Consequently, it is the defendant who usually moves for *summary judgment* in order to dismiss some or all of plaintiff's claims. As noted above, this is a remedy that can be requested in state or federal court, and the *motion* is typically made after the close of *discovery*, which means the plaintiff and the defendant have exchanged all the information they will introduce at trial.

B. Example Demonstrating How *Summary Judgment* Works

Let's work through a simple example step-by-step of what happens when a defendant moves for *summary judgment* in a slip and fall case. A "slip and fall" case is more or less what it sounds like: when someone falls, suffers an injury, and then alleges that the fall occurred because of an unsafe condition—for example, an icy sidewalk, slippery floor, or uneven step. This is a negligence case, with the four elements of 1) duty, 2) breach of duty, 3) causation, and 4) damages. The plaintiff is typically alleging that the landowner has breached its duty (element 2) to keep its property in reasonably safe condition.

One of the critical issues for the landowner is whether it knew about the dangerous condition. For example, let's say your property, such as a grocery store, is open to the public, and it has a huge yawning hole in the middle of the cereal aisle. There are no warning signs, no orange cones, no fences or tape—there is just a huge, three feet deep hole. If the hole happened suddenly at noon on a Saturday, and a customer fell into the hole a few seconds later, it might not be your fault. You might not have breached your duty of reasonable care if there was nothing you could do to prevent the hole, the hole happened suddenly, and someone fell into the hole right after it appeared. On the other hand, if the hole appeared on a Sunday at noon, and three days later it was still there and someone fell into it, there is a good chance you have breached your duty of reasonable care because you failed to fix the hole—or at least warn people about it—promptly.

For another more realistic example that might involve a *summary judgment motion*, let's say that plaintiff Martina slipped and fell on some grapes that were on the floor of the Publico Bodega (a small convenient store). She broke her leg, needed surgery, and was laid off at her job. Martina sued the bodega, alleging that the grapes must have been on the floor for a while, since they were mashed into the floor and jelly-like, so the bodega owner breached its duty to keep its floors reasonably safe. During *discovery*, Publico Bodega produced its cleaning records which showed that the aisle floor had been cleaned five minutes before Martina's fall.

After the close of *discovery*, the defendant Publico Bodega could move for *summary judgment*, arguing that it didn't know about the grapes, and that the grapes hadn't been there long enough for it to know. Defendant can argue that there is no factual issue—both sides agree about the facts—and that therefore as a matter of law—the legal rule, when applied to the undisputed facts, says it did not breach the duty of care—it should get *summary judgment*.

Various outcomes for defendant's *motion* are possible. The trial court could grant the *motion*, which would mean that plaintiff's complaint is dismissed, there is no trial, and defendant doesn't have to pay any damages.

But the plaintiff could appeal this grant of *summary judgment*, which has ended its case, and argue on appeal that there is an issue of fact that should be determined by a jury. If the plaintiff succeeds on appeal, and the appellate court reverses the trial court's decision, then the case goes back down to the trial level, and there is a trial on plaintiff's cause of action.

Or, if the court *denied* defendant's *motion*, in some jurisdictions, defendant could appeal the denial of its *motion*, and on appeal, the appellate court could 1) affirm the trial court and the denial of *summary judgment*, which means the case still proceeds to trial, or 2) reverse the trial court and grant the *summary judgment motion*, which then means there is no trial and defendant has won the case.

However, note that in some jurisdictions, including federal court, the defendant cannot appeal when it loses a *summary judgment motion*. After all, if the only "bad" thing that will happen is a trial, it's not really that bad—or more importantly, it's not *dispositive* (the end of the case). The rule makes sense when you consider the idea (again, fundamental to many jurisdictions) that only *dispositive*, or final, judgments can be appealed. If defendant has to go through a trial, it might win (and the appellate court's time will not have been wasted on an unnecessary appeal). And if it loses at trial, it can appeal what will then be a final judgment.

To summarize, one of the key things to remember is that the "win" or "loss" of a *summary judgment motion* doesn't necessarily align with a "win" or "loss" of the case. You have to look a little more closely so you can determine the consequence of the "win" or "loss" of the *motion*.

CHAPTER 8 LEGAL SKILLS

* **Recognize rule application**
* **Recognize and articulate the *substantive holding***
* **Recognize and articulate the *procedural holding***
* **Understand *summary* judgment**
* **Draft a case holding sentence**

CHAPTER 8 VOCABULARY

- Affirm
- Application
- Deny
- Dicta
- Discovery
- Dismiss
- Dispositive
- Doctrine
- Explicit reasoning
- Granted
- Holding sentence
- Implicit reasoning
- Issue of material fact
- Judgment
- Legal reasoning
- Litigation
- Material
- Modify
- Motion
- Motion to dismiss
- Procedural holding
- Procedure
- Relief
- Remand
- Reverse
- Rule application
- Rule-based reasoning
- Set aside
- Standards
- Substantive holding
- Summary
- Summary judgment motion

CHAPTER 8 RESEARCH AND ANALYSIS EXERCISES

I. **Researching and identifying federal and state procedural rules:**

The following exercises will help you locate and use procedural rules as needed.

1. Look up your state's procedural rules for conducting litigation at the trial level and at both appellate levels.

a. What are the rules called? Are there separate sets of rules for appeals to a mid-level appellate court and appeals to the court of last resort, or are such appeals covered by the same rules?

b. According to <u>The Bluebook</u> or your state citation rules, how would you cite to each set of procedural rules?

c. Are there any special or separate rules of procedure for limited jurisdiction courts, such as City Courts, Town Courts, or Surrogate's Courts?

d. What is the trial court rule for summary judgment?

e. Find and brief a mid-level or court of last resort case in your jurisdiction that discusses the application of the summary judgment rule.

2. Look up the procedural rules for conducting litigation at the trial level and at both appellate levels in your federal jurisdiction.

a. What are the rules called? Are there separate sets of rules for appeals to the mid-level appellate court and appeals to the court of last resort, or are such appeals covered by the same rules?

b. According to <u>The Bluebook</u> or your jurisdiction's citation rules, how would you cite to each set of procedural rules?

c. What is the trial court rule for summary judgment?

d. Find and brief a mid-level or court of last resort case in your jurisdiction that discusses the application of the summary judgment rule.

Methods of Rule Application

Legal Skills:
- Understand comparisons and draft analogies and distinctions
- Construct the legal rule broadly or narrowly
- Understand and use the reason behind the legal rule
- Understand and use the legislative history behind a statute

---

Sometimes the application of the legal rule to the facts is relatively straightforward; sometimes the process requires more time and effort. In this chapter, we will look at some different ways to approach rule application in the law. We will look at how you can actually interpret or define the rule differently, depending on your goals (and the case law, of course); how you can make *analogies* and *distinctions* by comparing your facts to the facts in precedent cases; and how you can use the purpose or *policy* behind a rule, as well as its legislative history (if it is a statute or regulation), as support for applying the legal rule in a certain way.

Remember, the fundamental rule application or legal reasoning process is applying the legal rule to facts. We look to the elements and see what facts match the elements. We will use a famous example of a rule to illustrate how the process can be straightforward:

No vehicles in the park.[1]

---

[1] This hypothetical rule was created by famous legal philosopher H.L.A. Hart in his article *Positivism and the Separation of Law and Morals,* 71 Harv. L. Rev. 593, 607 (1958). For many reasons,

Now, apply this rule to a fictitious factual situation (otherwise known as a hypothetical):

> Bill and Johnny wanted to test out their new Land Rover SUV to see whether it could really drive off-road, through hilly areas and through brush. They took their Rover on a midnight drive through their town's Wilcox Park. The "No Vehicles in the Park" rule applies. Have Bill and Johnny violated the rule?

The first step is identifying the elements of the rule, and there are two: vehicles and park. The next step is determining whether the facts meet the elements; is there a vehicle? Yes, the Land Rover SUV is a vehicle. Is there a park? Yes, Wilcox Park. Has the rule been violated? Yes. This is rule-based reasoning in its simplest form.

Using the same rule, let's look at another factual situation:

> Quinn is 7 years old, and her babysitter brought her to Wilcox Park. Quinn brought her favorite toy, a miniature toy fire truck, which was small enough to hold in her hand. The "No Vehicles in the Park" rule applies. Has Quinn violated the rule?

Since we know the elements are vehicle and park, the question is whether Quinn's toy fire truck is a vehicle. Probably not. Without any more context about the purpose of the rule, it is hard to imagine how it would make any sense to forbid children to bring their miniature toy trucks to a park.

That's the basic rule application; now let's look at the variations.

PART I. CONSTRUING THE RULE *BROADLY* OR *NARROWLY*

Part of the rule application process can include how you define and explain the rule. Although talking about rule construction sounds

---

this rule has been much discussed. *See, e.g.,* Frederick Schauer, *A Critical Guide to Vehicles in the Park*, 83 N.Y.U. L. Rev. 1109 (2008).

like we are talking about building a rule, what we are really talking about is how to construe or interpret a rule. *Broad* versus *narrow* construction means what it sounds like—a *narrow* definition means not much fits into it. A *narrow* definition is smaller and less inclusive than a *broad* definition. In contrast, a *broad* definition is wider and more inclusive. So if you want your facts to fit into a rule, you may have to construe the rule *broadly*, so that the rule is more inclusive. If you don't want your facts to fit into a rule, then the opposite is true—you want to construe the rule more *narrowly*.

A.   Everyday Examples of *Broad* Versus *Narrow* Construction

Interpreting the rule differently is probably something many of us have done instinctively. After all, if there is a strict "No underage drinking" rule on your college campus, has the 20-year-old college student who sipped wine at the college president's dinner violated the rule? How about the 20-year-old student who hosted an all-night keg party on campus (before it was discovered and shut down by the campus police)? Many would argue that the rule shouldn't be interpreted so strictly or literally as to find the sipper AND the keg party host guilty of violating the rule to the same degree. This argument is basically an argument that the "No underage drinking" should not be interpreted so *broadly* as to include the sipper of wine. An argument that the rule should not apply to the sipper is an argument that the rule should be applied more *narrowly*, or restrictively, and should NOT include absolutely every instance of underage drinking.

Let's return to the example of "No Vehicles in the Park" and look at how *broad* versus *narrow* construction of the rule plays out in the following examples.

Example 1

Susan and Janis go on 20-mile bike rides every morning. One morning they decide to take a short cut on their bicycles through Wilcox Park. Then they see the "No

Vehicles in the Park" sign. Have Susan and Janis violated the rule with their bicycles?

Remember that the two elements are "vehicle" and "park." Can you identify the factual issue here? The issue is whether the bicycles Susan and Janis are riding come under the definition of "vehicle" and are therefore not allowed in the park.

Whether the definition of "vehicle" includes bicycles depends on whether we define vehicles *broadly* and expansively, say, to include everything with wheels, or whether we define it *narrowly,* and include only motorized vehicles, such as cars and trucks. So, if we define vehicles *broadly*, to include anything with wheels, then Susan and Janis did violate the rule, because a bicycle would be considered a vehicle. If we define vehicles more *narrowly*, and less inclusively, then bicycles would NOT be vehicles because they are not motorized.

Let's say that Susan and Janis DID violate the rule, and the definition of vehicles includes bicycles. Now we will look at another hypothetical:

Example 2

Keeley is a babysitter for Arlo, a 7-month-old baby who is very smiley. Arlo likes the outdoors, so Keeley decided to put him in his three-wheeled jogging stroller and take him for a walk through Wilcox Park. Keeley reads the "No Vehicles in the Park" rule on a park sign. Have Keeley and Arlo violated the rule with the baby stroller?

The issue becomes even easier to identify because we have the same rule, and with a baby stroller we know the element at issue is vehicle, so the issue is: Whether "vehicle" includes baby stroller under the "No Vehicles in the Park" rule?

If we stretch the definition wider—more *broadly*—so that in addition to motor vehicles, we include not only bicycles but also baby carriages, then Keeley and Arlo have violated the rule. You can see how this would lead to what we call in law a *"slippery slope"* problem: taken to the most extreme point, if vehicle includes everything with wheels, then we get ourselves into the ridiculous position of wondering whether Quinn's toy truck would be included in "vehicle" as well. Of course, that seems absurd. How could a rule like "No Vehicles in the Park" apply to toys? It seems likely that the aim of the rule was to keep the park safe by keeping out cars or motorcycles, not toys.

You can use the *slippery slope* argument to show that if you take a proposition to an absurd extent, the rule simply does not make sense. In law, we typically don't want our rules to be absurd, so we don't interpret them that way. Construing the rule overly *broadly* to include absolutely everything with wheels makes little sense, assuming the purpose of the rule was simply to keep the park safe.

B. Recognizing Broad Versus Narrow Construction in Case Law

Let's work with another example here to see how a court might interpret a statute broadly—but the exception narrowly. The court in this example interprets a remedial statute, the Dram Shop Act, broadly, which makes sense because the purpose of the statute is to provide recovery for someone hurt by an intoxicated person. Many times when there is a remedial statute put in place to help people, the courts will be sensitive to that purpose. In interpreting the Dram Shop Act *broadly* in the example below, the court allows a path to recovery for the plaintiff, Yvonne, who is suing the restaurant. This is an example of a *broad* interpretation (for reasons that will become apparent when you read the example).

On the other hand, in refusing to adopt an exception to the Dram Shop Act that would foreclose recovery for Yvonne, the court interprets the proposed exception *narrowly*. Because the defendant restaurant does not want to be liable, it urged the court to adopt an exception to the Dram Shop Act that would deny Yvonne's recovery because she became drunk as part of the same situation in which the intoxicated person who injured her did. The court examined the proposed exception—no recovery.

As noted before, many states have what is called a "Dram Shop" act, which imposes liability on a bar or host who serves liquor to a visibly intoxicated guest (or an underage guest) who then injures someone. Here is the New York statute being applied in our example case, General Obligations Law § 11–101 (1) (McKinney 2017):

> *Any person who shall be injured in person, property, means of support, or otherwise by any intoxicated person, or by reason of the intoxication of any person, whether resulting in his death or not, shall have a right of action against any person who shall, by unlawful selling to or unlawfully assisting in procuring liquor for such intoxicated person, have caused or contributed to such intoxication; and in any such action such person shall have a right to recover actual and exemplary damages.*

Looking at the statute in terms of the elements, it allows a <u>person</u> who is <u>injured</u> by an <u>intoxicated person</u> to sue <u>any person</u> who <u>has caused or contributed to the intoxication</u> by <u>unlawfully selling OR unlawfully assisting in procuring alcohol</u>. In other words, if you illegally sell or illegally help to obtain alcohol which causes intoxication, you can be sued by someone who is injured by the intoxicated person.

You may be wondering—what is "unlawfully selling"? According to the New York Alcohol Beverage Control Law § 65 (McKinney 2017), an illegal sale includes a sale not only to an underage drinker, but also to those who are "visibly intoxicated" as well as those who are "habitual drunkards."

So, synthesizing our rules, the statute gives an injured person the right to sue a bartender, for example, who sold alcohol to a "visibly intoxicated" person who then becomes an "injurer" or tortfeasor. In law, the "tortfeasor" is someone who causes the harm—injury—to another. If there is a car accident, we know the injured person can sue the person at fault, like the driver; but the Dram Shop Act gives the injured person the right to also sue a bar if too much liquor was served to a visibly intoxicated person.

Now we will look at our example case, *Mitchell v. Shoals, Inc.*, 9 N.Y.2d 338, 280 N.Y.S.2d 113 (1967), slightly adapted, which interpreted and applied New York's Dram Shop Act. It provides us with examples of both *broad* and *narrow* statutory construction.

In *Mitchell*, a couple named Robert Taylor (the injurer or tortfeasor) and Yvonne Mitchell (intoxicated plaintiff) went to the Shoals restaurant for drinks and dancing. After Yvonne had several drinks, she passed out. Her date, Robert Taylor, had already enjoyed a series of double bourbons. The bartender continued to serve Robert despite his intoxication, even after being told not to serve him after Robert fell to the floor. When Robert drove Yvonne (who was still sleeping) home, he lost control of the car and crashed. Robert was killed, Yvonne was seriously injured, and she sued the restaurant under the Dram Shop Act. The issue was whether the plaintiff (Yvonne) could sue the restaurant for illegally serving Robert (given that the bartender served him even though he was visibly intoxicated) when she herself was intoxicated.

The Court evaluated the plaintiff's cause of action under the Dram Shop Act. This is what the Court stated, complete with citations (note the Court also refers to the purpose of the statute):

> *Although the statute—its forerunner goes as far back as 1873 (L.1873, ch. 646; see Note, 8 Syracuse L.Rev. 252)—does not give the inebriated person a cause of action if he is himself injured (see Moyer v. Lo Jim Cafe, 19 A.D.2d 523, 240 N.Y.S.2d 277, affd. 14 N.Y.2d 792, 251 N.Y.S.2d 30, 200 N.E.2d 212; Scatorchia v. Caputo, 263 App.Div. 304, 32 N.Y.S.2d 532), it does entitle any one else injured 'by reason of the intoxication' of such person to recover damages from the party dispensing the liquor.* **There is no justification, either in the language of the legislation or in its history, for exonerating the latter simply because he had also served, and brought about the inebriety of, the third person who was hurt.**

Note the bolded section in gray in which the Court concluded that there is "no justification" for "exonerating [the person dispensing the liquor]" when he also causes the intoxication of the "third person"—

in this case, Yvonne. In other words, the person who illegally served the liquor—the bartender—is still liable even if he illegally served not only the drunk party who injured the plaintiff (Robert) but also the plaintiff (Yvonne).

So if two people go to a bar and BOTH get drunk, the injured party can sue the bar even though that injured party was drunk, too. The statute is trying to get at the wrongful conduct of a bar for selling alcohol to those who are visibly intoxicated. The Court therefore explains that even though Yvonne was also drunk, that does not let the bartender (or the bar) off the hook for illegally serving Robert Taylor, who injured Yvonne. In other words, in order to achieve the statute's purpose of preventing wrongful conduct of bars, the Court interpreted the coverage of the statute broadly so as to include even drunk plaintiffs.

Now, let's look at the narrow aspect of the Court's holding. The defendant bar, unhappy with the notion that someone who was actually the drinking companion to the tortfeasor could actually recover damages, still sought a way out. The defendant urged the Court to adopt a "guilty participation" exception to the statute based on the specific circumstances. The Court concluded, however, that as long as the plaintiff, Yvonne, was not the one to "cause or procure" the intoxication of the tortfeasor, "there is no basis under the statute, for denying . . . recovery." The court reasons that it would defeat the purpose of the statute to disallow Yvonne's recovery just because she was Robert's drinking companion. The court holds that her drinking and passing out did not amount to "a guilty participation in his [Robert's] intoxication."

In other words, even though Yvonne had participated in the events surrounding Robert's intoxication, it would be interpreting the "guilty participation" exception too broadly to disallow her recovery when she had not caused the intoxication. Or, worded the other way around, the court interpreted the "guilty participation" exception narrowly to include only truly "guilty" participants.

Here is the Court's decision and reasoning:

In the case before us, the plaintiff had herself become drunk while drinking with Taylor but she had not, in any sense, caused or procured his intoxication. She had neither purchased the drinks nor encouraged him to take more than he could weather. The plaintiff had simply had a few drinks and passed out before her escort's inebriety became really serious. This did not amount to a guilty participation in his intoxication. To deny her a remedy because her own alcoholic capacity was limited would impair, if not go a long way toward defeating, the purpose of the statute.

[The above paragraph tells us that Yvonne, the injured person, "simply had a few drinks and passed out" but "had not, in any sense, caused or procured his (Taylor's) intoxication" which is not enough for "guilty participation."]

In two or three states, the courts have held that the plaintiff's mere participation in drinking with the person whose drunkenness caused the injury may be sufficient to prevent recovery under the Dram Shop Acts of those states. (See, e.g., Holcomb v. Hornback, 51 Ill App 2d 84; Guardado v. Navarro, 47 Ill App 2d 92, 96; Morton v. Roth, 189 Mich. 198, 202.) We need not, and do not, go that far. It is our view that the injured person must play a much more affirmative role than that of drinking companion to the one who injures him before he may be denied recovery against the bartender or tavern keeper who served them. The plaintiff before us comes within the coverage of the statute and the defendant was properly held accountable.

[The court notes that other jurisdictions have not allowed recovery when the plaintiff has participated in the drinking. The court reasons that participation in drinking—having a few drinks and passing out, or being the "drinking companion" is not enough to disqualify someone from relief.]

It is only necessary to add that, although the trial court was in error in casting its charge in terms of contributory negligence on the part of the plaintiff, it is apparent from what has already been written that the error was harmless and may be disregarded (CPLR 2001, 2002).

The order appealed from should be affirmed, with costs.

This case is also an example of a court considering a statute that had also been created in other states—notice the citation in the second paragraph to an Illinois case and a Michigan case. Because this case is from New York's top court, the Court could indeed develop its own construction of the statute. It chose not to adopt the *broad* construction of the exception that defendants presented, based on construction in some other states, that a plaintiff's "mere participation" in drinking with the intoxicated tortfeasor was enough to bar her recovery, instead holding that the injured person "must play a much more active role." Note that the court's interpretation of "guilty participation" is therefore *narrow*, or restricted—it's not just drinking, but drinking PLUS urging the other to drink more, etc.

The moral of the story is that any legal rule can be construed *narrowly* or *broadly*. Be on the lookout for instances to argue for a *narrow* versus a *broad* interpretation of a legal rule. Also, be aware that when dealing with an exception to a rule, there is an opportunity to make arguments about whether that exception should be interpreted *narrowly* or *broadly,* which likewise impacts whether the rule is interpreted *narrowly* or *broadly.*

SKILLS DEVELOPMENT

Constructing a Rule Narrowly or Broadly

Step 1: Choose broad versus narrow—Determine whether your facts fall squarely into the legal rule, and if not, whether you need a broad or expansive interpretation of the rule or a narrow and restrictive interpretation of the rule.

Step 2: Support—Find support and examples for the interpretation you want, whether from one other case, from synthesizing precedent, or from any mention of general purpose or goal of legal rule.

Step 3: Explain—Be clear and deliberate about HOW and WHY you are choosing a narrow versus a broad rule construction.

PART II. USING COMPARISONS TO MAKE *ANALOGIES* OR *DISTINCTIONS*

Given that we are using *precedent* to help us apply the rule, another method of rule application is to simply make a *comparison* between your facts and the facts in the *precedent*. The *comparison* can either be between facts that are alike—these facts are similar and therefore the outcome of the case should be the *same* (*analogizing*); or between facts that are different—these facts are different and therefore the outcome of the case should be *different* (*distinguishing*). Reasoning by *analogy* is so fundamental to legal reasoning that there is even a definition in an older version of Black's Law Dictionary: "Where there is no precedent on point, in cases on the same subject, lawyers have recourse to cases on a different subject-matter, but governed by the same general principle. This is reasoning by *analogy*." Black's Law Dictionary (2d ed. 1910) (italics added).

A. Everyday Examples of Analogies and Distinctions

For example, in our "No Vehicles in the Park" hypothetical, remember our friends Bill and Johnny violated the rule in Wilcox Park when they drove their new Land Rover all-terrain truck through the park. Let's assume they were arrested and convicted of this rule violation. As discussed in Part I, it seems pretty straightforward that a truck is a vehicle and that driving a truck through the park violates the rule. However, let's say a young man named Sawyer wanted to practice riding his unicycle in the park. You can probably spot the issue right away: is the unicycle a "vehicle" for the purposes of the rule?

If you represent Sawyer, and if you want Sawyer to be able to practice riding his unicycle in the park (since he has nowhere else to practice), then you would want a *different* result from the one in Bill and Johnny's case. So you would try to *distinguish* the unicycle and the all-terrain Land Rover. Not too hard a job: if Sawyer were to get arrested, you could argue that a unicycle is not a vehicle because a unicycle only has one wheel. You would essentially argue that vehicles have to have four wheels and a motor, as well as the purpose of transportation; a unicycle doesn't have a motor, doesn't have four wheels, and its purpose isn't usually transportation—its purpose is closer to entertainment or exercise.

You would thoroughly explain the *distinction* and the desired result as follows:

1. First, start out with your conclusion, or desired result, from comparing your case to the *precedent*:

> Unlike Bill and Johnny, who violated the "No Vehicles in the Park" rule by driving their Land Rover through Wilcox Park, Sawyer did not violate this rule.

2. Second, compare the specific facts of your case to the specific facts of the *precedent* (note that the facts fulfill/don't fulfill an element):

Bill and Johnny drove a car, which is a vehicle because it has four wheels and a motor, but Sawyer was just riding a unicycle, which only has one wheel and no motor. Also, a car seems to be the quintessential example of a vehicle.

3.   Finally, explain the legal consequence of the *comparison*:

Since a unicycle is not the same as a car, and is therefore not a vehicle, Sawyer did not violate the "No Vehicles in the Park" rule.

In making this argument, can you tell whether you are arguing for a *narrow* or a *broad* interpretation of the rule? Because you are arguing that the definition of vehicle *not include* something (unicycle), you are arguing for a more restrictive definition, which is therefore a more *narrow* definition.

On the other hand, let's say you are the park police, and you believe you have to arrest Sawyer for riding his unicycle in violation of the "No Vehicles in the Park" rule. To justify the arrest, you would *analogize* the Land Rover and the unicycle, arguing that a unicycle is a vehicle because it has a wheel and carries people, and that Sawyer has therefore violated the rule. Such a definition of vehicle is *broad* compared to the above argument on behalf of Sawyer because it is more inclusive.

Again, let's go through the same steps to explain the *analogy* and the desired result.

1.   First, start out with the conclusion or desired result from comparing your case to the *precedent*:

Like Bill and Johnny, who violated the "No Vehicles in the Park" rule by driving their Land Rover in Wilcox Park, Sawyer also violated this rule.

2.   Second, compare the specific facts of your case to the specific facts of the *precedent* (note that the facts fulfill/don't fulfill an element):

Just as Bill and Johnny's truck is a vehicle because it has wheels and carries people, Sawyer's unicycle is also a vehicle because it carries Sawyer and has a wheel. (Note that depending on whether we are *analogizing* or *distinguishing*, we choose different facts to emphasize, and we may characterize the facts differently.)

3.   Finally, explain the legal consequences of the *comparison:*

Both a car and a unicycle qualify as a vehicle because they have a wheel or wheels and they transport people. Therefore, Sawyer should be arrested for violating the rule.

Unlike the *distinction* above, when you argued that a unicycle was NOT a vehicle because it was unlike a Land Rover truck, which was a more *narrow* definition of vehicle, here you are arguing for a *broad* definition of vehicle, one that includes both all-terrain Land Rover trucks AND unicycles.

SKILLS DEVELOPMENT

Drafting Analogies and Distinctions

Step 1: Start out with your conclusion to inform the busy reader of where you are going; in other words, start out with the desired result from comparing your case to the precedent.

Step 2: Compare the specific fact(s) of your case to the specific fact(s) of the precedent—specifically note that the fact fulfills or doesn't fulfill an element.

Step 3: Explain the legal consequence of the comparison.

B. Recognizing *Analogies* and *Distinctions* in Case Law

A famous example of a court using an *analogy* to assist it in the process of applying the rule to facts is *Adams v. N.J. Steamboat*, 5 E.H.

Smith 163 (N.Y. Court of Appeals 1896). See if you can find the *analogy* that the Court made and relied on:

(slightly edited version with page references omitted)

Opinion.

O'BRIEN, J.

On the night of the 17th of June, 1889, the plaintiff was a cabin passenger from New York to Albany on the defendant's steamer Drew, and for the usual and regular charge was assigned to a stateroom on the boat. The plaintiff's ultimate destination was St. Paul, in the state of Minnesota, and he had upon his person the sum of $160 in money for the purpose of defraying his expenses of the journey. The plaintiff, on retiring for the night, left this money in his clothing in the stateroom, having locked the door and fastened the windows. During the night it was stolen by some person, who apparently reached it through the window of the room. The plaintiff's relations to the defendant as a passenger, the loss without negligence on his part, and the other fact that the sum lost was reasonable and proper for him to carry upon his person to defray the expenses of the journey, have all been found by the verdict of the jury in favor of the plaintiff. The appeal presents, therefore, but a single question, and that is whether the defendant is, in law, liable for this loss without any proof of negligence on its part. The learned trial judge instructed the jury that it was, and the jury, after passing upon the other questions of fact in the case, rendered a verdict in favor of the plaintiff for the amount of money so stolen. The judgment entered upon the verdict was affirmed at general term, and that court has allowed an appeal to this court.

As an aside, notice again the common organizational pattern of court opinions: starting with the facts. The court is helpful in telling us that this is an appeal, and that the issue is whether the defendant steamer can be liable for the theft of money from a passenger. We also know how the trial judge instructed the jury, and that this is an appeal from a verdict for the plaintiff—in other words, the plaintiff won at the trial level.

The defendant has, therefore, been held liable as an insurer against the loss which one of its passengers sustained under the circumstances stated. The principle upon which innkeepers are charged by the common law as insurers of the money or personal effects of their guests originated in public policy. It was deemed to be a sound and necessary rule that this class of persons should be subjected to a high degree of responsibility in cases where an extraordinary confidence is necessarily reposed in them, and where great temptation to fraud and danger of plunder exists by reason of the peculiar relations of the parties. Story, Bailm. § 464; 2 Kent, Comm. 592; Hulett v. Swift, 33 N. Y. 571.

The court then explains the rule that innkeepers are responsible for the money and property of their guests.

The relations that exist between a steamboat company and its passengers, who have procured staterooms for their comfort during the journey, differ in no essential respect from those that exist between the innkeeper and his guests. The passenger procures and pays for his room for the same reasons that a guest at an inn does. There are the same opportunities for fraud and plunder on the part of the carrier that was originally supposed to furnish a temptation to the landlord to violate his duty to the guest. A steamer carrying passengers upon the water, and furnishing them with rooms and entertainment, is, for all practical purposes, a floating inn, and hence the duties which the proprietors owe to the passengers in their charge ought to be the same. No good reason is apparent for relaxing the rigid rule of the common law which applies as between innkeeper and guest, since the same considerations of public policy apply to both relations. The defendant, as a common carrier, would have been liable for the personal baggage of the plaintiff, unless the loss was caused by the act of God or the public enemies; and a reasonable sum of money for the payment of his expenses, if carried by the passenger in his trunk, would be included in the liability for loss of baggage. Merrill v. Grinnell, 30 N. Y. 594; Merritt v. Earle, 29 N. Y. 115; Elliott v. Rossell, 10 Johns. 7; Brown, Carr. § 41; Redf. Carr. § 24; Ang. Carr. § 80. Since all questions of negligence on the part of the plaintiff, as well as those growing out of the claim that some notice was posted in the room regarding the carrier's liability for the money, have been disposed of by the verdict, it is difficult to give any good reason why the measure of liability should be less for the loss of the money, under the circumstances, than for the loss of what might be strictly called baggage.

Aha! Here we have it: the *analogy*. The court explains that it is applying the rule about innkeepers to the steamboat and compares inns to steamboats (which seem about equivalent to today's cruise ships). Notice how the court makes the *comparison*:

- First sentence is the conclusion—the two items are like one another: the relationship between a steamboat and its passengers is like the relationship between an inn and its guests;

- The court compares: passengers versus inn guests; carrier versus innkeeper ("same opportunities for fraud and plunder");

- The BIG *analogy*: a steamer housing passengers is basically a floating inn!

A little later in the case, the Court distinguishes a sleeping coach on a train from a passenger's room on a steamboat or "carrier":

. . . It was held in Carpenter v. Railroad Co., 124 N. Y. 53, 26 N. E. 277, that a railroad running sleeping coaches on its road was not liable for the loss of money taken from a passenger while in his berth, during the night, without some proof of negligence on its part. That case does not, we think, control the question now under consideration. Sleeping-car companies are neither innkeepers nor carriers. A berth in a sleeping car is a convenience of modern origin, and the rules of the common law in regard to carriers or innkeepers have not been extended to this new relation. This class of conveyances are attached to the regular trains upon railroads for the purpose of furnishing extra accommodations, not to the public at large, nor to all the passengers, but to that limited number who wish to pay for them. The contract for transportation, and liability for loss of baggage, is with the railroad, the real carrier. All the relations of passenger and carrier are established by the contract implied in the purchase of the regular railroad ticket, and the sleeping car is but an adjunct to it only for such of the passengers as wish to pay an additional charge for the comfort and luxury of a special apartment in a special car. . . .

A *distinction*, like an *analogy*, compares two items—but finds them to be different. The court reasons that "sleeping-car companies are neither innkeepers nor carriers" by pointing out the following facts about sleeping cars in the excerpt above:

- Sleeping berths on a train are newer than the common law rule for carriers

- Berths are for some special passengers wanting to pay extra, not for "public at large"

- Contract is with railroad, the "real carrier," not the sleeping-car company

As the court continues its discussion, it also points out that the railroad berths are open and shared while the state rooms are private with an expectation of some privacy or security.

So, to make an item fit within a rule, you may have to *analogize* (or *distinguish*)—but as you can see from the court's discussion, making comparisons is not difficult. And of course, use the substantive holding to report the *analogy*, and use and explain the *analogy* in the reasoning section of your legal writing.

PART III. UNDERSTANDING AND USING THE PURPOSE BEHIND THE RULE

Lawyers often talk about *policy* arguments in law; consequently, students have to ask—what is *policy*? One way to think about *policy* is the reason behind a legal rule. For example, when a statute is passed by the legislature, there is often evidence of the purpose behind that statute, such as an officially stated purpose that may be included in the notes after a statute, committee meeting transcripts or notes, or other statements. Sometimes the purpose or intent behind a statute is included in the preamble of the statute itself. We call this *legislative intent*. Sometimes the court derives the purpose from the surrounding circumstances or context. In applying a statute, a court will sometimes look at *legislative intent* as another *factor* in helping it determine the meaning of the statute.

Courts will look at not only the reasons behind a statute to determine its proper application, but also will look at the reasons behind other legal rules—including *case law, administrative regulations, or constitutional provisions*—to determine their proper application. In their decisions, courts will discuss the purpose of a rule as a reason for how it should be applied. These reasons, or policies, can sometimes provide compelling arguments. So you should know how to identify a *policy* argument, and *policy* arguments should be in your arsenal of legal tools.

Note that the *policy* behind a rule can be either a general purpose, such as the remedial purpose of a statute, or a more specific purpose, such as achieving a specific goal of legislative intent.

A. Everyday Examples of Recognizing the Purpose Behind a Rule

Let's return to our "No Vehicles in the Park" rule, and the following (fictional) case, *Town of Westerly v. Tedith*, which is the only published case on the rule and contains the following reasoning and holding:

> *In this case we have to apply the "No Vehicles in the Park" statute. This law was enacted by our state legislature to promote the use of parks for recreation, exercise, and relaxation. The statute also promotes safety for the recreational users of the park by keeping out vehicles, as they could pose a danger to people enjoying the park. Therefore, we hold that Jill Tedith, who was riding a bicycle in the park, did not violate the rule.*

In a real case, a discussion about the reasons behind a statute might include a discussion about its legislative history that cites to committee reports or other statements stating or suggesting what the legislature intended to accomplish by enacting the statute (*legislative intent*)—or it might include a court's musings based on the holdings of other cases. Here, we have kept it simple, and the court has made a one-line reference to the purpose behind the rule with no citation.

If we represent Sawyer, the young man who wants to practice his unicycle, which might be a "vehicle" under the statute, we can make a *policy* argument that he should be allowed to practice in the park because it is consistent with the purpose behind the rule. Practicing a unicycle is a form of recreation and relaxation, and therefore can and should be done in a public area devoted to recreation. Also, as we learned in Part II, we can make an *analogy* by comparing the unicycle to the bicycle: if a bicycle is allowed in the park, then a similar recreational but non-motorized vehicle like a unicycle should also be allowed. Both are used for recreation and neither will endanger people in the park, so using these items in the park should not be a violation of the rule.

B. Recognizing the Purpose Behind the Rule in Case Law

As you read more and more cases, you will sometimes see courts similarly refer to the purpose behind a legal rule, especially a statute. A court might note that the purpose behind a criminal statute is to punish, so the criminal statute should be interpreted *narrowly* so as not to improperly punish people, or a court might note the remedial purpose of a statute, as we saw in the example (Part I) regarding the Dram Shop Act.

In the Dram Shop case discussed in Part I, the court mentioned that the general purpose of the statute was remedial—to remedy harm—and used that purpose as a justification to refuse the defendants' suggestion of a *broad* interpretation of the "guilty participant" exception to liability. In *Mitchell* when the court was deciding whether it would adopt the "guilty participant" exception, which would have disallowed recovery for the plaintiff injured when her drunk escort crashed the car simply because she also became drunk as part of the events that led to the tortfeasor's drunkenness, the Court of Appeals stated:

> *There is no justification, either in the language of the legislation or in its history, for exonerating the [defendant Shoals bar] simply because he had also served, and brought about the intoxication of, the third person who was hurt. As long as the [drunk plaintiff] does not himself cause or*

procure the intoxication of the other, there is no basis, under the statute,
for denying him a recovery from the party unlawfully purveying the liquor.

Mitchell v. Shoals, 19 N.Y.2d at 341.

The Court went on to state that although the injured plaintiff had herself become drunk, she did not cause the drunkenness of her escort. The Court did not cite any specific legislative intent, but rather, seemed to be alluding to an overall remedial purpose of the statute. The Court specifically mentioned the remedial purpose of the statute in *Oursler*, again without any citation to legislative intent, stating:

> *The Dram Shop Act is remedial in nature and serves the dual purposes*
> *of deterring bar owners and their employees from selling alcoholic*
> *beverages to intoxicated persons and of compensating individuals injured*
> *as a result of the unlawful sale of alcohol.*

Oursler v. Brennan, 67 A.D.3d at 40, 884 N.Y.S.2d at 538 (citing *Bartlett v. Grande*, 103 A.D.2d 671, 672, 481 N.Y.S.2d 566).

The Court further elaborated on the importance of the legislative intent:

> *In our view, the appropriate rule in cases that do not involve minors is*
> *one that balances the dual purposes of the Legislature in enacting the*
> *Dram Shop Act, i.e., to deter the sale of alcoholic beverages to visibly*
> *intoxicated persons and to compensate those injured as a result of the*
> *unlawful sale of alcohol, with the fundamental common law principle*
> *that a person may not profit from his or her own wrongdoing (see*
> *generally Barker v. Kallash, 63 N.Y.2d 19, 24–25, 479 N.Y.S.2d*
> *201, 468 N.E.2d 39).*

The Court balanced the purpose of the Act, which is to deter bars from serving alcohol to the visibly intoxicated, with the idea that you should not be able to benefit from your own wrongdoing, by adopting a bar on recovery for "guilty participation" but interpreting it narrowly to include only those who were guilty of promoting the drunkenness of the tortfeasor.

In both *Oursler* and *Mitchell*, the courts looked at the underlying purpose of the Dram Shop Act in order to make sure that the injured party is compensated. The courts also discussed a basic principle of fairness in noting that if the injured party was actively responsible for the intoxication, then it would not make sense to allow that party to recover.

When it comes to looking specifically at legislative intent behind a statute, not all courts and judges agree that this is proper, and the practice has evoked a spirited debate.[2]

A famous instance of the Supreme Court looking at legislative intent to interpret a statute (or, some might argue, to interpret a statute the way it wanted to) is *Holy Trinity Church v. United States*, 143 U.S. 457 (1892). In *Holy Trinity*, the Holy Trinity Church was prosecuted by the U.S. for entering into a contract with an English rector to serve as the church's pastor, in violation of the U.S. Statute, 23 Stat. 332, which made it unlawful to "assist or encourage the importation or migration, of any alien or . . . any foreigner . . . into the United States." *Holy Trinity*, 143 U.S. at 457–58.[3]

After quoting the act in full, the court first noted:

> *It must be conceded that the act of the corporation is within the letter of this section, for the relation of rector to his church is one of service, and implies labor on the one side with compensation on the other.*

---

[2]   *Compare, e.g.,* Robert A. Katzman, Judging Statutes (Oxford Univ. Press 2014) (explaining the history of "purposivism" versus "textualists" and arguing for the appropriate use of legislative history given the enormous increase in new statutes) *with* Antonin Scalia, A Matter of Interpretation: Federal Courts and the Law (Princeton Univ. Press 1997).

[3]   In case you were wondering, here is a quote of the statute as quoted in the case:

Be it enacted by the senate and house of representatives of the United States of America, in congress assembled, that from and after the passage of this act it shall be unlawful for any person, company, partnership, or corporation, in any manner whatsoever, to prepay the transportation, or in any way assist or encourage the importation or migration, of any alien or aliens, any foreigner or foreigners, into the United States, its territories, or the District of Columbia, under contract or agreement, parol or special, express or implied, made previous to the importation or migration of such alien or aliens, foreigner or foreigners, to perform labor or service of any kind in the United States, its territories, or the District of Columbia.

In other words, the Court began its discussion by stating that the statute clearly applied to the contract between the church and the rector.

However, throughout the rest of its discussion, the Court openly consulted sources outside the statute, including the context of "contemporaneous events," the title of the act, and, most notably, the *intent of the legislature* when it passed the act. The Court was unapologetic in deciding that "we cannot think Congress intended to denounce with penalties a transaction like that in the present case." *Holy Trinity*, 143 U.S. at 459. The Court went on to explain why the statute's prohibition against hiring foreign labor did not apply to a church hiring a rector. The Court justified its review of surrounding circumstances and surrounding text by stating: "It is a familiar rule that a thing may be within the letter of the statute and yet not within the statute, because not within its spirit nor within the intention of its makers"—in other words, everyone knows that legislators don't always mean what they say, or perhaps, that the literal meaning of the statute is not always intended. The Court further justified its reliance on *legislative intent*:

> *This is not the substitution of the will of the judge for that of the legislator; for frequently words of general meaning are used in a statute, words broad enough to include an act in question, and yet a consideration of the whole legislation, or of the circumstances surrounding its enactment, or of the absurd results which follow from giving such broad meaning to the words, makes it unreasonable to believe that the legislator intended to include the particular act.*

After detailing some *precedent* in which other courts likewise looked outside the language of the statute in order to determine its meaning, the court went on to explain that the title of the Act—"An act to prohibit the importation and migration of foreigners and aliens under contract or agreement to perform labor in the United States, its territories, and the District of Columbia"—suggests manual labors, not "ministers of the gospel" because "labor" does not typically include "any class whose toil is that of the brain." Then, the Court discussed the "motives" of the Act, and, relying on the history of the Act contained in another court decision, concluded that given the "contemporaneous events," held that the real purpose of the act was to prevent "capitalists" from importing cheap labor from other countries that would "break down" the labor market. *Holy Trinity*, 143 U.S. at 464.

The Court then pointed to committee proceedings (specifically a petition, reports, and testimony) to support its conclusion (that the statute should not apply to pastors), stating:

> *[t]hat it was this cheap, unskilled labor which was making the trouble, and the influx of which congress sought to prevent. It was never suggested that we had in this country a surplus of brain toilers, and, least of all, that the market for the services of Christian ministers was depressed by foreign competition.*

Ultimately, the Supreme Court concluded that given the intent of Congress and the political events around the time of the act's passage— in other words, the context—the act did NOT apply to prohibit the Holy Trinity's "importation" of the rector.

Do you agree with this decision? You should understand the pros and cons of the Court's strategy in relying on legislative intent and historical context. As you have probably deduced, in some ways this was a bit of a leap by the Court, for it essentially declared that it was not going to apply the statute as written, but would instead apply the statute *as it thought it should*. In a way, by using surrounding circumstances, you could argue that the Court wrote its own statute.

On the other hand, given the historical context and the many reliable statements in the legislative history about the intent of the statute, the Court's application of the statute makes sense. It is probably correct that Congress had no intention of forbidding a church from hiring and "importing" highly-paid rectors, because this was not the problem Congress was addressing.

The important thing for you to remember is that courts will sometimes use these *policy* reasons to interpret a legal rule (as well as the other sources of law), which can be either the general purpose of the rule or, in the case of a statute, the specific *legislative intent*. This is also a strategy for you to remember when you compose your rule application.

CHAPTER 9 LEGAL SKILLS

- **Understand comparisons and draft analogies and distinctions**
- **Construe the legal rule broadly or narrowly**
- **Understand and use the reason behind the legal rule**
- **Understand and use the legislative history behind a statute**

CHAPTER 9 VOCABULARY

- Analogy
- Broad construction/interpretation
- Comparison
- Distinction
- Factor
- Jury instructions
- Legislative intent
- Mandatory precedent
- Narrow construction/interpretation
- Persuasive precedent
- Policy
- Slippery slope
- Tortfeasor

CHAPTER 9 RESEARCH AND ANALYSIS EXERCISES

I.   Practicing analogies and broad vs. narrow rule construction:

Remember that an analogy is a specific tool of legal reasoning, and that the key to drafting a thorough and convincing analogy is to be specific and direct in your comparison of the facts. Apply all three steps from this chapter's **Skills Development: Drafting Analogies and Distinctions** to do the following exercises:

1.   Starting out with Fruit:[4]

Consider a basket and three pieces of fruit: a red McIntosh apple, a green Granny Smith apple, and a green pear. One court has held that the red McIntosh apple **belongs in** the basket. In a separate ruling, the same court held that the green pear **does not belong** in the basket. Now the Granny Smith apple is before the court.

a.   What analogies and distinctions can you make?

b.   What should the court hold and why?

c.   What if, in addition to its holding, the court considering the red McIntosh apple supplied the reasoning that the McIntosh goes in the basket because only fruit goes in the basket?

d.   How would you construe the court's rule narrowly? Broadly?

2.   Laptops in the Law School Classroom:

Law professors at the University of Sitcom School of Law were upset about the increasing use of laptops in their classes, which they believed was causing lower grades in their classrooms. Professor Monica and Professor Chandler both believed that laptops in the classroom cause major distractions because of the screens and the internet access. On the other hand, when these professors asked for input from law students Joey

---

[4]   Jane Kent Gionfriddo, *Using Fruit to teach Analogy*, Digital Commons @ Boston College Law School (1997).

and Ross, the students explained that the laptops were an important tool for taking and organizing notes.

> a.   If you wanted to help the law professors develop an argument for banning laptops from the classroom, what could you analogize the laptops to?
>
> b.   If you wanted to help the law students develop an argument for allowing the use of laptops in the law school classroom, what could you analogize laptops to?
>
> c.   Should laptops be banned from law school classrooms? Why or why not?
>
> d.   If laptops were forbidden in law school classrooms, and we added the facts that law students then started using their smart phones, how could the laptop ban rule be interpreted broadly? Narrowly?

3.   Trucks Versus Buses:

On Route 66 in Illinois, there is a big sign that states: "No Trucks Allowed according to Illinois law." A police officer stops a school bus and gives the driver a ticket for violating that Illinois law.

> a.   If you worked for an attorney representing the bus driver, how would you argue that a bus is NOT the same as a truck for purposes of this law?
>
> b.   If you worked for the county or town prosecutor, how would you help the prosecutor argue that a bus IS the same as a truck for purposes of this law?
>
> c.   How would the Illinois law be interpreted broadly? Narrowly?
>
> d.   Suppose that you researched traffic citations given on Route 66 and learned that tickets were issued to: 1) a 110-ton oil truck carrying oil for delivery to a residence, 2) an 89-ton car transporter, carrying cars to a nearby car dealership, and 3) a 101-ton truck carrying groceries to a nearby Stop and Shop. But

a 26-ton Zoots dry cleaning van, while stopped, was not issued a ticket.

> i.   How would you synthesize those examples? Consider using a chart to help you.

> ii.   How would you use the information to argue for a broad interpretation of the rule? For a narrow interpretation of the rule?

4.   Possible Battery:

FACTS: Stevie Wander, a musician who is blind, was walking on the sidewalk with a cane. A group of teenagers approached him, and one named Steely Tom approached Wander and complimented him on the cane, which was shiny, silver, and studded with rhinestones. Steely Tom then knocked the cane out of Wander's hand. While Wander was searching for his cane, he tripped over the curb and broke his ankle. Wander has asked the attorney you work for whether he can bring a lawsuit based on battery, and the attorney has asked you your opinion.

> RULE: Intention to come into offensive contact with a person's body is battery.

> a.   Can you make an analogy that would give Wander a cause of action under the battery rule?

> b.   How would the defendant in such a case (Steely Tom) have to construe the statute in order to come up with a defense?

Conclusion: Putting It All Together

In Section III, you will use everything you have learned to put together two instructive and helpful legal writing products, a legal memo and a motion. Chapter 10 takes you through the structure of a legal memo step-by-step, and Chapter 11 introduces the skill of writing persuasively in another basic legal writing product, the motion. Memos and motions are typical writing products for beginners in legal work, and give you an opportunity to practice and apply the skills you learned in Sections I and II.

The Legal Memo

Legal Skills:

- Summarize facts
- Synthesize facts
- Recognize link between IRAC and legal memos
- Draft a legal memo following the organization and using headings
- Draft a Discussion section of a memo following the IREAC organization (Issue, Rule, Rule Explanation, Application, and Conclusion)

Before we begin talking about legal memos, please preview this topic by reading one. You can read the memo at the end of this chapter straight through, or read one of the other samples in the Appendix. As you read the sections in the memo, ask yourself two questions: 1) what is the purpose of each section? and 2) can you recognize any of the skills you learned in the past chapters being demonstrated here? You can also try to make observations on the format, the organization, and the substance.

Since you don't have the "raw materials" for this memo—the information from the client, a copy of the statute or case law—you are more or less in the position of the supervising attorney who is now reviewing the paralegal's work. So, in addition to asking yourself the two questions above, jot down your reactions, thoughts, and questions so you could communicate them to the memo writer if you were a supervising attorney.

Now that you have some context, we will walk through a memo step by step, starting with the purpose and background of a memo.

PART I. BACKGROUND ON LEGAL MEMOS

So what is all this for, anyway? One of the classic written products that is taught in law school and in undergraduate legal studies is the standard legal memo—also called an "interoffice" memo (with "interoffice" meaning that it is circulated within an office). Just like the word *brief,* *memo* has different meanings in different contexts. Some courts and jurisdictions use the word *memo of law* to mean the persuasive document that you submit in support of your case—whether that's at the trial court level to "win"[1] a summary judgment motion, or at the appellate level to win on appeal.

Remember that "memo" is short for "memorandum," which according to <u>Black's Law Dictionary</u> means, among other things, "An informal written communication used esp. in offices." So *memo* really has a broad meaning (remember Chapter 9); in this chapter we will use it to describe informal (or some would say very formal) interoffice communication about how the law applies to a certain set of facts. Given the broad meaning of memo, a memo can also be for relating facts or factual research; or for simply updating a supervising lawyer or paralegal on the status of a client file.

You will meet many attorneys that, if you tell them you are working on a legal memo, will laugh and say they never did a legal memo after they left law school. That may be true. Whether or not your law office uses legal memos is a matter of practice area and law office culture. It may depend on the formality of that law office or whether that office (private firm, organization, agency, court, or government

---

[1] The word "win" is in quotes because if the plaintiff, the party usually defending a summary judgment motion, actually "wins," it still means that the plaintiff must go through a trial process—where anything could happen (see Chapter 8). For the plaintiff, getting to go to trial is "winning."

office) has attorneys that will actually get paid for researching, writing, and reading that memo.

However, even if you never write another memo after you leave your paralegal or legal studies program, this certainly doesn't mean that the exercise of writing a legal memo is useless. To the contrary, the process of writing a legal memo teaches students quite a lot about what is expected of work products in the legal profession: clear and helpful *topic sentences*; clear support in the law and the facts for a legal conclusion (and a clear conclusion); clear organization; the use of *headings* and *sub-headings* to promote clear organization; attention to detail when it comes to ALL things, including grammar, punctuation, word choice, and above all, citation; and, well, as you can guess, general overall CLARITY. Most importantly, however, writing a legal memo requires you to develop and write down your legal analysis.

Any time you write something, you need to figure out who your audience is so that you can write your document with your audience in mind. When it comes to legal documents that you are writing for class, often your audience is not really your professor, who has probably come up with the problem, gently guided you through it, and helped you research it and write it. The professor would be very familiar with the facts, the law, and the analysis. And while your professor will read your memo, the professor will be assessing your memo from the perspective of a different kind of reader.

In fact, the idea behind the assignment is that you are writing for a practicing attorney—someone who may have a vague recollection of the law and the facts, but who assigned you this project so that he or she does not have to do it. This person is quite different from your professor, who has most likely thought through and perhaps even written out the assignment in order to know where the pitfalls and trouble spots are. So it's probably safe to call your audience (your reader)—"the busy reader." If you think of your audience as "the busy reader," that will help you understand the memo's organization and why there may seem to be a lot of repetition in the memo.

Because you have a "busy reader," there is also another rule of thumb that helps to explain some of the repetition—the "don't make the reader look back" rule. It may seem to you that you don't have to really explain your analysis because, after all, you have summarized the facts so beautifully and laid out the law so clearly, and it's SO OBVIOUS. But that's not true. Your job is to spell out your analysis and make it so clear and so easy to read that there is no question in the mind of the reader as to how you got from Point A to Point B. And, remember, analysis means application (see Chapter 8)—applying the rule to the relevant facts. So analysis should be a discussion that references both law and facts.

The "busy reader" rule explains why the legal memo offers a conclusion up front, and again, at the end. The reader needs to know where you end up in order to understand your path. This might be much different from other types of writing—but in law you absolutely have to know your conclusion before you start your final draft. The repetitive sections of the legal memo are therefore explained by the two rules of thumb: the "busy reader" rule and the "don't make the reader look back" rule.

So now that we know the audience for a legal memo, let's think about the purpose. In general, the purpose of the memo is to inform someone on your legal team about your legal analysis. Sometimes, depending on the legal practice and the culture and time constraints of the legal practice, the purpose of the memo is simply to *memorialize* your own legal analysis so you don't have to re-do it. That's right, sometimes you write a legal memo "to the file" so that when you pick up that file in three months, you can consult the memo in order to know not only the answer to your legal question, but also how you got there.

Because the memo is an internal document, you should definitely point out any arguments the other side can make, or any weaknesses or issues that you see as you develop your analysis. Often in law we talk about analysis in terms of argument. That is, we set out the argument that is beneficial for our side, and then examine the argument of the "other side." Depending on the legal issue, it may be a relatively straightforward matter, where one side has a clear and strong argument and there really is no argument on the other side (such as whether one has complied with the statute of limitations or not); or, it may be a matter in which both sides have solid arguments. But either way, remember to NEVER omit the negative authority or the arguments on the other side. The attorney will need to know the full picture in order to develop an effective strategy for representing the client. In addition, attorneys actually have an ethical duty to point out to the court any legal authority that opposes their position.[2] So eventually, for any future court submissions, opposing arguments and opposing authority will be something your supervising attorney needs to know. Additionally, attorneys always have the duty to be truthful.

The importance of the memo being internal is that it will not be seen by the other side, opposing counsel, the judge, the jury, or the (opposing) client. There are two principles at play here. First, all the work you do for a client is protected by attorney-client privilege, meaning that you may not divulge your work, your opinion, or the facts of the client's case to a third party. The attorney-client privilege is an ethical rule that in most states is codified in state statutes or administrative regulations.[3] Second, the work you do is protected from disclosure by the attorney work-product doctrine, an evidentiary rule in the Federal Rules of Civil Procedure and parallel state evidentiary rules.[4] Generally, in all states and federal courts there are rules of

---

[2]   *See* Model ABA Rule 3.3.

[3]   *See* ABA Rule 1.6.

[4]   Federal Rule of Civil Procedure 26(b)(3) provides:

(a) A lawyer shall not reveal information relating to the representation of a client unless the client gives informed consent, the disclosure is impliedly authorized in order to carry out the representation or the disclosure is permitted by paragraph (b).

(b) A lawyer may reveal information relating to the representation of a client to the extent the lawyer reasonably believes necessary:

(1) to prevent reasonably certain death or substantial bodily harm;

(2) to prevent the client from committing a crime or fraud that is reasonably certain to result in substantial injury to the financial interests or property of

evidence that specifically protect attorney work-product. Because the memo is internal, and because you want the memo to be truthful and helpful, you can include the opposing side's arguments or note any weaknesses or concerns in your argument.

Although some may buck at legal writing conventions like *headings*, strict organization, and brevity, the legal memo format is a good building block for learning how to present a legal writing and analysis product. After you learn this structure and are comfortable with it, you can create whatever variations your legal work or legal environment may need. But only after you understand the fundamental structure can you go beyond it.

PART II. WORKING THROUGH AN EXAMPLE

Now, let's walk through a sample memo. You will now see for yourself some of the hallmarks of legal writing mentioned above: clear and helpful *topic sentences*; clear support in the law and the facts for a legal conclusion (and a clear conclusion); clear organization; the use of

---

another and in furtherance of which the client has used or is using the lawyer's services;

(3) to prevent, mitigate or rectify substantial injury to the financial interests or property of another that is reasonably certain to result or has resulted from the client's commission of a crime or fraud in furtherance of which the client has used the lawyer's services;

(4) to secure legal advice about the lawyer's compliance with these Rules;

(5) to establish a claim or defense on behalf of the lawyer in a controversy between the lawyer and the client, to establish a defense to a criminal charge or civil claim against the lawyer based upon conduct in which the client was involved, or to respond to allegations in any proceeding concerning the lawyer's representation of the client;

(6) to comply with other law or a court order; or

(7) to detect and resolve conflicts of interest arising from the lawyer's change of employment or from changes in the composition or ownership of a firm, but only if the revealed information would not compromise the attorney-client privilege or otherwise prejudice the client.

(c) A lawyer shall make reasonable efforts to prevent the inadvertent or unauthorized disclosure of, or unauthorized access to, information relating to the representation of a client.

headings and sub-headings to promote clear organization; attention to detail when it comes to ALL things, including grammar, punctuation, word choice, and above all, citation; and, well, as you can guess, general overall CLARITY.

Here, we will go step by step through each section of a memo and examine the format and purpose of each section. Remember that one of the cardinal rules in legal writing is that the different sections of the memo are each limited to one specific purpose. The boundaries between the sections are firm: the Facts section is just facts, the Question Presented section is just the issue statement, and the Conclusion is just the conclusion. Of course, as with any paradigm or structure, there can be variations; this example is a classic memo format, but variations on it are not necessarily wrong.

A. The *Heading*

Perhaps the simplest part of the memo is the very beginning, the *heading*, which is essentially a label indicating who it is to, who it is from, the date, and the subject matter. The only tricky thing about the *heading* is making it conform to expectations—whether those expectations come from a law office or a professor. This is one place in which following directions and observing the details of the required format come in handy. Typically, a *heading* goes like this (explanatory notes are in italics):

MEMORANDUM *(this is the name of the document)*

TO: Professor Phillips

FROM: Smart student

RE: File #: 6514; People vs. Andrews *(identify the client matter for your "busy attorney")*

DATE: January 1, 2000 *(don't forget the year—the case could easily be around for more than one year)*

Notice the details such as the centering and bolding of "**MEMORANDUM**"; the left-hand alignment of the **TO**, **FROM**, **RE** and **DATE**, and that those words are double-spaced. If you have not seen a "Re" line before, it is Latin for "in the matter of" or "in the case of."[5] Finally, notice that the information about the memo is all justified on the left. The spacing and the left-justification help give the appearance of space, and provide neat, clean lines. Because of the spacing, the *heading* is easy to read. If these are the directions or the sample you are given for an assignment, then you should follow them precisely.

B. Question Presented or Issue

This section contains the issue. In our example there will be only one question in this section. There can be multiple issues, in which case there would be multiple, separate questions. This section can be called "Question Presented," "Issue," "Issue Statement," or the like. It all means the same thing. The definition of issue, as we saw in the last chapter and Chapter 6, is the intersection of the legal rule and facts that presents a question, or more precisely, the element of the legal rule that may or may not be fulfilled.

In a memo, the issue is the first thing you communicate because it shapes everything. If the reader knows what the issue is, then the reader knows which facts are important. The issue provides necessary context.

Just like there is formality in the presentation of a legal memo, there is likewise a bit of formality in the presentation of the issue. The more information you can communicate with the issue, the better. Typically, you can communicate at least the legal rule and hopefully, the element at issue, if possible. In the best-case scenario, you can communicate the legal rule, the element at issue, the question, and

---

[5]   Many people think that "Re" is an abbreviation for "Regarding" but there is not actually any support for that in Black's Law Dictionary or the Oxford English Dictionary.

some of the relevant facts that give rise to the issue. All this occurs after a *heading*, like this:

QUESTION PRESENTED

Whether Mark Andrews was "sleeping" in violation of N.Y. Penal Law § 10.10.10 (McKinney's 2014), which prohibits sleeping in the picnic area of a state-owned park, when he was woken up by a policeman after he was observed lying down and snoring at 1:00 p.m. in the picnic area of a park?

To encourage yourself to include all three components of the issue, it is helpful to remember the prompts from Chapter 6: Whether, under, when. After "whether" comes the question; after "under" (or the variation here, "in violation of") comes the legal rule, or when possible, the specific element at issue (sometimes there is room to include both), and after "when" come the legally relevant facts. Remember, the *legally relevant facts* are defined as the facts that make a difference. That is, facts that, if they were changed, would change the outcome of the question. In the issue example above, as we shall see, if it turns out that the policy behind the statute is to keep people from spending the night there and to promote using the park for rest and relaxation, then the time of day that Mark Andrews was found sleeping could be relevant—that's why the time of day is included.

Of course, there are always multiple ways to frame the issue and still include the maximum amount of information. You can also use different prompts. Here are some additional examples:

QUESTION PRESENTED

Whether Mark Andrews violated § 10.10.10 of New York Penal Law, which prohibits sleeping in the picnic area of a state-owned park, when he was woken up at 1:00 p.m. by a police officer who found him lying on the grass, next to an empty lunch bag, with his eyes closed and snoring?

Notice that this question doesn't specifically identify the element.

QUESTION PRESENTED

Whether defendant Andrews violated N.Y. Penal Law § 10.10.10, and was "sleeping" within the meaning of the statute, when he was lying down with his eyes closed, snoring, and appeared to be napping after lunch at 1 p.m. in the afternoon?

Notice that this example doesn't quote the entire statute.

QUESTION PRESENTED

Under N.Y. Penal Law § 10.10.10, which forbids sleeping in the picnic areas of state-owned parks, was Mark Andrews "sleeping" in violation of that statute when he was napping after lunch in the middle of the day?

This example doesn't use the "whether" prompt, but still includes all three sections and gives a good picture of the issue.

C. Short Answer

Another indicator of the organized nature of legal writing is that the answer does not come at the end; it comes at the beginning. That way, no doubt can be left in the mind of the reader. Unlike other types of writing, such as fiction, that lead you down a path with suspense, there should be no suspense in legal writing. Think of this type of writing as an "answer first" type of writing. When the reader has the answer first, it should be a little easier to follow the analysis.

Hence, the next section after "Question Presented" is "Short Answer." This section doesn't include facts or background. This section just allows the reader to know your destination. Given that the "Question Presented" section is simply a question, the "Short Answer" section is simply the answer to that question, with a brief identification of the key reason for the answer. This section should be as short and simple as the following examples:

SHORT ANSWER

No. Mr. Andrews did not violate N.Y. Penal Law § 10.10.10 (McKinney's 2014) because napping in the park during the day is consistent with the way the park should be used.

SHORT ANSWER

No. Mr. Andrews did not violate N.Y. Penal Law § 10.10.10 (McKinney's 2014) because he was not using the park as a place to sleep.

SHORT ANSWER

No. Although Mr. Andrews was sleeping, he did not violate N.Y. Penal Law § 10.10.10 (McKinney's 2014) because the statute was intended to prevent sleeping in the park overnight, not napping for a short time during the day.

Notice that in all these examples the question is answered right away with a "No." Sentences can have just one word in them, and the reader needs to know what that one word is. Choosing a "yes" or "no" does not necessarily mean there are no possible opposing arguments, but it does mean that on balance—considering those opposing arguments and any flaws in your argument—your choice of "yes" or "no" is the best answer.

Note also that there is a "because"—so you are providing the reason, or at least one reason, for your answer. Making sure you use "because" helps you avoid *conclusory* statements. A *conclusory* statement contains a conclusion with no explanation, often using the very language at issue. For example, in the above example, a *conclusory* statement would be: "No. Mr. Andrews did not violate the statute because he was not sleeping." Well, the first thing a reader would wonder is WHY he was not sleeping. Instead, if you review the three examples above, you can see that in each answer, some real insight—in the amount of only a handful of words—is provided.

D. Facts

The next section is for a summary of the facts. This is where you tell the story of your case. You have to make sure you include the legally relevant facts—those that give rise to the issue. There should not be any omissions here. A good rule of thumb is there should be no fact that you mention in the Question Presented, the Short Answer, or the Analysis/Discussion that is not included in the "Facts" section. The only thing you cannot include is conjecture that has no basis in the facts—such as "Maybe Mr. Andrews was sleeping in the park because he gets drowsy after he eats." If the fact that Mr. Andrews gets drowsy after he eats was not provided to you—in the hypothetical, for example, or by the client—then you should not speculate or create a list of "maybes."

Writing a summary is a skill (see the Skills Development box on page 329). Because telling a factual story does not include any legal analysis, it may seem like writing a factual summary is an easy task. That is not necessarily so. First, writing a summary requires choices. You must choose the organization: will you use a chronological organization; a topical organization that organizes the story by each witness; or an issue-by-issue organization?

Many times, because of the organization you choose, you will have to do some synthesis of your factual sources. Your factual source(s) could be just a client interview. But they could range from expert reports, police reports, medical records, contracts, and *deposition transcripts* to multiple other items exchanged in *discovery*. It is almost never helpful for your "busy reader" to read a summary of each source separately—first a summary of the client's or opposing party's *deposition transcript*, then a summary of the accident report, then a summary of the private investigator's report.

Rather, the "busy reader" needs to know how all these facts fit together. If the client testimony is different from the accident report or another source of evidence, those differences should be front and center, and mentioned in the same spot in your factual summary. For example, if your client testified that the light was green, but the police report indicates that a witness stated the light was red, instead of putting those facts in two different places (like the summary of the accident report and then, in another spot, the summary of the client's testimony from a deposition), you should have a *topic sentence* that goes something like this: "There are different accounts of what color the traffic light was when Mr. Joe Client went through it" or "While Mr. Joe Client testified at his *deposition* that the light was green, a witness statement in the accident report indicates the opposite—that the light was red." This way, the "busy reader" knows right away that there is a factual issue here because you have done your job of succinctly presenting it. For a review of synthesizing, see Chapter 7.

Second, writing a summary requires that you are very clear on the *legally relevant facts*, and above all, requires that you include them. It is actually a great practice to draw the reader's attention to the *legally relevant facts* by featuring them in *topic sentences*. Therefore, you should not write the "Facts" section first. Rather, start by writing the "Discussion" section first so you can think through the analysis. Remember, considering that this is an internal document only, and considering the attorney's ethical duty, you must include any facts or law that may harm or go against a client's position.

Third, writing a summary requires *topic sentences*. A *topic sentence* is the first sentence of a paragraph that provides a bit of a summary of what is to come in the paragraph. Think of it as a "head's-up" sentence (see explanation of *topic sentences* in Chapter 7). Your facts are not a novel that unwinds slowly down a path, revealing a bit of information at a time. Your facts are meant to deliver a clear, unambiguous, and succinct message. In order to write apt and descriptive *topic sentences*, you will need to do AT LEAST two drafts of the facts.

Fourth, you need to include a citation every time—yes, every time—you refer to or rely on a source. Essentially, there should be a citation after every sentence. The citation should include a specific page reference. Although the format for citations to factual sources can vary for products like internal office memos that will never be turned in to a court, it is always best to follow a predictable system that supplies enough information so that the "busy reader" can locate the source and the exact spot in the source that you are referring to. For example, if we use a "citation sentence" (which starts after the period at the end of a sentence), you could use a citation like this: (Client's Interview.) or, without parentheses, like this: Client's Interview. For items with page numbers, the citation would look like this: (Dep. Tr. at 16.) or, without parentheses, like this: Dep. Tr. at 16. Note that at the end of the factual citation there is a period, just like at the end of a citation to a legal source.

Fifth, when you are thinking about your "busy reader," you should also think about facts that cannot be well-summarized and that are so important they may need to be quoted. For example, if your client equivocated in the client interview about whether the light was red or green, you can certainly introduce that fact with an apt description and then include the quote, like this:

> Mr. Joe Client went back and forth about whether the light was red or green. He stated: "Well, I'm quite sure the light was green. Well, almost sure. There is a possibility it was red, but I'm pretty sure it was green."

With a statement like that, it would be important to convey to your "busy reader" the entirety of the statement, because it indicates the client's lack of clarity.

Quoting is not just for client statements, although those may be especially helpful to quote. You can also use quotations for any other highly relevant statement, regardless of source. Remember that there is almost never a reason to use a long block quote. Using short quotes that contain essential facts, or *legally relevant facts*, is helpful not only for clarity but also for color. In other words, there is no reason a factual summary has to be boring. Give it life!

Finally, of course, to check your Facts section, review your summary against your checklist and against each and every source. Students often want to rush through writing the Facts section, either because they have saved it for last and are approaching a deadline, or because they want to "get it out of the way," or simply because they are in a rush. Rushing or not re-checking almost always results in missing facts. Another way to check that you have covered all the important events is to read just the first sentence of each paragraph (just like we reviewed *topic sentences* when reading case law in Chapter 5).

SKILLS DEVELOPMENT

TIPS: Writing Process for a Summary of Facts

You should think about your method for writing a summary of facts. In general, as noted above, it is good to remember that the FACTS section does not have to be—and should not be—the first section you write. Because the legal rule and issue are so critical to defining legally relevant facts, write the DISCUSSION section first—this is where the analysis takes please. After you lay out your analysis, you will know the legally relevant facts. Additionally, for most people, it is helpful to have a method so that you can be sure you have written an accurate and complete factual statement. For example:

1. FIRST—**read** every piece of information **carefully**. Information can come in the form of hypothetical fact situations from your professor, a summary of a client statement or interview, reports (such as an accident report), or deposition transcripts.

2. SECOND—as you read each piece of information, or immediately after you have read each piece of information, **make a list** of each fact that you must include.

3. THIRD—based on the analysis or DISCUSSION section of the memo that you have already written, **highlight the legally relevant facts** on your list. Remember, "legally relevant facts" means facts that, if different, would change the outcome. Highlight both the legally relevant facts that support your client and those that support your opponent. In your FACTS section, you will need many facts to accurately tell the story, in addition to the legally relevant facts. Think of these facts as background facts that glue together your story.

4. FOURTH—decide on the **organization** that is most helpful for someone who is reading the facts for the first time. Remember, your choices include chronological organization: starting with the earliest event first and then moving through the facts according to a timeline (earliest to last). This is probably the most common approach. You can also organize by witness or party, starting with party 1 and the events that happened to party 1, then moving on to party 2, party 3, etc. Or finally, you can organize by legal issue (for example, in a memo about a car accident, you might have facts about negligence, insurance coverage, passenger liability, etc.) Any method of organization will require synthesis, so review Chapter 7 and use a synthesis chart.

5. FIFTH: **compose an outline** using **topic sentences**—make sure the legally relevant facts are in the topic sentences (see Skills Development box in Chapter 7 for a review of how to write topic sentences). A good test of whether you have drafted true topic sentences is to remove the first line of each paragraph and place the sentences in the same order on a separate page. Those sentences should be an outline of your facts.

6. SIXTH: **complete by filling in the outline** and **checking the summary** to make sure you have not forgotten any legally relevant facts. There should not be any facts that you discuss elsewhere in the memo that are not mentioned in the FACTS section.

Here are some examples of FACTS sections:

FACTS

We represent Mark Andrews, a 40-year-old white male who was issued a ticket on May 4, 2018, for sleeping in City Park. Mr. Andrews works for a local bank. To date, we have had just one short conversation with Mr. Andrews, which this factual statement is based on.

On May 4, 2018, Mr. Andrews decided to eat his lunch in the park. At 1 p.m., a police officer found him lying in the grass next to his empty brown bag with his eyes closed. The police officer observed him for five minutes, and then charged him with violating Penal Law § 10.10.10.

Mr. Andrews hired us to represent him in the criminal proceedings.

FACTS

We represent Mark Andrews, a 40-year-old white male who was issued a ticket on May 4, 2018, for sleeping in the park. This summary is based on our interview with him (summarized in Client Interview Memo, dated May 5, 2018) and the police report (Police Report, dated May 4, 2018).

According to both the Police Report and our client interview, Mark Andrews was lying on the grass in a picnic area at 1:15 p.m. on May 4, 2018. (Client Memo, page 1; Police Report, page 1.) Mr. Andrews stated that on sunny spring days he sometimes brings a picnic lunch that he likes to eat outside. (Client Memo, page 1.) On May 4th, Mr. Andrews decided to eat his lunch at City Park. (Client Memo, page 1.) Since all the picnic tables were full, he sat on the ground under a tree. (Client Memo, page 2.) After he finished his bag lunch, there was a sunny patch of grass right next to him, and, feeling sleepy, he lay down and ended up dozing off. (Client Memo, page 2.)

Police Officer James Cricket reported that he first noticed Mr. Andrews at about 1:08, lying down, with his eyes closed, in the picnic area of City Park. (Police Report, page 1.) The Police Report contains a sketch that shows Mr. Andrews' location in the park. (Police Report, page 2.) Officer Cricket stated in his report: "Sleeping/eyes closed/ laying down in picnic area—City Park." (Police Report, page 2.) Mr.

Andrews told us that after finishing his lunch, he lay down and dozed off for just a "couple minutes." (Client Memo, page 2.) He reports that after he closed his eyes, the next thing he knew there was a police officer next to him saying loudly "Sir, sir, wake up." (Client Memo, page 2.) After Officer Cricket woke up Mr. Andrews, he issued him a ticket for violating Penal Law § 10.10.10. (Police Report, page 2.) Mr. Andrews came to see us the following day, on May 5th. (Client Interview, page 1.)

You have asked me to look at the statute and any case law interpreting the statute to determine whether there is any reasonable argument that Mr. Andrews did not violate Penal Law § 10.10.10: "It is unlawful for any person to sleep in the picnic areas of a state, county or city owned park."

———————

Both Facts sections convey the essential information succinctly. The first example does not contain any citations; there will be situations where you are not provided with supporting documents or when you are just given a factual summary by your supervising attorney or professor. You can see in the second section that the supporting documents were provided, and therefore there is a bit more detail, as well as citations after every sentence. Notice that the exact language of the officer was quoted. Here, using the quote of Officer Cricket's exact language is more precise, more informative, and more succinct than attempting to summarize it. Also, in the second example, notice the synthesis—the writer does NOT first summarize the Client Memo and then summarize the Police Report. Instead, the writer synthesizes the two documents and chooses a chronological organization, starting with the start of the sleeping in the park episode, and ending with the officer giving Mr. Andrews the ticket. You know there is synthesis because the *topic sentence* of the second paragraph references both documents, and then proceeds to rely on and cite to both documents. Likewise, the second paragraph contains references to both the Client Memo and Police Report.

Finally, notice that both Facts sections use the first person ("we" in the first paragraph) and that the sections start out with the writer providing some context for the "busy reader"—the client, the client's name, and the reason for the legal representation. This type of preview is often a helpful way to start the Facts section for an office memo because it provides context for the busy reader.

Your Facts section should be simple and straightforward—but remember, that doesn't make it easy to write. Make sure you spend enough time, and check and double-check your Facts section.

E. The Discussion

The Discussion section is the most fun to write, and it is really the heart of the interoffice legal memo. This section contains both facts and law, and most importantly, it contains your application of the law to the facts. In other words, this is where you will present your legal analysis. You will present it in a clear and detailed manner for your busy reader. Remembering the busy reader is especially important in this section, because it is easy to skip articulating one part of the analysis, and that omission then renders your analysis hard to understand.

It's also especially important to remember the "don't make the reader look back" rule. There can be a tendency to leave out facts or factual details about case holdings. Leaving out facts requires the reader to look back at the Facts section, thereby violating the "don't make the reader look back" rule. Leaving out factual details about case law requires the reader to find and review the case, thereby violating the "busy reader" rule. Don't make either mistake! Sometimes it helps to think of yourself as the teacher who is teaching the analysis step-by-step for the first time. That way, it's harder to leave something out. Therefore, do not be afraid, when you are applying the legal rule to the facts of the case, to lay out the specific facts you are relying on.

The organization of the Discussion section is based on what you learned when you did IRACs—Issue, Rule, Application, and Conclusion. Considering the prior sections of your memo, relating the issue and rule, and composing the application and conclusion, all involve using facts and law previously mentioned in your memo. In other words, you must repeat—yes, REPEAT—the law, issue, and facts already mentioned. Why? Because it's necessary to do so to perform a careful and orderly analysis, AND because you can't compose your analysis without mentioning and using ALL those items. However, you don't repeat the issue, rule and facts in exactly the same way. There is no cutting and pasting. Rather, in the Discussion portion, you reference, explain, apply, discuss, and expand these elements.

The one addition to IRAC that you will see in this section of the memo is the Rule Explanation section (note that rule explanation was also discussed in Chapter 7). Notice that the quote of the statute provides the rule, and then following this quote, we see how this rule—the statute—has been applied by the mid-level appellate courts in New York. Once we know how the courts have interpreted and applied the statute, we can better predict what may happen in our case. In more advanced legal documents, such as an inter-office memo or a persuasive piece, such as a memorandum in support of a motion, there is often a Rule Explanation section. This section is very useful in explaining the previous applications and any necessary synthesis before (and separate from) the application of the rule to the facts of our case. It also provides the material you will need to explain analogies and distinctions when you apply the law to the facts in your analysis.

One thing to be careful of in the Rule Explanation section is your case holding sentences that you learned to write in Chapter 8. Remember, case holding sentences include the substantive holding of the court AND the *legally relevant facts*. Your Rule Explanation should include strong case holding sentences with both elements in order for it to be helpful.

Here is an example (with the topic sentences in bold so you can easily see how topic sentences outline the analysis):

DISCUSSION

The issue is whether Mr. Andrews violated the Penal Law prohibiting sleeping in the park (N.Y. Penal Law § 10.10.10), when he was napping in the picnic area of a state-owned park after eating his lunch one afternoon.

New York Penal Law § 10.10.10 provides: "It is unlawful for any person to sleep in the picnic areas of a state, county or city owned park." The elements of the statute are: person, sleep, picnic area, and state, county or city-owned park. Since we have established that our facts fulfill all of the elements except "sleep," the issue in this case is what constitutes "sleep" under the statute.

The Fourth Department has upheld convictions for sleeping in the park when the defendant was found in the park in the early morning lying down under a covering. For example, in *People v. Matthews*, 100 A.D.2d 99, 100, 98 N.Y.S.2d 97, 98 (4th Dep't 2000), the court affirmed the defendant's conviction under Penal Law § 10.10.10 because he was found under a picnic table, in a sleeping bag, snoring, with his eyes closed, at 1:00 a.m. Additionally, a police officer observed him like this for five minutes before arresting him. *Id.*

Likewise, in a case where the defendant was not actually sleeping at the time of arrest, the Fourth Department upheld a conviction because the defendant was found lying down, under a blanket, with his head on a knapsack, in the early morning. *People v. Wilson*, 96 A.D.2d 95, 95, 94 N.Y.S.2d 93, 93 (4th Dep't 1997). At trial the defendant, who was observed at 3:00 a.m., testified that he suffers from insomnia and only sleeps one or two hours a night, but that he "may have fallen asleep for a short time on the night he was arrested." *Id.* at 96, 94 N.Y.S.2d at 94. The court accordingly held that "[t]he evidence is . . . consistent with a finding that at some time that night the defendant had been asleep on the bench." *Id.*

In both *Matthews* and *Wilson* the defendants used the park as a place to sleep, which courts have held is not the intended use of state parks. In *Wilson*, the Fourth Department noted that Penal Law

§ 10.10.10 was enacted to make sure the parks were used for recreation—"to picnic, play, and relax"—and not as a place to sleep. 96 A.D.2d at 96, 94 N.Y.S.2d at 94. Arguably, the surrounding circumstances of the defendants' arrests—the time of night, where they were lying down, and the blanket or sleeping bag covering them—were more important than whether the defendant was actually sleeping at the time of arrest.

For example, the court in *Wilson* noted: "even if the defendant did not actually sleep in the park, he was using the park as a place to sleep, and this is unlawful under the statute." 96 A.D.2d at 96, 94 N.Y.S.2d at 94.

Thus, the courts' holdings in *Wilson* and *Matthews* indicate that in addition to the physical act of sleeping, the surrounding circumstances are also important, such as the time of day or night, where the defendant is found, and whether the defendant appears to be settling in for a long time. *Matthews*, 100 A.D.2d at 100, 98 N.Y.S.2d at 98; *Wilson*, 96 A.D.2d at 96, 94 N.Y.S.2d at 94. These circumstances indicate whether the defendant is using the park as a place to sleep, contrary to the intent behind the statute.

Although Mr. Andrews was sleeping at the time of arrest, he was not using the park as a place to sleep. First, unlike the defendants in *Matthews* and *Wilson*, who were found lying down in or near the middle of the night under a blanket, Mr. Andrews was arrested in the middle of the day. *Matthews*, 100 A.D.2d at 100, 98 N.Y.S.2d at 98; *Wilson*, 96 A.D.2d at 96, 94 N.Y.S.2d at 94. Because he was arrested at 1:00 p.m. and was found lying down next to an empty lunch bag, it's likely that he was napping after finishing his lunch. A short nap after lunch in the park is much different from using the park as a place to sleep at night.

In fact, by using the park as a place to eat his lunch, Mr. Andrews was using the park as a place to picnic—which, according to *Wilson*, the state legislature has sought to protect. 96 A.D.2d at 96, 94 N.Y.S.2d at 94. Indeed, simply using the park in the afternoon suggests a recreational use, while using the park in the early morning hours does not. Thus, one of the most important factors distinguishing this case from *Matthews* and *Wilson* is the time of day Mr. Andrews was found sleeping.

Second, Mr. Andrews was not in a sleeping bag or under a blanket. The defendant in *Matthews* was found lying down in a sleeping bag under a picnic table. 100 A.D.2d at 100, 98 N.Y.S.2d at 98. Similarly, in *Wilson*, the defendant was found lying on a park bench under a blanket with his head on a knapsack. 96 A.D.2d at 96, 94 N.Y.S.2d at 94. Unlike either of these defendants, Mr. Andrews was not using a blanket or a sleeping bag as a covering, which further suggests that Mr. Andrews was not using the park as a place to sleep. Additionally, he did not have a pillow, and simply lying down on the grass does not imply the same intent to sleep as lying under a picnic table like the defendant in *Matthews* or lying on a park bench like the defendant in Wilson. *Matthews*, 100 A.D.2d at 100, 98 N.Y.S.2d at 98; *Wilson*, 96 A.D.2d at 96, 94 N.Y.S.2d at 94. Rather, lying on the grass is consistent with picnicking, which is the intended use of state parks.

Of course, the prosecution could argue that Mr. Andrews was sleeping within the meaning of the statute because he was observed snoring, with his eyes closed, for five minutes. Like Mr. Andrews, the defendant in *Matthews* was observed lying down, with his eyes closed, and snoring, for five minutes. *Matthews*, 100 A.D.2d at 100, 98 N.Y.S.2d at 98. Since the defendant's conviction in *Matthews* was affirmed, arguably Mr. Andrews could be convicted under the statute as well.

However, although Mr. Andrews was actually sleeping, prosecuting him does not seem consistent with the legislative intent behind the statute. As the Fourth Department noted, "New York State sought to ensure that its parks would be used only for the purpose for which they were intended: The picnic areas of parks are designed as a place where people can picnic, play, and relax and not as a place for people to sleep." *Wilson*, 96 A.D.2d at 96, 94 N. Y.S.2d at

94. Mr. Andrews ate his lunch in the park in the middle of the day, after which he happened to take a nap, which is entirely consistent with the legislative intent of protecting picnicking and relaxing. In this case, the overall purpose of the statute is more significant than whether he was actually sleeping at the time of arrest.

———————

First, let's look at the big picture and the general ideas you get after reading this analysis. When reading it, did you have enough information about the case law that you didn't have to look up the case yourself?

Second, let's look a little more closely at the organization and at what is happening in each paragraph. Just as we did when we read the case law, we will take the first sentence of each paragraph to see what our *topic sentence* outline is:

1. The issue is whether Mr. Andrews violated the Penal Law prohibiting sleeping in the park (N.Y. Penal Law § 10.10.10), when he was napping in the picnic area of a state-owned park after eating his lunch one afternoon.

Here, we start off—again—with the issue. Although your busy reader has just read your rendition of the issue in the **ISSUE** section above, this is still a good place to start the Discussion, and again, we must remember the "don't make the reader look back" rule. Remember, when possible, you want to isolate and identify the specific element that is at issue. Here, that element is "sleep." Knowing which element is at issue is also key for keeping your research focused. Notice that in the Rule Explanation section below, the focus is on how courts have interpreted "sleep."

2. New York Penal Law § 10.10.10 provides: "It is unlawful for any person to sleep in the picnic areas of a state, county or city-owned park."

This paragraph provides the rule, which is easily quotable since it is one simple line. As you know from previous chapters, many times a statute is not self-explanatory, so we must look to case law to see how it has been applied. Hence, we have the Rule Explanation section that directly follows the rule, and that does nothing but explain how the rule has been applied. Notice in the following rule explanation, there is no mention of our facts. You should try to remember that the sections of the Discussion are discrete, and not intermixed—in fact, the sections should be easily recognizable. When starting to use this structure, it's easy for students to mix in the Rule Explanation with the Application. But if the sections are not separate, then it gets confusing for the writer. Can you identify which of the following *topic sentences* are part of the "rule explanation" in IRAC?

3.   The Fourth Department has upheld convictions for sleeping in the park when the defendant has been found in the park in the early morning lying down under a covering.

4.   Likewise, in a case where the defendant was not actually sleeping at the time of arrest, the Fourth Department upheld a conviction because the defendant was found lying down, under a blanket, with his head on a knapsack, in the early morning.

5.   In both *Matthews* and *Wilson* the defendants used the park as a place to sleep, which courts have held is not the intended use of state parks.

6.   For example, the court in *Wilson* noted: "even if the defendant did not actually sleep in the park, he was using the park as a place to sleep, and this is unlawful under the statute." 96 A.D.2d at 96, 94 N.Y.S.2d at 94.

7.   Thus, the courts' holdings in *Wilson* and *Matthews* indicate that in addition to the physical act of sleeping, the surrounding circumstances are also important, such as the time of day or night, where the defendant is found, and whether the defendant appears to be settling in for a long time. *Matthews*, 100 A.D.2d at 100, 98

N.Y.S.2d at 98; *Wilson,* **96 A.D.2d at 96, 94 N.Y.S.2d at 94.**

Correct—the above five *topic sentences,* all of which concern case law and none of which mention the facts of our case or Mr. Andrews— all start out paragraphs that explain not only how the mid-level appellate court has applied the statute in general, but also, specifically, how the court applied and interpreted the statute regarding the "sleep" element. These paragraphs are all Rule Explanation paragraphs. The paragraphs contain discussions about how the statute has been applied, but they do NOT contain discussion about how the case law applies to the facts. That is why the *topic sentences* contain only references to the case law, and do not contain any references to the facts of our case.

Also, notice the synthesis in paragraphs 5 and 7, in which the cases are compared and discussed. The synthesis allows the reader to see the commonalities between the two cases—again, this is helpful for the busy reader.

Finally, notice that the first sentence in the Rule Explanation is a *topic sentence* that explains and summarizes the paragraphs that follow. The writer probably didn't write this sentence first. Rather, the writer probably first figured out what the two cases had in common, and what, taken together, they would mean about the element of "sleep," and then, after all that figuring out, composed a "head's up" sentence. This "head's up" sentence tells the reader what is coming in the following paragraphs.

Now we will review the subsequent *topic sentences.* Notice, again, that the Rule Explanation paragraphs made no mention of our facts regarding Mr. Andrews, but the paragraphs below those paragraphs, which make up the Application section, focus on him and his sleeping. In fact, every *topic sentence* in the following Application section mentions Mr. Andrews.

8.   Although Mr. Andrews was sleeping at the time of arrest, he was not using the park as a place to sleep.

Similar to the Rule Explanation above, which started with a *topic sentence* explaining the gist of the two cases, the Application section also starts with a *topic sentence* summarizing the overall analysis. In other words, the gist of the case law, after it was synthesized, was that perhaps more important than the physical act of sleeping are the acts of using the park as a place to sleep by going there in the middle of the night and bringing sleep "equipment" like pillows, blankets, and backpacks, together with sleeping for periods of time.

9.   In fact, by using the park as a place to eat his lunch, Mr. Andrews was using the park as a place to picnic— which, according to *Wilson*, the state legislature sought to protect. 96 A.D.2d at 96, 94 N.Y.S.2d at 94.

Here, the *topic sentence* supports the overall idea expressed in the *topic sentence* above, and expands upon it by introducing the idea that Mr. Andrews' actions were consistent with the legislative intent behind the statute.

10. Second, Mr. Andrews was not in a sleeping bag or under a blanket.

This sentence indicates the *absence* of something—in this case an important and legally relevant fact for one of the past cases.

11. Of course, the prosecution could argue that Mr. Andrews was sleeping within the meaning of the statute because he was observed snoring, with his eyes closed, for five minutes.

Just as we practiced in the IRAC exercises in Chapter 5, this paragraph deals with the opposing arguments. We can never ignore the arguments that can be made by opposing counsel. These opposing arguments are not the main feature of our analysis, but they absolutely must be dealt with clearly and succinctly. Remember, the busy reader will not want to figure out the opposing arguments and a response, and needs to have it all laid out clearly. The busy reader will want to clearly see what the opposing counsel will argue, and the weak points of our case, in order to prepare a strong and thorough response. The busy reader wants to be thoroughly prepared.

12. However, although Mr. Andrews was actually sleeping, prosecuting him does not seem consistent with the legislative intent behind the statute.

Now, in the final paragraph before the conclusion, the writer effectively responds to the opposing argument (see above paragraph) again relying on the legislative intent. This is what the busy reader needs: to fully understand the opposing argument, and all the legal support for the opposing argument, AND then to fully understand the logical response.

Remember to review the example of the complete memo at the end of this chapter, which is preceded by an IRAC exercise on the same problem with the same authorities. You should be able to see the similarity in the content and the organization, and the expansion and added detail in the Memo. This is especially so because of the Rule Explanation section. In the next chapter, you will see how to alter the basic IRAC organization slightly in order to create a persuasive document.

Before we move on to Conclusions, a word about quotes. At some point in your life, you may have been allowed to use long block quotes in your written work. You may be tempted to use them when you are relating case law. However, long block quotes are not at all useful to the busy reader. In general, you shouldn't use them. Long block quotes are hard to read, and busy readers will also need to be supplied with your thought process, and a context, before we can make sense of them. Short pithy quotes, of a sentence or two, can be used to relay a court's reasoning or holding when it is just too difficult to summarize well, or when the exact words from the court are significant for some reason.

F. The Conclusion

Students are often pretty tired of a memo project by the time they get to the Conclusion section. But, now is not the time to hurriedly jot some random thoughts onto the page at 1 a.m. just so you can finish the project. Like each portion of the memo, the Conclusion should be a planned, measured, and carefully composed section.

Just as summarizing might be a new skill, so might be writing a true conclusion. A true conclusion in an interoffice memo does the following: 1) clearly and succinctly sets out your decision on how the issue should be decided—without hedging; and 2) summarizes, without repeating verbatim, your reasons. A true conclusion does NOT: 1) cut and paste from other portions of the memo, or repeat any prior portions of the memo verbatim; 2) restate every element of the memo; 3) introduce your analysis for the first time; 4) introduce any facts or law for the first time; 5) hedge, with statements like "it will be up to the judge to decide" or "the jury could go either way." The Conclusion should be shorter than any other section, and should highlight the best reasons for your recommendation as well as the *legally relevant facts*.

Here are some examples:

CONCLUSION

Mr. Andrews did not "sleep" in the park in violation of Penal Law § 10.10.10. A nap in the middle of the day is completely distinct from sleeping in the middle of the night under a blanket or sleeping bag. Specifically, Mr. Andrews' behavior differs from that of the *Matthews* defendant and the *Wilson* defendant because Andrews was napping in the middle of the day, not at night, and because he had no blanket or sleeping bag.

Because his nap was casual and connected to the recreational use of picnicking, Mr. Andrews was not using the park as a place to sleep, which is what the New York legislature sought to avoid when it enacted Penal Law § 10.10.10.

Notice that the first sentence is a declarative sentence stating a position, and not a repetition of how the facts developed. This first sentence is an apt *topic sentence* for a conclusion—a conclusion that is a final decision for the preceding analysis. In the first paragraph, after the *topic sentence*, the writer goes on to reiterate the distinction between Mr. Andrews' behavior versus the defendants' behavior in *Matthews* and *Wilson*, where the defendants were convicted of sleeping in the park. The final sentence—also the final paragraph—again states that Mr. Andrews' use of the park was congruent with the legislative intent.

The above Conclusion reminds the reader of the analysis. Let's read the following Conclusion for a slightly different approach:

CONCLUSION

Although there are two Appellate Division cases from our jurisdiction that affirmed convictions of defendants because they had slept in the park in violation of Penal Law § 10.10.10, both those cases are easily distinguishable from Mr. Andrews' case. The facts of those cases both involve men using backpacks, pillows, or sleeping bags to sleep in the park for the night, as opposed to Mr. Andrews, who was just lying down napping in the sun without any of those items. Additionally, since Mr. Andrews had just eaten his lunch and was relaxing, arguably his behavior is consistent with the legislative intent behind the statute. Therefore, Mr. Andrews should not be convicted under the statute.

———————

This Conclusion, instead of reiterating the analysis, weighed the authorities and suggested a result based on legislative intent. Same basic idea as the other conclusion, but worded differently, with a different emphasis.

Can you see what both Conclusions have in common? The discussion is authoritative and does not hedge; the discussion reiterates and emphasizes the important points from the analysis; there is nowhere in either discussion that repeats verbatim, or cuts and pastes, from other portions of the memo; and finally, there is not really a rushed quality to either Conclusion. Aim for something like this!

SKILLS DEVELOPMENT

DOs and DON'Ts for Writing Legal Memos

DOs:

- Follow the structure provided, either by your law firm or by your teacher.

- Use IRAC to organize your Discussion section.

- Remember the busy reader and the "don't make the reader look back" rules.

- Synthesize the law and synthesize the facts whenever you can.

- Use citations—either factual or legal—at the end of EVERY sentence that contains a factual or legal reference.

- Use pithy, colorful quotes when available.

- Spell-check AND proofread.

- Use correct citation format.

- Include and respond to negative authority AND opposing arguments.

DON'Ts:

- Take shortcuts on format.

- Use block quotes.

- Copy from one part of the memo and paste in another part of the memo.

CHAPTER 10 LEGAL SKILLS

- **Summarize facts**
- **Synthesize facts**
- **Recognize link between IRAC and legal memos**
- **Draft a legal memo following the organization and using headings**

- • Draft a Discussion section of a memo following the IREAC organization (Issue, Rule, Rule Explanation, Application, and Conclusion)

CHAPTER 10 VOCABULARY

- • Conclusory
- • Deposition
- • Deposition transcript
- • Discovery
- • Headings
- • Legally relevant facts
- • Topic sentence

CHAPTER 10 RESEARCH AND ANALYSIS EXERCISES

I.   Comparing IRAC to a memo:

Read and compare the full IRAC based on the sleeping in the park exercise, to the full, uninterrupted legal memo. What are the commonalities and what are the differences?

IRAC

ISSUE: Whether Mr. Andrews can be convicted for "sleeping" in the park when his eyes were closed and he was snoring but it was the middle of the day and he was napping after lunch?

RULE: New York Penal Law § 10.10.10 provides: "It is unlawful for any person to sleep in the picnic areas of a state-owned park."

APPLICATION: Mr. Andrews was not guilty of "sleep" in violation of the statute because he was taking a short-term nap in the middle of the day after eating his lunch outside. This behavior is different than that of the defendants in *Matthews* and *Wilson* where the defendants were found sleeping in the park in the middle of the night and appeared to be using the park as a place to sleep. The prosecution could argue that the surrounding circumstances don't matter, and that just because he was sleeping during the day doesn't mean he wasn't violating the statute.

However, considering the legislative intent behind the statute mentioned in *Wilson*, that the legislature wanted the public to use the parks to picnic and relax, and Mr. Andrews' use was consistent with that, he should not be guilty of its violation.

CONCLUSION: Based on the legislative intent behind the statute that the public use the parks to relax and picnic, and that Mr. Andrews was napping after his lunch in the middle of the day, Mr. Andrews should not be found guilty.

* * *

MEMORANDUM

TO: Professor Phillips

FROM: Smart Student

RE: *People v. Andrews*

DATE: September 12, 2006

ISSUE

Whether Mark Andrews violated Penal Law § 10.10.10, which prohibits sleeping in the picnic area of a state-owned park, when he was woken up at 1:00 p.m. by a police officer who found him lying down on the grass next to his empty lunch bag, with his eyes closed, and he was snoring?

OR

Under Penal Law § 10.10.10, which forbids sleeping in the picnic areas of state owned parks, was Mark Andrews "sleeping" in violation of the statute when he was napping after lunch in the middle of the day?

SHORT ANSWER

No. Mr. Andrews did not violate Penal Law § 10.10.10 because he was not using the park as a place to sleep.

FACTS

We represent Mark Andrews, a 40-year-old white male who was arrested on May 4, 2006, for sleeping in the park. Mr. Andrews works for a local bank.

On May 4th, Mr. Andrews decided to eat his lunch in the park. At 1:00 p.m., a police officer found him lying in the grass next to his empty brown bag with his eyes closed, snoring. The police officer observed him for five minutes, and then woke him up and charged him with violating Penal Law § 10.10.10.

Mr. Andrews hired us to represent him in the criminal proceedings.

DISCUSSION

New York Penal Law § 10.10.10 provides: "It is unlawful for any person to sleep in the picnic areas of a state-owned park." The issue in this case is what constitutes "sleep" under the statute.

The Fourth Department has upheld convictions for sleeping in the park when the defendant has been found in the park in the early morning lying down under a blanket. For example, in *People v. Matthews*, 100 A.D.2d 99, 100, 96 N.Y.S.2d 97, 98 (4th Dep't 2000), the court affirmed the defendant's conviction under Penal Law § 10.10.10 because he was found under a picnic table, in a sleeping bag, snoring, with his eyes closed, in the early morning. Additionally, a police officer observed him like this for five minutes before arresting him. *Id.*

Likewise, in a case where the defendant was not actually sleeping at the time of arrest, the Fourth Department upheld a conviction because the defendant was found lying down, under a blanket, with his head on a knapsack, in the early morning. *People v. Wilson*, 96 A.D.2d 95, 95, 94 N.Y.S.2d 93, 93 (4th Dep't 1997). At trial the defendant testified that he suffered from insomnia and only sleeps one or two hours a night, but that he "may have fallen asleep for a short time on the night he was arrested." *Id.* at 96, 94 N.Y.S.2d at 94. The court accordingly held that "[t]he evidence *is* . . . consistent with a finding that at some time that night the defendant had been asleep on the bench." *Id.*

In both *Matthews* and *Wilson* the defendants used the park as a place to sleep, which is certainly not the intended use of state parks. In *Wilson*, the Fourth Department noted that Penal Law § 10.10.10 was enacted to make sure the parks were used for recreation—"to picnic, play, and relax"—and not as a place to sleep. 96 A.D.2d at 96, 94 N. Y.S.2d at 94. Arguably, the surrounding circumstances of the defendants' arrests—the time of night, where they were lying down, and the blanket or sleeping bag covering them—were more important than whether the defendant was actually sleeping at the time of arrest. For example, the court in *Wilson* noted: "even if the defendant did not actually sleep in the park, he was using the park as a place to sleep, and this is unlawful under the statute." 96 A.D.2d at 96, 94 N.Y.S.2d at 94. Thus, the courts' holdings in *Wilson* and *Matthews* indicate that in addition to the physical act of sleeping, the surrounding circumstances are also important, such as the time of day or night, where the defendant is found, and whether the defendant appears to be settling in for a long time. *Matthews*, 100 A.D.2d at 100, 98 N. Y.S.2d at 98; *Wilson*, 96 A.D.2d at 96; 94 N.Y.S.2d at 94. These circumstances indicate whether the defendant is using the park as a place to sleep, contrary to the intent of the statute.

Although Mr. Andrews was sleeping at the time of arrest, he was not using the park as a place to sleep. First, unlike the defendants in *Matthews* and *Wilson*, who were found lying down in the middle of the night under a blanket, Mr. Andrews was arrested in the middle of the day. *Matthews*, 100 A.D.2d at 100, 98 N.Y.S.2d at 98; *Wilson*, 96 A.D.2d at 96, 94 N.Y.S.2d at 94. Because he was arrested at 1:00 p.m. and was found lying down next to an empty lunch bag, it's likely that he was napping after finishing his lunch. A short nap after lunch in the park is much different from using the park as a place to sleep at night. In fact, by using the park as a place to eat his lunch, Mr. Andrews was using the park as a place to picnic—which, according to *Wilson*, the state legislature sought to protect. 96 A.D.2d at 96, 94 N. Y.S.2d at 94. Indeed, simply using the park at 1:00 p.m. in the afternoon suggests a recreational use, while using the park in the early morning hours does not. Thus, one of the most important factors distinguishing this case from *Matthews* and *Wilson* is the time of day Mr. Andrews was found sleeping.

Second, Mr. Andrews was not in a sleeping bag or under a blanket. The defendant in *Matthews* was found lying down in a sleeping bag under a picnic table. 100 A.D.2d at 100, 98 N. Y.S.2d at 98. Similarly, in *Wilson*, the defendant was found lying on a park bench under a blanket with his head on a knapsack. 96 A.D.2d at 96, 94 N. Y.S.2d at 94. Unlike either of these defendants, Mr. Andrews was not using a blanket or a sleeping bag, which further suggests that Mr. Andrews was not using the park as a place to sleep. Additionally, he did not have a pillow, and simply lying down on the grass does not imply the same intent to sleep as lying under a picnic table like the defendant in *Matthews* or lying on a park bench like the defendant in *Wilson*. *Matthews*, 100 A.D.2d at 100, 98 N. Y.S.2d at 98; *Wilson*, 96 A.D.2d at 96, 94 N. Y.S.2d at 94. Rather, lying on the grass is consistent with picnicking, which is the intended use of state parks.

Of course, the prosecution could argue that Mr. Andrews was sleeping within the meaning of the statute because he was observed snoring, with his eyes closed, for five minutes. Like Mr. Andrews, the defendant in *Matthews* was observed lying down, with his eyes closed, and snoring, for five minutes. *Matthews*, 100 A.D.2d at 100, 98 N.Y.S.2d at 98. Since the defendant's conviction in *Matthews* was affirmed, arguably, Mr. Andrews could be convicted under the statute as well. However, although Mr. Andrews was actually sleeping, prosecuting him does not seem consistent with the legislative intent behind the statute. As the Fourth Department noted, "New York State sought to ensure that its parks would be used only for the purpose for which they were intended: The picnic areas of parks are designed as a place where people can picnic, play, and relax and not as a place for people to sleep." *Wilson*, 96 A.D.2d at 96, 94 N. Y.S.2d at 94. Mr. Andrews ate his lunch in the park in the middle of the day, after which he happened to take a nap, which is entirely consistent with the legislative intent of protecting picnicking and relaxing. In this case, the overall purpose of the statute is more significant than whether he was actually sleeping at the time of arrest.

CONCLUSION

Mr. Andrews was not "sleeping in the park" in violation of Penal Law § 10.10.10. A nap in the middle of the day is completely distinct from sleeping in the middle of the night under a blanket or sleeping bag. Specifically, Mr. Andrews' behavior differs from that of the *Matthews* defendant and the *Wilson* defendant because he was napping in the middle of the day, not at night, and because he had no blanket or sleeping bag. Because his nap was casual and connected to the recreational use of picnicking, Mr. Andrews was not using the park as a place to sleep, which is what the New York legislature sought to avoid when it enacted Penal Law § 10.10.10.

Onward and Upward—Persuasion

Legal Skills:

* Shift from IRAC to CREAC or CRAC
* Compose a legal argument
* Draft a motion

In some ways, persuasion is at the crux of understanding law. When you read a case, you are reading the legal argument that the court found most persuasive. There was a dispute, two (or more) sides went to court, they argued, and the best argument won. Even when you compose a legal analysis presented in an office memo, you are making choices about what law applies, what facts are legally relevant, and how all of that fits together in a cogent analysis. Although you are not necessarily trying to persuade your audience, the supervising attorney, you are certainly presenting one view of how the law should be interpreted and applied. That legal analysis is essentially a legal argument. Even when participating in a transaction, although legal argument may play a less overt role—after all, the two parties are trying to agree on a deal, not necessarily trying to "win"—but choosing the best application of law to facts is still part of the way you think about the transaction.

You are called upon to make legal arguments directly in the litigation process when you make a request to a court, which is called a motion. There are a variety of motions typically made in both the civil and criminal litigation processes—motions to dismiss, motions to amend pleadings, motions to compel (in the discovery process), motions to suppress the introduction of evidence at trial, and motions for summary judgment, to name a few. You also make legal arguments in appeals. In other words, if you lose at the trial level, you take an appeal and make arguments to the appellate court about why you should not have lost.

Of course, legal arguments can regularly be made in the course of law practice, without a submission to court, whether in letters or settlement demands or offers proposed to an opposing party, contract negotiations, or any other type of negotiations incident to a legal agreement or transaction.

When making arguments to a court, either for a motion at the trial level or for an appeal, you are not only dealing with how the rule should be applied to the facts, you are also dealing with the rule—or *standard*—that the court must follow in order to grant the relief you want. Remember in Chapter 8 when you learned about *summary judgment motions* in civil cases, for example, you also learned that when parties make a motion, there is typically a *standard* that the court uses as a lens through which to view the facts and the law of the case. For summary judgment, a defendant can argue that judgment should be granted as a matter of law because there is no issue of material fact. In a criminal case, a criminal defendant can move for dismissal of the charges (called an indictment or information, depending on the level of crime) in the interest of justice or for failure to state an offense.[1]

When submitting a motion to court, there are certain required components—think of them as legal "ingredients." First, you have to tell the court what you are submitting—you do this is in the Notice of Motion, a document that, at a minimum, tells the court what case the motion concerns, what the case docket or index number is, and what you are asking for. Second, you will have to tell the court about your

---

[1]   Federal Rules of Criminal Procedure 12(b)(3)(B)(v) provides for the criminal defendant's motion for "failure to state an offense." Typically, in state jurisdictions, criminal procedure or case law also allows a motion to dismiss in the interest of justice.

client's facts, so you need a way to document and authenticate those facts—for example, an attorney *affidavit* with exhibits or a client affidavit (or both), both of which are called "*affirmations*" in some jurisdictions. Third, you have to submit a legal argument to support the request you are making—done in a Memorandum of Law. This chapter focuses on that type of memo of law because knowing how to make a legal argument is a fundamental legal skill.

PART I. BACKGROUND ON LEGAL ARGUMENT

Although there is a fundamental commonality between legal analysis and legal argument, they are not exactly the same, nor are they written in exactly the same way.

For one thing, there's the audience. You are no longer speaking to a supervising attorney in a frank and matter-of-fact way as part of strategizing and developing the case for your client. You are now writing to the court and trying to convince that reader to rule in favor of your client. That reader is a judge—not a jury, not your client, not a layperson. Therefore, notwithstanding what you may have seen on TV or in movies, pleas to emotion, highfalutin pleas to justice, and any exaggeration or hyperbole in general are mistakes. In other words, your *tone* should be direct, forceful, and informed. In writing, "*tone*" means the mood or impression that is not expressed directly with words, but rather, is conveyed indirectly through choice of words, sentence structure, and punctuation. You are striving for a professional and persuasive *tone*.

Second, there is the organization. You are asking for something, not merely explaining something. You must focus on your request and the reasons for your request. Your client, your client's arguments, your client's requests—NOT the opponent's—ALWAYS come first. You still deal with the opposing arguments, but you explain why they are weak, wrong, or why your arguments are better. You must be assertive and definite as you propose that the court see the law and the facts as you see the law and the facts. Your topic sentences should clearly assert the relief and findings that you want the court to make.

The structure of your presentation is similar to IRAC. But because you need to assertively request relief, and not explore an issue, you will use the *C-R-A-C* organization (or the *C-R-E-A-C* organization—Rule and Rule Explanation) instead of the I-R-A-C organization. That is, instead of starting off by stating the "I" or "Issue," you start off by stating the *"C"* or *"Conclusion"*—your affirmative request, the conclusion about the issue that you want the court to agree with. The organization must stay focused on your request. Each of the topic sentences, put together, should outline your argument.

Third, you can't forget the "because." It is easy to say your client should get the desired result, but it's also easy to forget to include the reason. You can't say the reason only once—you have to state it multiple times, although you may be stating many reasons, and you may be stating the same reason multiple times. Including the reason can be the hardest part, so you want to be sure to ask yourself—did you answer the question "Why?" that the judge will be asking while reading the memo of law? This is what your busy reader—now the judge that the supervising attorney will submit the memo of law to—expects.

Finally, and by no means the least important, is the *theme*. Although perhaps not as important for simple motions, a *theme* can really unite your ideas so that they are easy for the busy reader to grasp. A *theme* is an idea that connects all the individual arguments into a bigger, all-encompassing idea. One reliable *theme* that is often at the heart of a dispute is fairness and justice. But developing a *theme* doesn't mean you have to repeat the actual words "fairness" and "justice" in a petulant manner. Rather, it means that you are arguing that your client's position is the most fair, and the best position to take, in order to get a just result. How do you make your client look good? And reasonable? What facts do you emphasize?

Let's see what this all looks like in our "sleeping in the park" example.

SKILLS DEVELOPMENT

Tips on Developing Legal Argument

Step 1: Focus on what you are asking for—put your arguments first.

Step 2: Yes, definitely address the opposing argument— clearly articulate what the other side argues, and clearly spell out why you have the better argument. But do this only AFTER you have put forward your own argument.

Step 3: Keep the tone assertive, but not angry—never any personal attacks.

Step 4: Ask directly and clearly for what you want. Then back it up.

Step 5: Find a theme—create an accurate story about justice and fairness with your client's facts.

PART II. WORKING THROUGH AN EXAMPLE

Like a legal memo, a memo of law in support of a motion has specific and discrete sections. The format for a memo of law will vary according to your jurisdiction and your jurisdiction's norms. However, although information may be put together in slightly different ways, there will definitely be a format, and courts usually require—or at least, enjoy—receiving documents in uniform formats. Therefore, one of your assignments at the end of the chapter is to find the forms and formats for different motions and memos of law used in your state.

Keeping in mind that there will be variations according to the procedural rules in your jurisdiction, let's work through the "sleeping in the park" example using all the typical components.

A. The *Caption*

Here, since this is a document to be submitted to the court, you include the *caption* of the case and any identifying information necessary for your jurisdiction, such as a docket number, an index number, or other identifying information. The *caption* is also where you give the document an identifying title, such as "Motion to Compel" or "Motion for Summary Judgment."

We will use the "sleeping in the park" example to construct a sample motion to dismiss the charges against Mark Andrews. Keep in mind as we go through this example that the different sections are models that are subject to variation depending on the jurisdiction.

Here is an example of a *caption* for a memo of law to be submitted in a mythical state:

The People of the State of Myrna

MEMO OF LAW
IN SUPPORT OF
vs.   MOTION TO
DISMISS

Index No. 45CR

Mark Andrews

Note that the components of a *caption* are the names and roles of the parties—in a criminal case, prosecution (representing "The People") and defendant, and in a civil case, plaintiff and defendant; the identifying number from the court (in this case an index number, but can also be called a docket number); and a title identifying the type of document. Note that the case caption here has similar components to the *caption* at the beginning of the appellate decisions you read.

B. The Introduction or Summary of Argument

Much like a legal memo, the start of the document should contain its essence—the relief you are requesting, the legal rule you are relying on, and a summary of the argument. The busy reader in law always wants to know where she is going, and this type of a loaded beginning tells the reader the point of the document and lets the reader know what direction she is going.

Here is an example:

INTRODUCTION

Pursuant to Criminal Procedure Rule 10, the defendant requests a dismissal of the criminal charge for violating Penal Law § 10.10.10, which prohibits sleeping in the park, because the evidence cannot support a finding beyond a reasonable doubt that Mr. Andrews was violating the true purpose and intent of the statute. The purpose of Penal Law § 10.10.10 is to prohibit people using the park as a place to sleep at night. Mr. Andrews was not using the park as a place to sleep, but rather, was taking a short nap during the day after his lunch. Mr. Andrews' use of the park was consistent with the purpose of the park to provide a place for people to enjoy nature and relax.

Notice that the Introduction includes a specific *request for relief*—"dismissal of the criminal charge for violating Penal Law § 10.10.10." This *request* necessarily requires the criminal procedural rule that allows a defendant to *request* dismissal, referred to here as Criminal Procedure Rule 10. The *Introduction* (sometimes called the *"Summary"* or *"Summary of Argument"*) also includes the argument "Mr. Andrews was not using the park as a place to sleep." So right from the beginning, the court knows the what and the why of this motion.

C. Statement of the Facts

Although including a factual section may seem just like a mirroring of the office memo of law format in Chapter 10, the Statement of Facts in a memo of law submitted to a court is written with the end goal of persuasion in mind. The same guideline of using well-crafted topic sentences applies, but for a court you want to be mindful of topic sentences that construct an argument or present the facts in a helpful or beneficial way.

Note the differences between the Statement of Facts below, written to support the defendant's motion to dismiss, and the Facts written for the office memo in Chapter 10. First, the audience is different. No longer are you writing for your supervising attorney, and speaking in a friendly but professional *tone*. Now, your *tone* should be a bit more formal, since you are presenting your case to a judge. Also, since you want the judge to decide the case in your favor, you are summarizing the facts in way that is accurate and honest—and doesn't leave anything relevant out—but, wherever possible, describes the facts in a way that benefits your client or puts your client in a good light.

Second, because the audience is a court and not your supervising attorney, you are not including any information from the attorney-client interview that is not already known to the prosecution. This information is completely confidential and protected by the ethical rule that attorneys must keep all information learned in the course of client representation confidential.[2] So, for a motion in a criminal case, prior to any additional discovery or hearings, and therefore before your client has given any statements, you would likely stick to the evidence that would be admissible at trial, which is usually the police report in a simple case like this one. In other words, you would not really have the liberty of providing the client's own statements or his personal point of view.

Finally, note that the absence of something can be a fact worthy of inclusion in the Statement of Facts, especially when your opponent has the burden of proof.

---

[2]   The ABA Model Rule on confidentiality is Rule 1.6; your state probably has a parallel rule that governs attorney conduct.

Here is an example:

STATEMENT OF FACTS

At approximately 1:08 p.m. in the afternoon on May 4, 2018, Officer James Cricket issued Mark Andrews a ticket for sleeping in City Park. (Police Report dated 1/1/16.) According to the Police Report, Cricket noticed Mr. Andrews lying down, with his eyes closed, sleeping, in the picnic area. (Police Report dated 1/1/16.) Mr. Andrews was not charged with any other crime, and there is no evidence of any inappropriate conduct such as public drunkenness or lewd behavior.

———————————

Notice that the example includes all the facts from the Police Report, as well as the suggestion that Mark Andrews is harmless and law-abiding because he was not breaking any other rules and was not charged with any other crime. There are no facts omitted—especially not "bad" facts that might be negative for the client. Similar to the ethical obligation to disclose any adverse authority to the court, the lawyer's duty (and consequently, the paralegal's duty) is to exercise candor at all times with the court.[3] Failing to disclose or discuss negative facts is therefore an ethical violation, and not something that will get the judge to trust you.

Note also that after each sentence, there is a citation to a source. The citation informs the court about where the information came from, and the judge or law clerk should be able to rely on the citation in order to easily find the information. Here, the sole source of facts is the Police Report. In a simple matter like this, the attorney may simply take the police report at face value, and use it as the source of evidence as long as that is permitted under the state evidence rules. In more complicated matters with additional evidence that the attorney needs to support the

---

[3] According the ABA Model Rule of Professional Conduct 3.3, a lawyer may not make a false statement of fact or law to a tribunal, or, as discussed in Chapter 4, fail to disclose adverse authority. Most states will have a parallel state rule—your primary authority—which will contain the same or similar provisions.

motion, the attorney could choose to submit an affidavit with the necessary records or items attached as exhibits.

D. Argument

In this section you see the importance of switching from IRAC, which is the organization used to explain a legal analysis in the safe zone of your legal office, to *CRAC*. Using the organization of *CRAC* (*Conclusion, Rule, Argument, Conclusion*) or *CREAC* (*Conclusion, Rule, Rule Explanation, Argument, and Conclusion*) means that you start out with your Conclusion. Starting out with your Conclusion means that you assert that what you want to happen is true: The charge against Mr. Andrews should be dismissed. This is different than starting out with a neutral legal Conclusion: Mr. Andrews was not violating the statute. Remember, you are *requesting relief* from the court, so you need to be very specific about what you think should happen.

Note also that the *tone* is different—you are asking for relief, and you have to explain why the relief you are asking for is justified. You cannot simply state your analysis and expect someone to agree with you.

See if you can recognize the difference between the sample Argument here and the more neutral legal analysis from the last chapter:

ARGUMENT (*CREAC*)

The charge against Mr. Andrews should be dismissed in the interest of justice and because the prosecution has failed to state a proper offense under the true meaning of the statute. Although Mr. Andrews was observed sleeping in the picnic area of City Park, he was hardly using the park as a place to sleep. He was not making a nuisance out of himself by napping in the middle of the day, nor was he substituting the park for a home or a camping site by using it as a place to spend the night.

Penal Law § 10.10.10 does prohibit sleeping in the park when it states: "It is unlawful for any person to sleep in the picnic areas of a state, county or city owned park." However, the statute has been applied only to itinerants who set themselves up to spend the entire night in the park. For example, in *People v. Matthews*, 100 A.D.2d 99, 98 N.Y.S.2d 97 (4th Dep't 2000), the defendant was convicted because he was discovered by the police officer in the early morning hours—at 1:00 a.m.—and observed snoring and sleeping in a sleeping bag. Likewise, in *People v. Wilson*, 96 A.D.2d 95, 94 N.Y.S.2d 93 (4th Dep't 1997), although the defendant was found with his eyes open, he was also found by the police officer in the early morning hours—at 3:00 a.m.—lying down, under a blanket, using a knapsack as his pillow. The court stated that the defendant "was using the park as a place to sleep," id. at 96, 94 N.Y.S.2d at 94, which is unlawful under the statute.

A person napping during the lunch hour should not be guilty of violating the same statute as defendants who are camping out in a public park with sleeping materials. Unlike the defendants in *Wilson* and *Matthews*, Mr. Andrews did not have a blanket, sleeping bag, or pillow, and he was not found by a police officer in the early hours of the morning. Mr. Andrews was simply napping, while the *Wilson* and *Matthews* defendants were spending the night. Mr. Andrews was not using the park as a place to sleep, unlike those defendants; he was just taking a casual daytime nap.

Additionally, by enjoying a mid-day nap, Mr. Andrews was using the City Park in a way that is consistent with the legislative purpose behind Penal Law § 10.10.10. According to the Fourth Department, the purpose behind the statute is to protect state parks and ensure they are used for recreation so people can "picnic, play, and relax." *Matthews*, 100 A.D.2d at 101, 98 N.Y.S.2d at 99. A daytime nap is consistent with relaxing, while sleeping at night with a blanket and a pillow is consistent with sleeping in violation of the statute.

Pursuing this prosecution of Mr. Andrews is in opposition to the basic protective purpose of the statute, and the violation of the statute cannot be proven beyond a reasonable doubt. Therefore, the charge should be dismissed.

Note that this persuasive memo of law consistently urges that the reader adopt a point of view. Note also that it is shorter than the more thorough explanatory legal memo. This difference results from the different audience. A busy criminal court judge who would be handling this type of low-level crime would likely be somewhat familiar with the statute, and would not necessarily welcome a long legal argument. Pointing out how the mandatory precedent supports the relief you are requesting in a persuasive way, and that the *standard* of proof is not met, are enough for this type of court and for this type of violation (low-level crime). On the other hand, an appellate brief to a mid-level state or federal appellate court would be much more developed and involved.

Notice that the present case with Mr. Andrews is distinguished from the two other cases in which convictions were sustained by using a thorough comparison: comparing specific facts (napping versus pillow and blanket), circumstances of arrest (mid-day versus middle of the night), and the different result desired (Mathews and Wilson convicted, Andrews should not be convicted).

Finally, let's take a look at how we would write a persuasive Conclusion.

E. Conclusion

The Conclusion is an important time to remind the court of your best and most persuasive points. This is especially important in a long brief, but here, in a short piece for a low-level court, it is a bit less important. In the Conclusion, you should aim to make the judge feel comfortable granting the relief you are requesting. A judge feels comfortable if the result is supported by precedent, seems reasonable, is consistent with the *standard*, and is within the power and/or discretion of the judge.

Here is an example:

CONCLUSION

Based on Criminal Procedure Rule 10, this Court can dismiss the pending charge against Mr. Andrews because it is outside the scope of the statute and cannot be proven beyond a reasonable doubt at trial. Rule 10 allows dismissal of criminal charges when there is "insufficient basis in fact or law" and the charges could not be successful at trial. If an arrest is entirely inconsistent with the meaning of a statute established by the Fourth Department, then the basis is "insufficient" under the rule and the charges should not be sustained. Mr. Andrews was not using the park as a place to sleep, but rather, was using the park in a way that is consistent with the purpose of the Penal Code—for rest and relaxation.

Here, the court is reminded that the arrest of Andrews was not consistent with past arrests, and not consistent with the purpose of the statute. The court is also reminded of its power to dismiss the charges.

As you can see, a legal argument is not a mysterious thing once you have the tools to use and apply the law in different ways. Remember that although it is rule-based, in the end, it is the facts that make your legal argument—no pillow, no blanket, no sleeping in the middle of the night. Even if you are never asked to write a motion, to do substantive legal work you should have the ability to frame an argument and to present a legal analysis in a persuasive manner.

CHAPTER 11 LEGAL SKILLS

- **Shift from IRAC to CREAC or CRAC**
- **Compose a legal argument**
- **Draft a motion**

CHAPTER 11 VOCABULARY

• Affidavit/affirmation
• Brief
• Caption
• CRAC
• CREAC
• Introduction/summary of argument
• Motion for summary judgment
• Standard
• Theme
• Tone

CHAPTER 11 RESEARCH AND ANALYSIS EXERCISES

I.   **Researching a motion to dismiss:**

1.   Researching the rule for a motion to dismiss:

a.   Find your state civil procedural rule governing motions to dismiss.

   i.   Compare this rule to the rule governing summary judgment.

   ii.   Find a case from an appellate court in your state discussing the motion to dismiss rule and how to apply it.

   iii.   Cite the rule.

b.   Find your state criminal procedural rule governing motions to dismiss.

   i.   Find a case from an appellate court in your state discussing the rule and how to apply it.

   ii.   Cite the rule.

2.   Using Forms to draft a motion:

a.   Find your state forms for motions to dismiss and motions for summary judgment.

b.   Can you find forms for all the documents needed: notice of motion, supporting affidavits, and briefs for both civil and criminal motions to dismiss?

c. Can you find the same for a civil motion for summary judgment?

II.   Recognizing differences between memos and motions:

1.   AUDIENCE: In writing, your writing differs depending on your audience—the person(s) who will read that piece of writing.

a.   Who is the audience for the memo versus the motion?

b.   What is the difference between those two audiences?

2.   TONE: Everything you write, from emails, to letters, to memos, to motions, has a "tone," which means implicit mood or attitude.

a.   Look up three definitions of tone as a writing/literary device, and synthesize them into one definition in your own words.

b.   What are some tools you can use to differentiate your tone in writing?

c.   Review the entire sleeping in the park memo and the sleeping in the park motion and compare the tone. How would you describe the difference in tone? What were some ways in which a difference in tone were accomplished?

3.   TOPIC SENTENCES: As you know, the topic sentence is the first sentence in a paragraph.

a.   Copy and paste EACH topic sentence from the sleeping in the park memo to EACH topic sentence from the sleeping in the park motion. What are the differences? Why is one more persuasive than the other?

Bibliography

Adelman, Belniak, Selby, and Detweiler, <u>New York Legal Research</u>, Third Edition (2015)

Berring and Levy, <u>The Legal Research Survival Manual</u> (2017)

Clermont, Hillman, Johnson and Summers, <u>Law for Society: Nature, Functions, and Limits</u> (2010)

Columbia Law Review, et al, <u>The Bluebook: A Uniform System of Citation</u>, Twentieth Edition (2015)

Coughlin, Rocklin, Patrick, <u>A Lawyer Writes: A Practical Guide to Legal Analysis</u> (2013)

Currier and Eimerman, <u>Introduction to Law for Paralegals: A Critical Thinking Approach</u> (2014)

Bryan Garner, <u>Black's Law Dictionary</u>, Eleventh Edition (2019)

Bryan Garner, <u>Black's Law Dictionary</u>, Fifth Pocket Edition (2016)

Bryan Garner, <u>Legal Writing in Plain English</u> (2001)

Jane Kent Gionfriddo, <u>Using Fruit to Teach Analogy</u>, The Second Draft: Bulleting of the Legal Writing Institute, Vol. 12 iss. 1 (1997)

Grise, <u>Critical Reading for Success in Law School and Beyond</u> (West Academic 2017)

Tracy McGaugh, The Synthesis Chart: Swiss Amy Knife of Legal Writing, 9 Perspectives: Teaching Legal Research and Writing 80 (2001)

Laurel Oates, <u>Leveling the Playing Field: Helping Students Succeed by Helping Them Learn to read as Expert Lawyers</u>, 80 St. John's L. Rev. (2006)

Mark Osbeck, <u>Impeccable Research, A Concise Guide to Mastering Legal Research Skills</u> (2015)

Shapo, Walter and Fajans, <u>Writing and Analysis In The Law</u>, Fifth Edition (2008)

Williams, Booth, Colomb, <u>The Craft of Research</u> (2008)

Richard Wydick, <u>Plain English for Lawyers</u>, Fifth Edition (2005)

Zimmerman, Creative Ideas and Techniques for Teaching Rule Synthesis 8 Perspectives: Teaching Legal Research and Writing 68 (Winter 2000)

CASES

Carlill v. Carbolic Smoke Company, EWCA Civ 1 (1892)

Carter v. Flaherty, 37 Misc.3d 46, 953 N.Y.S.2d 814 (App. Term. 2012)

Conti v. ASPCA, 77 Misc.2d 61, 353 N.Y.S.2d 288 (Queens Co. 1974)

In Re Castelli, 131 A.D.3d 29, 11 N.Y.S.3d 268 (2d Dept 2015)

Loving v. Virginia, 388 U.S. 1 (1976)

Lucy v. Zehmer, 196 Va. 493, 84 S.E.2d 516 (1954)

Negri v. Stop and Shop, 65 N.Y.2d 625, 491 N.Y.S.2d 151, 480 N.E.2d 740 (1985)

Obergefell v. Hodges, 576 U.S. ___ (2015)

Sussman v. Grado, 192 Misc.2d 628, 746 N.Y.S.2d 548 (Nassau Co. 2002)

Village of Skokie v. National Socialist Party of America, 69 Ill.2d 605, 373 N.E.2d 21 (1978)

Identifying Legal Sources Through Citation

Much of your legal research, if not all of it, may be on the computer screen. Therefore, much of the law that you read may be in your textbooks or, more likely, on the computer screen. Hopefully, you will take the time to experience the profundity of a law library, with its extensive shelves of secondary sources that make browsing so easy. However, the reality of today is that you have access to sophisticated search engines and free legal websites, and can research *statutes, regulations, constitutions* and *case law* from appellate courts.

So, if your research is performed on the screen and you do not have the physical book and its location in the library to help you identify the source of law, you will have to rely on observable characteristics to help you determine what kind of source you are looking at. Be careful to identify what type of source you are looking at—is the source a primary or a secondary one, and if primary, is it a *statute, regulation, constitution,* or *case law?*

In addition to the observable characteristics of the online source itself discussed in Chapter 1, Part I, another observable characteristic is the *citation*—meaning the identifying name and numbers for the *statutes,* the *regulation,* the *constitution,* and the *case law.* The citation is the "address" to the source—it is how you find the source, whether you are in the library or using the Find Function on an electronic database. In the old days when students of the law and lawyers did their research in a law library, it would have been hard to mix up the sources of law: the secondary sources were in one spot, with the state encyclopedia having a place of honor; the statutes were in another spot—and could easily be identified by the color of the books, and the labels on the book spine; and the state case law was in yet another spot, depending on the jurisdiction (whether it was your state, federal case law, or case law from other states). Now, you are looking at one thing and one thing only—a computer screen. You will have to take more care in keeping your sources straight.

Given the ease of electronic searches and the amount of cross-referencing in sources, you need to be able to distinguish one source from another. For example, the body of a case can refer to statutes, administrative regulations, a constitution, or other cases; reference to a statute can be followed by cross-references to a secondary source (remember, not "the law," as explained in Part I), such as comments in which scholar-practitioners explain the workings of the statute or highlight a unique or recently-litigated point. When looking at the text of an *annotated* statute, information following the statute can include additional cross-references to relevant secondary sources, related statutes, regulations, and case law. The federal statutes come in an annotated version, as do many states; some states have annotated versions of their administrative code, too. As we saw above, a regulation often refers to the statute from which it is derived.

Think of a citation as the key—the key not only to identifying the source of law but the key to locating that source. When you have the citation to a legal source, the citation will allow you to locate the source in a library, and nearly always allow you to find the source online as well. Most databases have a "Find" function in which you can simply enter the citation and the legal source will be pulled up.

In general, every citation has three important clues:

1.   An abbreviation or other indication of the type of source;

2. The geographic jurisdiction of that source—meaning whether it is federal or state, and if it's state, which state, and sometimes, for appellate court decisions, which region of the state;

3. A relevant date—usually the year—for the source (Note that this is the date of decision for cases; for statutes and regulations, there are different citation rules regarding the proper year to include depending on whether you are looking at an actual volume or a screen.)

All these clues give you information for helping you to judge how much weight to give the legal precedent you are citing. For example, is the source in your jurisdiction? Is it really old? And what type of source is it? Additionally, each legal source also has other unique characteristics in its citation, which we will now explore.

One last piece of advice when thinking about citations: know what citation guide you should be using. Currently, although there are alternatives, the citation guide most used by lawyers and paralegals is The Bluebook: A Uniform System of Citation (20th Edition) (2015 Harvard). However, your region or the legal subject in which you land up working may have a different citation convention. The citations here are all according to the format prescribed by the Bluebook, and assume that you are using a digital source and viewing your resources on the screen.

A. Statutes

Statutes generally have all three clues of a citation: an abbreviation indicating type of source (such as Code, Stat., Rev. Stat., Law, etc.); the jurisdiction (either state or U.S.); and a relevant year.

Additionally, in many cases of state statutes we will see both the reference to the state (N.Y.) as well as the subject matter (Penal). For example, one of the burglary statutes in New York would be referenced as N.Y. Penal Law § 140.20 (McKinney's 2015). The subject matter—such as "Penal"—is not something we would see in a case citation. The case citation won't identify the subject matter of the case as "civil" or "torts" or "intellectual property." In many state codes, after legislation is passed it is then "codified," which means the legislation is assigned a subject area. Most state statutes are organized by the topic area, not by the date they were passed. All state statute citations include an indication to the state.

However, federal statutes would be referenced without any helpful subject-area indication, but would include "U.S.C." or "U.S.C.A." For example, the citation to a federal statute, 42 U.S.C. § 1983 (2001), does not indicate that it is a Civil Rights statute, but you can clearly see that the jurisdiction is the United States. Note that U.S.C. stands for United States Code, and U.S.C.A. stand for United States Code Annotated. We will review why the latter is a more helpful research tool, but in either case, note that there is a "C" for "Code" and therefore a helpful hint that this is a statute.

Both state statutory and federal statutory citations end with the relevant year in parenthesis, which according to the Bluebook for practitioners in Rules B.12.1.1 and B12.1.2 is "the year of the cited code edition (not the year the code was passed)." This rule assumes that you are looking at a printed volume when you are reading the statute. Since today's practitioner may not take the time to travel to the library to ascertain the edition of the code, they may instead choose to use the effective date of the statute. On subscription databases there is usually a hyperlink labeled "Currentness" which will take you to the effective date of the statute; in Lexis at the top of the statute there will usually be a statement "Current through ___ date" included when you pull up the statute. You should be able to use those years as the "effective date" for your statutory citations (but to be on the safe side, you can find out what is acceptable in your jurisdiction). The most important thing is that there is no red flag or red stop sign showing that the statute has been overturned.

It is important to know how you might recognize a citation to a statute if you come across one in a secondary source. Many times, beginning researchers start research with secondary sources like legal encyclopedias. Most secondary sources, especially legal encyclopedias, explain the law and in so doing, have lots of citations to primary sources, including citations to statutes. It's good to know whether the citations you are looking at are citations to a statute, a case, a constitution, an administrative regulation, or another secondary source.

One notable aspect of many (but not all) statutory citations is the "section" sign—what some students call the "squiggly 's' "—§. This is the symbol signifying "section." Statutes on one general topic are divided into sections and subsections; we usually see this denoted by numbers, section signs and letters in an outline format. However, beware: both aspects can also be seen in regulations AND in some secondary sources. Read carefully.

Because statutes are codified, that is, organized by topic, the statutory citation also usually includes the subject—Penal Law, Social Security Law, Civil Rules, etc.

Finally, the last thing to remember about statutes is to look for both annotated and unannotated versions, as well as both official and unofficial versions. The federal government, and many states, have separate sets of codes—the law is the same, but one set of volumes is annotated, and one set of volumes is not annotated. The idea of annotations or "stuff" is introduced in Chapter 1 to help you distinguish between primary sources and secondary sources, and to alert you to the fact that when you are reading a case or reviewing a statute, you may come across citations, quotations or references to secondary sources. Annotations following a statute usually intend to explain the statute and its application, and can consist of notes, cross-references, hyperlinks to other sources (such as corresponding regulations, or Westlaw or Lexis sources), legislative history, commentaries by scholars, and case law. Therefore, the better research tool is the annotated version of the statutes.

Sometimes, as in the case of the United States statutes, the annotated version is clearly indicated. For example, these first two citations to a federal statute are to a well-known federal civil rights law:

- 42 U.S.C. § 1983 (1996)

- 42 U.S.C.A. § 1983 (West 1996)

You can see that the volume numbers (42) and the section or "§ " number is the same (1983); the only difference is that one abbreviation is "U.S.C." for "United States Code" and one is "U.S.C.A." for "United States Code Annotated."

The concept of annotation is sometimes linked to whether the publication is considered "official" or "unofficial." In general, whether a primary source—a statute—is the "official" version depends on the publisher. If the publisher is the government, then that source is the official source. Typically, (but not always) the official version of a source is NOT annotated. Rather, the extra work of annotating a set of statutes falls to a private publisher, and makes their product a better tool for doing research.

For example, the U.S.C. is the "official" version of the United States statutes because it is published by the federal government. Likewise, when states have both official and unofficial compilations of statutes, official means that it is published by that state, and unofficial means the publisher is not the government, but rather, a private company. Some states do not have an official code; you will have to investigate the practice in your region and your state as to which compilation of statutes should be cited. In general, when there is an official code, the official code should be cited. For example, when researching and citing United States law, always cite to the official (unannotated) version—U.S.C.

Again, rest assured that the actual text of the statute is the same (same goes for official versus unofficial publication of cases).

Here are some sample statutory citations from different states, as found on a website listing each states' statutes on social host liability[1], both civil and criminal:

State statutes:

- Cal. Civil Code § 1714 (Deering 2019), or Cal. Civil Code § 1714 (West 2019)

- Fla. Stat. § 856.015 (2019), or Fla. Stat. Ann. § 856.051 (West 2016), or Fla. Stat. Ann. § 856.015 (LexisNexis 2016)

- Ill. Rev. Stat. ch. 235, § 5/6–21 (2019), or

- Mich. Comp. Law § 436.1801 (2019), or Mich. Comp. Laws Ann § 436.1801 (West 2019), or Mich. Compl. Laws Serv. Section § 436.1801 (LexisNexis 2019)

- N.J. Rev. Stat. § 2A:15–5.6 (2019)

- N.Y. Gen. Oblig. Law § 11–101 (McKinneys 2019)

- Ohio Rev. Code Ann. § 4301.69

- Pa. Cons. Stat. tit. 18, § 6310.1

- S.C. Code Ann. § 45–2–40

- Tex. Alcoholic Beverage Code Ann. § 2.01 *et seq.*

B.   Administrative Regulations

State and federal administrative regulations generally have all three clues: an abbreviation indicating type of source (tends to be "Code" and/or "Regulations"); the jurisdiction (either a state or U.S.); and the year. For regulations, according to Bluebook Rule B14, the year included in the parenthetical is simply "the date of the rule or the regulation." Because there is no further explanation, it seems to make sense that in Westlaw this can be the year of the effective date (listed at

---

[1]   National Conference of State Legislatures, at http://www.ncsl.org/research/financial-services-and-commerce/social-host-liability-for-underage-drinking-statutes.aspx (last checked May 23, 2018).

the top for federal regulations) or for state regulations, any year that is listed that indicates the currency of the regulation.

For example, the federal code is the Code of Federal Regulations, or when abbreviated, C.F.R. A full citation would likewise include a section sign—29 C.F.R. § 1625.5 (2019). We can at least see the "F" for federal, and the "R" for regulations.

Note that like statutes, regulations can be printed in official vs. unofficial versions, and in annotated or unannotated versions.

Here is a list of some sample state and federal regulatory citations, following the Bluebook conventions. Note, again, that states may have their own citation format for practice-related or court-related documents.

Federal regulations:

- 29 C.F.R. § 1625.5 (2019)

State regulations:

- Cal. Code Regs. Tit. 14, § 1270.01 (2019)

- Fla. Admin. Code Ann. R. 69A–37.060 (2019)

- Ill. Admin. Code tit. 17, § 4000.435 (2019) or 17 Ill. Code. R. 4000.435 (Weil 2019)

- Mich. Admin. Code r. 281.426 (2019)

- 7 N.J. Reg. 18–1.3 (2019)

- N.Y. Comp. Codes R. & Regs. Tit. 6, § 617.7 (2019), or 6 N.Y.C.R.R. 617.7 (2019)

- Ohio Admin. Code 3745:1–05 (2019)

- 61 Pa. Code § 158.6 (2019)

- S.C. Code Ann. Regs. R. 61–112 (2019)

- 37 Tex. Admin. Code § 455.5 (2019)

C.   Constitution

The U.S. Constitution, or your state constitution, will not necessarily come up as often as other cases, statutes, and administrative regulations. Look for capitalization that is odd in today's world, as well as long paragraphs that are labeled "Articles," or a "Bill of Rights"; a constitution may also have section signs and statutes, but the subject matter of the constitution will usually be about the structure of the government, including the structure of the legislatures, courts and the executive branch.

In citation, according to the Bluebook's Rule 11, all the constitutions are abbreviated as Const., and all citations include the jurisdiction—either U.S. or the state. States are abbreviated according to Bluebook's Table 1. In addition, the section of the constitution should be abbreviated according to Bluebook's Table T16. Here are some examples of federal and state constitutional citations:

Federal constitution:

- U.S. Const. amend. XIV, § 2

State constitutions:

- Cal. Const. art. XXXV

- Fla. Const. pmbl.

- Ill. Const. art. X

- Mich. Const. art. II

- N.J. Const. art. XI, sec. I

- N.Y. Const. art. I

- Ohio Const. art. XVIII

- Pa. Const. art. I, § 28

- S.C. Const. art. I, sec. 2

- Tex. Const. art. 1, sec. 3a

D. Cases

In case law, the single most obvious identifying criteria is the case name, meaning the names of the parties, which will always be included in the citation. For example, the name of the case we read in Chapter 1 was *Carr v. Buss*. Two names, separated by a "v." A case name could also be "In Re," which means "in the matter of," or it could include a reference to the government if a government body is a party, such as "Secretary of Health and Human Services," or "U.S." or "State of New Jersey." After the case name, you will see some numbers and letters which may appear indecipherable, but if you look closely, you will see there is a pattern, and there are three parts to the pattern.

The first number is the volume number for the reporter. A reporter is the name we give the books in which court opinions appear. The next group of letters is the abbreviation for the reporter. This abbreviation usually, if not always, indicates the jurisdiction—whether it's a specific state or federal jurisdiction. For example, this abbreviation could be N.Y.S., for New York Supplement, or F.Supp, for Federal Supplement.

The last number is the page number in the reporter where you will find the case. So, again, the citation has three components: volume, name of reporter (usually an abbreviation), and page number. These pieces of information tell you specifically where you can find the case.

Sometimes, depending on the citation rules of your state, you will see another "parallel" group of numbers and letters, like this: 145 A.D.2d 341, 42 N.Y.S.3d 34 (1990). Note that this second citation follows the same pattern: volume number, reporter name, and page number.

Finally, the case citation ends with the year the court decision was decided—in the above case, 1990. So, just from looking at a case citation, you can usually identify the jurisdiction (the state or the U.S.) and the year. In other words, the citation always gives you specific and important information.

Also, note that there are specialized reporters that are not reviewed here, such as the Federal Rules Decisions, Tax Court, and Bankruptcy Court. Even though a reporter may have a specialized name, the format still has the same components as other case citations, and the abbreviation will indicate this unique reporter.

Here are some examples of citations from the top court of the federal and state jurisdictions—the court of last resort in the United States, and the courts of last resort for some states:

U.S. Supreme Court:

- *Loving v. Virginia*, 388 U.S. 1 (1967)

State courts (highest court; note that these examples are to give you a general idea of what high court citations may look like, but be sure to double-check your state rules in the Bluebook):

- *City of San Jose v. Superior Court of Santa Clara*, 2 Cal.5th 608, 389 P.3d 848, 214 Cal.Rptr.3d 274 (2017)

- *Hitchcock v. Florida*, 226 So.3d 216 (2017)

- *Jarrett v. Jarrett*, 78 Ill.2d 337, 400 N.E.2d 421 (1979)

- *Moning v. Alfono*, 400 Mich. 425, 254 N.W.2d 759 (1977)

- *State v. Novembrino*, 105 N.J. 95, 519 A.2d 820 (1987)

- *ITC Limited v. Punchgini, Inc.*, 9 N.Y.3d 467, 850 N.Y.S.2d 366, 880 N.E.2d 852 (2007)

- *Scott v. News-Herald*, 25 Ohio St. 3d 243, 496 N.E.2d 699 (1986)

- *Com. v. Carroll*, 412 Pa. 525, 194 A.2d 911 (1963)

- *Abbeville County School District v. State*, 410 S.C. 619, 767 S.E.2d 157 (2014)

- *Rogers v. Bradley*, 38 Tex. Sup. Ct. J. 1168, 909 S.W.2d 872 (1995)

Instructions and Rubrics for Case Briefing

This explanation and rubric is a good place to start when you are learning to do a case brief. Think of it as a checklist to remind yourself of all the different parts of a case brief. Notice the emphasis on relevant facts.

A SUMMARY OF INSTRUCTIONS

A case brief is an organized and active way of taking notes and summarizing a judicial opinion.

FACTS: All cases deal with stories. What is the story of this case? What happened with the people? Think about what People magazine would report.

Check: Did you identify legally relevant facts and summarize them in your own words?

PROCEDURAL HISTORY: There is always another story: what has happened so far in the courts? What court decided this case—a trial court, a mid-level appeals court, or a court of last resort? How did the case get to the court where it is now?

Check: Did you accurately describe what the trial court and mid-level appellate court decided?

RULE: The court will always rely and cite to the legal rule the court used to solve the problem. Hint: look for the citation—just like you have to provide a citation for legal authority, so does the court.

Check: Did you identify the legal rule that the court relied on to resolve this issue?

ISSUE: How does the legal rule apply to the "story" (facts) of the case? What element is at issue? The issue is a question that begins with "Whether." There may be more than one issue.

Check: Did you identify just one legal issue? If there is more than one issue, number each one.

HOLDING: What is the court's answer to each issue? Start out by stating: The court held . . .

Check: Did you avoid cutting and pasting and instead summarize what the court decided in your own words? If there is more than one issue, then include a holding for each issue.

REASONING: Why did the court decide how it did? Think about what goes after "because." Sometimes the court's reasons are implicit—or sometimes the court just lists the facts viewed as most relevant to answering the question.

Check: Did you identify the reasons for the court's holding in your own words? Did you avoid "cutting and pasting"? If there is more than one issue and corresponding holding, did you also identify the corresponding reasoning?

CASE BRIEF INSTRUCTIONS WITH RUBRIC

What is a case brief?

A case brief is an organized and active way of taking notes and summarizing a judicial opinion. It is a good tool because it requires you to identify the rule, the issue, and the holding.

FACTS: 20 points

All cases deal with stories. What is the story of this case? What happened with the people? Think about what People magazine would report. DO NOT CUT AND PASTE FROM THE COURT OPINION. Instead, try to summarize the facts in your own words.

Identified legally relevant facts and summarized in own words?

PROCEDURAL HISTORY: (optional)

There is always another story: what has happened so far in the courts? What court decided this case—a trial court, a mid-level appeals court, or a court of last resort? How did the case get to the court where it is now?

Accurately describe what the trial court and mid-level appellate court decided?

RULE: 20 points

The court will always rely and cite to the legal rule the court uses to solve the problem. Hint: look for the citation—just like you have to provide a citation for legal authority, so does the court.

Identified legal rule that court relied on in opinion?

ISSUE: 20 points

How does the legal rule apply to the "story" (facts) of the case? What element is at issue? The issue is a question which begins with "Whether." There may be more than one issue.

Identified the correct legal issue? * Included relevant facts?

HOLDING: 20 points

What is the court's answer to each issue? Start out by stating: The court held . . .

Summarize what the court decided in own words?

REASONING: 20 points

Why did the court decide how it did? Think about what goes after "because." Sometimes the court's reasons are implicit—or sometimes the court just lists the facts viewed as most relevant to answering the question.

Identified the reasons for the court's holding in own words? * Included relevant facts?

* * *

<h2 align="center">CASE BRIEF RUBRIC</h2>

The following rubric is another good tool for instructors and students, along with whatever variation the class material requires, to check and grade work. This rubric provides a bit more concrete guidance on the necessary components for each part of the brief.

	Professional	Competent	Developing	Beginner
FACTS	Shows synthesis and summarizes without repeating verbatim; Includes all legally relevant facts; clear prose and easy to read	Includes all legally relevant facts; Clear; Some mistakes in grammar, usage, and/or awkward summarizing	Uses bullet points instead of full sentences; Some lack of clarity; Some missing facts	Cutting and pasting from decision instead of summarizing; Missing relevant facts; Includes components that don't belong in "Facts"
PROCEDURAL HISTORY	Demonstrates understanding of any lower court proceedings; clear prose and easy to read	Demonstrates basic understanding of procedural disposition	Some confusion between substantive and procedural holding	Does not include or confuses with substantive holding

RULE	Includes correct rule for each issue; Includes all elements for each rule; demonstrates understanding that legal rule can be from any primary legal source	Basic and accurate understanding; may not include all elements of all rules	Demonstrates confusion or lack of completeness; does not include rule for EACH issue; includes incorrect rule or demonstrates some confusion	Includes only one rule, incorrect rule, or missing some elements of the rule
ISSUE	Includes ALL issues; identifies element(s) at issue and includes legally relevant facts	Does not include all necessary elements of issue statement (rule, elements at issue, legally relevant facts)	Does not include each issue; does not include legally relevant facts for each issue	Issue phrasing is too basic or unclear
SUBSTANTIVE HOLDING	Includes substantive holding for EACH issue; does not confuse with procedural holding	Includes basic holding but some lack of clarity	Does not include holding for each issue or confuses with procedural holding	Not complete and/or not clear
REASONING	Deduces or summarizes ALL of the court's reasons for EACH issue; thorough and not conclusory	Reasoning not fully summarized or explained for EACH issue	Lack of understanding of substantive holding in case	Not complete and/or not clear

Sample Case Briefs and Case Holding Sentences

CASE

(edited; based on 27 N.Y.2d 397, 318 N.Y.S.2d 467,
267 N.E.2d 251 (1971))

Edwin S. LOWE, Appellant,

v.

Jayne D. QUINN, Respondent

Opinion

FULD, Chief Judge.

The plaintiff, a married man, sues for the return of a diamond 'engagement' ring which he gave the defendant in October of 1968 upon her promise to wed him when and if he became free; he had been living apart from his wife for several years and they contemplated a divorce. About a month after receiving the ring, the defendant told the plaintiff that she had 'second thoughts' about the matter and had decided against getting married. When he requested the return of the ring, she suggested that he 'talk to (her) lawyer'. Convinced of the futility of further discussion, he brought this action to recover the ring or, in the alternative, the sum of $60,000, its asserted value.

Following a motion by the defendant for summary judgment dismissing the complaint and a cross motion by the plaintiff to amend his complaint 'to include causes of action for fraud, unjust enrichment and monies had and received,' the court at Special Term denied the defendant's application and granted the plaintiff's. The Appellate Division reversed and granted the defendant's motion, directing summary judgment against the plaintiff.

An engagement ring 'is in the nature of a pledge for the contract of marriage' (*Beck v. Cohen*, 237 App.Div. 729, 730, 262 N.Y.S. 716, 718) and, under the common law, it was settled—at least in a case where no impediment existed to a marriage—that, if the recipient broke the 'engagement,' she was required, upon demand, to return the ring on the theory that it constituted a conditional gift. (See, e.g., *Wilson v. Riggs*, 267 N.Y. 570, 196 N.E. 584, affg. 243 App.Div. 33, 276 N.Y.S. 232; *Beck v. Cohen*, 237 App.Div. 729, 262 N.Y.S. 716, Supra; *Goldstein v. Rosenthal*, 56 Misc.2d 311, 288 N.Y.S.2d 503; *Jacobs v. Davis* (1917), 2 K.B. 532; see, also, Note, 24 A.L.R.2d 579.)

However, a different result is compelled where, as here, one of the parties is married. An agreement to marry under such circumstances is void as against public policy (see, e.g., *Haviland v. Halstead*, 34 N.Y. 643; *Williams v. Igel*, 62 Misc. 354, 116 N.Y.S. 778; *Davis v. Pryor*, 8 Cir., 112 F. 274), and it is not saved or rendered valid by the fact that the married individual contemplated divorce and that the agreement was conditioned on procurement of the divorce. (See, e.g., *Smith v. McPherson*, 176 Cal. 144, 167 P. 875; *Leupert v. Shields*, 14 Col.App. 404, 60 P. 193; *Noice v. Brown*, 38 N.J.L. 228; see, also, 49 Harv.L.Rev. 648.)

Based on such reasoning, the few courts which have had occasion to consider the question have held that a plaintiff may not recover the engagement ring or any other property he may have given the woman. (See *Malasarte v. Keye*, 13 Alaska 407, 412; *Morgan v. Wright*, 219 Ga. 385, 133 S.E.2d 341; *Armitage v. Hogan*, 25 Wash.2d 672, 171 P.2d 830.) Thus, in *Armitage v. Hogan*, 25 Wash.2d 672, 171 P.2d 830, Supra, which is quite similar to the present case, the high court of the State of Washington declared (pp. 683, 685, 171 P.2d):

'* * * if it be admitted for the sake of argument that (defendant) respondent did agree to marry (plaintiff) appellant, and that the ring was purchased in consideration of such promise, such agreement would be illegal and void, as appellant was, at that time, and in fact has at all times since been, a married man. (p. 683, 171 P.2d 837).

'Regardless of the fact that appellant states this action is based on fraud and deceit, we are of the opinion that, under the facts in the case, appellant's claimed cause of action is based upon an illegal and an immoral transaction, and that this court should not lend its aid in furthering such transaction. (p. 685, 171 P.2d 838).

There are cases, it is true, which refuse to apply the doctrine of 'unclean hands'—invoked by the courts in the cited decisions—when the conduct relied upon is not 'directly related to the subject matter in litigation' (*Weiss v. Mayflower Doughnut Corp.*, 1 N.Y.2d 310, 316, 152 N.Y.S.2d 471, 474, 135 N.E.2d 208, 210; see also *National Distillers Corp. v. Seyopp Corp.*, 17 N.Y.2d 12, 15–16, 26 N.Y.S.2d 193, 194–196, 214 N.E.2d 361, 362, 363; *Furman v. Krauss*, 175 Misc. 1018, 26 N.Y.S.2d 121, affd. 262 App.Div. 1016, 30 N.Y.S.2d 848, mot. for lv. to app. den. 287 N.Y. 852, 39 N.E.2d 308; *Brooks v. Martin*, 2 Wall (69 U.S.) 70, 17 L.Ed. 732; 2 Pomeroy, Equity Jurisprudence (5th Ed., 1941), s 399, pp. 97–99) but it is difficult to see how the delivery of the ring or the action to procure its return may be deemed unrelated to the contract to marry.

There can be no possible doubt that the gift of the engagement ring was part and parcel of, directly related to, the agreement to wed.

· · ·

The order appealed from should be affirmed, with costs.

BURKE, BREITEL and GIBSON, JJ., concur with FULD, C.J.

Order affirmed.

CASE BRIEF

FACTS: A married man gives an engagement ring worth $60,000 to his mistress; the mistress eventually calls off the wedding but refuses to give the ring back.

RULE:

- An engagement ring is a pledge for the contract of marriage, and if the recipient breaks the contract, she must give the ring back.

- An agreement to marry where one of the parties is already married is void as against public policy

PROCEDURAL HISTORY: Plaintiff, a married man, sued for the return of an engagement ring from defendant. The trial court denied defendant's motion for summary judgment and granted plaintiff's motion to amend his complaint to include a cause of action for fraud and unjust enrichment. The Appellate Division reversed, and granted the defendant's motion for summary judgment against the plaintiff.

ISSUE: Whether the defendant mistress must give the engagement ring back to the plaintiff when the plaintiff is already married?

HOLDING: No, the defendant mistress can keep the engagement ring.

REASONING: The court reasoned that where a promise to marry is void as against public policy because one of the parties is already married, the usual rule that the recipient of the ring has to give the ring back when she breaks off the engagement does not apply.

CASE HOLDING SENTENCE

In *Lowe v. Quinn*, 27 N.Y.2d 397, 318 N.Y.S.2d 467, 267 N.E.2d 251 (1971), the Court of Appeals held that the plaintiff was not entitled to the return of a $60,000 engagement ring because he was already married and his pledge to marry was therefore void.

OR

The New York Court of Appeals denied recovery to a married plaintiff and precluded him from getting a $60,000 engagement ring back from his paramour because he was already married and therefore any promise to marry was illegal as against public policy. *Lowe v. Quinn*, 27 N.Y.2d 397, 318 N.Y.S.2d 467, 267 N.E.2d 251 (1971).

CASE

(based on 144 Cal.App.3d 827, 192 Cal. Rptr. 635 (1983))

THE PEOPLE, Plaintiff and Respondent,

v.

CATHERINE ANN McCABE, Defendant and Appellant

Court of Appeals of California, First District, Division Four.

COUNSEL

Carmen J. Newby for Defendant and Appellant.

George Deukmejian, Attorney General, Robert H. Philibosian, Chief Assistant Attorney General, William D. Stein, Assistant Attorney General, Eugene Kaster and Laurence K. Sullivan, Deputy Attorneys General, for Plaintiff and Respondent.

OPINION

THE COURT.

Catherine McCabe was charged with possession of cocaine for sale (Health & Saf. Code, § 11351) based on cocaine the police found in her purse. Appellant pleaded not guilty. After her motion to suppress evidence was denied, she pleaded guilty to the lesser included offense of possession of cocaine. (Health & Saf. Code, § 11350.) The court placed her on probation on the condition that she serve 12 days in the county jail and that she pay a $1,000 fine. On appeal, the issue is whether the police lawfully seized the cocaine from appellant's purse where they searched the purse under the authority of a search warrant providing for the search of a residence where appellant was visiting at the time of the search.

Frank Luis, Brennan Pang, and Sarah Bush shared a house at 838 Rorke Way in Palo Alto. Luis and Pang sold small amounts of cocaine to an undercover police officer at the residence. The police obtained a search warrant providing for the seizure of cocaine, marijuana, and narcotics paraphernalia on the premises of 838 Rorke Way.

When the police arrived at the house to execute the search warrant, the officer in charge demanded entry, waited 20 to 25 seconds and entered. Appellant, who was not a resident at 838 Rorke Way, was on the kitchen floor when the police entered. Bush was found hiding in the shower. Pang was found in the living room. The police found appellant's purse on a table in the living room.

One of the police officers opened appellant's purse and found her driver's license and bindles of cocaine. The police also found quantities of cocaine, marijuana, and drug-related paraphernalia in the bedrooms of the residents.

Appellant contends that the search of her purse was unlawful because the police may not rely on a search warrant to search the personal effects of a visitor who happens to be present on the premises at the time of the execution of the search warrant. Respondent contends that the search warrant authorized the search of the purse because the police may rely on a search warrant to search anywhere that the contraband which is the object of the search warrant might be concealed.

During the execution of a search warrant for fixed premises, the police may lawfully search the personal effects of a resident of the premises subject to search where the personal effects are plausible repositories of contraband. (*People* v. *Saam* (1980) 106 Cal. App.3d 789, 794 [165 Cal. Rptr. 256]). Today we hold that, during the execution of a search warrant, the police may, under specified conditions, lawfully search the personal effects of nonresidents found on the premises subject to search.

The police may ordinarily assume that all personal property which they find while executing a search warrant is the property of a resident of the premises subject to search. (*State* v. *Nabarro* (1974) 55 Haw. 583 [525 P.2d 573, 577]). (5) Thus, the police may search any personal property of a visitor which might serve as a plausible repository of the contraband which is the object of the search where they have no knowledge of the fact that the item searched is the personal property of a visitor. (*Id.*) If the police have actual knowledge that the property which is searched belongs to a nonresident, however, they may not, as a general rule, rely on the authority conferred by a search warrant to conduct a warrantless search of the nonresident's property, even though it is a plausible repository of contraband. (*Id.*; 2 LaFave, Search and Seizure (1978) Search Warrants, § 4.10(b), p. 154.). Seizure, *supra,* at p. 157.)

. . . .

. . . Thus, the search of the purse was lawful only if the police had no knowledge that the purse was the property of a nonresident.

Given the circumstances leading up to the search of the purse, the police knew of no facts which would have put them on notice that the purse belonged to a nonresident. The police officers were not told by appellant that the purse belonged to her. Appellant did not have possession of the purse at the time the police entered the house, nor did she subsequently take possession of the purse. (Cf. *State* v. *Nabarro, supra,* 525 P.2d at p. 577.) Moreover, the police were not compelled to infer from the fact that Luis and Pang, two males, were the suspects in the case that a purse, typically a woman's accessory, was beyond the permissible scope of the search warrant. The police knew that three people shared the premises subject to search: two men and a woman, Sarah Bush. The police could have reasonably assumed that the purse belonged to Bush, thereby bringing it within the scope of the search warrant. (Cf. *State* v. *Nabarro, supra,* 525 P.2d at p. 577). In the absence of any facts to suggest that the police knew that appellant owned the purse, the search of the purse did not exceed the permissible scope of the search warrant.

The judgment is affirmed.

CASE BRIEF

FACTS: While executing a search warrant for a residence, the police seized cocaine from a visitor's purse. Visitor was charged with possession of cocaine for sale.

RULE: Police may lawfully search "personal effects" of the residents when searching a home under a search warrant when the personal effects, like purses, are "plausible repositories" for contraband.

PROCEDURAL HISTORY: Criminal defendant pled guilty to cocaine possession, and on appeal, challenged the admissibility of the cocaine evidence seized from her purse on the basis that she was a visitor, not a resident, of the house searched.

ISSUE: Whether the evidence of cocaine found in a purse should be excluded because the police officers found it while acting under a search warrant to search a home and the purse belonged to a visitor?

HOLDING: No, police may lawfully search the purse of a nonresident while executing a search warrant at a house.

REASONING: The court reasoned that police may ordinarily assume that all personal effects they find in a home they are searching pursuant to a warrant belong to the residents. The police can therefore search the personal effects in the home as long as they don't know those items belong to a visitor. However, if they have actual knowledge that those personal effects belong to visitors, they cannot search them. In this case, there were no facts indicating that the purse belonged to a visitor. The defendant was not wearing the purse, and one of the house residents was a woman, so the police could have assumed the purse was hers.

CASE HOLDING SENTENCE

The First District California Court of Appeals denied the defendant's suppression motion and allowed the cocaine seized from defendant's purse to be used as evidence because the police had no knowledge that defendant was a visitor and not a resident of the house. *People v. McCabe*, 144 Cal.App.3d 827, 192 Cal. Rptr. 635 (1983).

OR

In *People v. McCabe*, 144 Cal.App.3d 827, 192 Cal. Rptr. 635 (1983), the court held that cocaine seized from the defendant's purse was admissible because, although the defendant was a visitor to the house that police were searching, the police had no actual knowledge of this so the search of her purse was lawful.

Sample IRACs

IRAC #1

Engagement Ring

HYPOTHETICAL FACTS: Jamal Washington and Maritza Martinez were engaged on Valentine's Day. Jamal surprised Maritza with a ring in a gluten free cupcake at their favorite vegan café, and Maritza joyfully exclaimed "Absolutely!" They planned their wedding for the following year, also on Valentine's Day. They were enjoying their engagement period until Jamal enrolled in a Paralegal Studies program. Jamal wanted to be a lawyer and go to law school, and thought Paralegal Studies would prepare him. After enrolling in the program, he spent all his time studying and realized he just loved the law. When he was not reading about it, he was visiting courts and networking through his local paralegal association. After many broken dates and three weeks of not seeing Jamal at all, Maritza confronted him. She wanted to know if he still wanted to marry her, and told him that he didn't have to spend ALL his time on law in order to be a good paralegal and later, a good lawyer. Jamal responded with an 1829 quote from Joseph Story, a Harvard law professor and Supreme Court Justice: "The law is a jealous mistress and requires constant courtship." Maritza asked him what he meant by that, but Jamal just answered her by reciting case holdings from English Common Law. Jamal then told her that yes, he would like to break the engagement. Maritza was heartbroken and refused to give

399

the ring back. Jamal, representing himself, sued her for return of the ring.

RULE: An engagement ring is a conditional gift, so if the marriage does not take place, the ring must be returned.

IRAC: The issue is whether Jamal is entitled to the return of the engagement ring, especially considering he is the one who broke the engagement. In this state, the rule is simply that the engagement ring is a conditional gift and must be returned if the marriage does not take place. Given that the rule does not have any provision for the reason the engagement was broken, and makes no mention that fault should be considered, Jamal is entitled to the return of the ring he gave Maritza because they are not getting married.

IRAC #2

False Imprisonment

HYPOTHETICAL FACTS: Samuel Webster, a young teenager, was hanging out with his hockey friends, and they decided they would give a prank gift to one of their buddies on the team. They went to a local convenient store and Sam was too embarrassed to buy condoms so he stole two packages off the shelves. The owner of the store, Mr. Wilson, saw Sam shoplifting, and immediately yelled: "Stop! You are caught red-handed!" Sam froze and turned red with embarrassment. Mr. Wilson ordered Sam into the back room storage room and told him he would have to wait there until the police arrived. Mr. Wilson was sure to lock the door. In the meantime, Mr. Wilson tried to call Sam's mother. However, Sam's mother, Ms. Webster, had turned her phone off while she was in a meeting and had forgotten to turn it back on. Although Mr. Wilson called her repeatedly, he just kept leaving messages. After an hour passed, Sam started banging on the door and asking to be let out. Mr. Wilson insisted that Sam wait in the storage room until his mother came to get him. Four hours later, Mr. Wilson finally got in touch with Sam's mother. When Mr. Wilson let Sam out of the storage closet, he was sweaty and shaking with hunger. Enraged,

Ms. Webster said she would sue Wilson for false imprisonment. She has asked you to consider her case based only on the facts above.

RULE: False imprisonment occurs when there is 1) intent to confine; 2) actual confinement not of the plaintiff's choosing; 3) a causal link; and 4) awareness of the confinement.

IRAC: The issue is whether Ms. Webster's case against Mr. Wilson and the store can satisfy all the elements of false imprisonment.

In this state, false imprisonment occurs when there is intent to confine; actual confinement; a causal link; and awareness of the confinement. Here, Ms. Webster would sue on behalf of her teenage son, Sam. First, it seems Mr. Wilson did have the intent to confine Sam because he ordered him to wait in the storage room and then locked the door.

Second, Sam experienced actual confinement when he was locked in the storage room of the convenient store by Mr. Wilson. Mr. Wilson locked the door, and Sam could not leave, which is why he was pounding the door asking to be released. Sam did not choose this confinement, but rather, was ordered into the storage room because he had shoplifted condoms. He was following Mr. Wilson's orders. Third, there is a causal link between the intent to confine and the confinement because Mr. Wilson ordered Sam into the storage room as a result of the shoplifting from Wilson's store.

Finally, given that the confinement lasted four hours and that Sam was banging the door asking to be released, Sam was aware of the confinement. Therefore, Ms. Webster does have an actionable claim against Wilson and his store for false imprisonment of Sam.

Sample IRAC, Memo and Motion

SLEEPING IN THE PARK IRAC

ISSUE: Whether Mr. Andrews can be convicted for "sleeping" in the park when his eyes were closed and he was snoring but it was the middle of the day and he was napping after lunch?

RULE: New York Penal Law § 10.10.10 provides: "It is unlawful for any person to sleep in the picnic areas of a state-owned park."

APPLICATION: Mr. Andrews was not guilty of "sleep" in violation of the statute because he was taking a short-term nap in the middle of the day after eating his lunch outside. This behavior is different than that of the defendants in *Matthews* and *Wilson* where the defendants were found sleeping in the park in the middle of the night and appeared to be using the park as a place to sleep. The prosecution could argue that the surrounding circumstances don't matter, and that just because he was sleeping during the day doesn't mean he wasn't violating the statute. However, considering the legislative intent behind the statute mentioned in *Wilson*, that the legislature wanted the public to use the parks to picnic and relax, and Mr. Andrews' use was consistent with that, he should not be guilty of its violation.

CONCLUSION: Based on the legislative intent behind the statute that the public use the parks to relax and picnic, and that Mr. Andrews was napping after his lunch in the middle of the day, Mr. Andrews should not be found guilty.

SLEEPING IN THE PARK MEMO

TO: Professor Phillips

FROM: Smart Student

RE: *People v. Andrews*

DATE: September 12, 2020

ISSUE

Whether Mark Andrews violated Penal Law § 10.10.10, which prohibits sleeping in the picnic area of a state-owned park, when he was woken up at 1:00 p.m. by a police officer who found him lying down on the grass next to his empty lunch bag, with his eyes closed, and he was snoring?

OR

Under Penal Law § 10.10.10, which forbids sleeping in the picnic areas of state owned parks, was Mark Andrews "sleeping" in violation of the statute when he was napping after lunch in the middle of the day?

SHORT ANSWER

No. Mr. Andrews did not violate Penal Law § 10.10.10 because he was not using the park as a place to sleep.

FACTS

We represent Mark Andrews, a 40-year-old white male who was arrested on May 4, 2006, for sleeping in the park. Mr. Andrews works for a local bank.

On May 4th, Mr. Andrews decided to eat his lunch in the park. At 1:00 p.m., a police officer found him lying in the grass next to his empty brown bag with his eyes closed, snoring. The police officer observed him for five minutes, and then woke him up and charged him with violating Penal Law § 10.10.10.

Mr. Andrews hired us to represent him in the criminal proceedings.

DISCUSSION

New York Penal Law § 10.10.10 provides: "It is unlawful for any person to sleep in the picnic areas of a state-owned park." The issue in this case is what constitutes "sleep" under the statute.

The Fourth Department has upheld convictions for sleeping in the park when the defendant has been found in the park in the early morning lying down under a blanket. For example, in *People v. Matthews*, 100 A.D.2d 99, 100, 96 N.Y.S.2d 97, 98 (4th Dep't 2000), the court affirmed the defendant's conviction under Penal Law § 10.10.10 because he was found under a picnic table, in a sleeping bag, snoring, with his eyes closed, in the early morning. Additionally, a police officer observed him like this for five minutes before arresting him. *Id.*

Likewise, in a case where the defendant was not actually sleeping at the time of arrest, the Fourth Department upheld a conviction because the defendant was found lying down, under a blanket, with his head on a knapsack, in the early morning. *People v. Wilson*, 96 A.D.2d 95, 95, 94 N.Y.S.2d 93, 93 (4th Dep't 1997). At trial the defendant testified that he suffered from insomnia and only sleeps one or two hours a night, but that he "may have fallen asleep for a short time on the night he was arrested." *Id.* at 96, 94 N.Y.S.2d at 94. The court accordingly held that "[t]he evidence *is* . . . consistent with a finding that at some time that night the defendant had been asleep on the bench." *Id.*

In both *Matthews* and *Wilson* the defendants used the park as a place to sleep, which is certainly not the intended use of state parks. In *Wilson*, the Fourth Department noted that Penal Law § 10.10.10 was enacted to make sure the parks were used for recreation—"to picnic, play, and relax"—and not as a place to sleep. 96 A.D.2d at 96, 94 N.Y.S.2d at 94. Arguably, the surrounding circumstances of the defendants' arrests—the time of night, where they were lying down, and the blanket or sleeping bag covering them—were more important than whether the defendant was actually sleeping at the time of arrest. For example, the court in *Wilson* noted: "even if the defendant did not actually sleep in the park, he was using the park as a place to sleep, and this is unlawful under the statute." 96 A.D.2d at 96, 94 N.Y.S.2d at 94.

Thus, the courts' holdings in *Wilson* and *Matthews* indicate that in addition to the physical act of sleeping, the surrounding circumstances are also important, such as the time of day or night, where the defendant is found, and whether the defendant appears to be settling in for a long time. *Matthews*, 100 A.D.2d at 100, 98 N. Y.S.2d at 98; *Wilson*, 96 A.D.2d at 96, 94 N.Y.S.2d at 94. These circumstances indicate whether the defendant is using the park as a place to sleep, contrary to the intent of the statute.

Although Mr. Andrews was sleeping at the time of arrest, he was not using the park as a place to sleep. First, unlike the defendants in *Matthews* and *Wilson*, who were found lying down in the middle of the night under a blanket, Mr. Andrews was arrested in the middle of the day. *Matthews*, 100 A.D.2d at 100, 98 N.Y.S.2d at 98; *Wilson*, 96 A.D.2d at 96, 94 N.Y.S.2d at 94. Because he was arrested at 1:00 p.m. and was found lying down next to an empty lunch bag, it's likely that he was napping after finishing his lunch.

A short nap after lunch in the park is much different from using the park as a place to sleep at night. In fact, by using the park as a place to eat his lunch, Mr. Andrews was using the park as a place to picnic— which, according to *Wilson*, the state legislature sought to protect. 96 A.D.2d at 96, 94 N. Y.S.2d at 94. Indeed, simply using the park at 1:00 p.m. in the afternoon suggests a recreational use, while using the park in the early morning hours does not. Thus, one of the most important factors distinguishing this case from *Matthews* and *Wilson* is the time of day Mr. Andrews was found sleeping.

Second, Mr. Andrews was not in a sleeping bag or under a blanket. The defendant in *Matthews* was found lying down in a sleeping bag under a picnic table. 100 A.D.2d at 100, 98 N. Y.S.2d at 98. Similarly, in *Wilson*, the defendant was found lying on a park bench under a blanket with his head on a knapsack. 96 A.D.2d at 96, 94 N. Y.S.2d at 94. Unlike either of these defendants, Mr. Andrews was not using a blanket or a sleeping bag, which further suggests that Mr. Andrews was not using the park as a place to sleep. Additionally, he did not have a pillow, and simply lying down on the grass does not imply the same intent to sleep as lying under a picnic table like the defendant in *Matthews* or lying on a park bench like the defendant in *Wilson*. *Matthews*, 100 A.D.2d at 100, 98 N. Y.S.2d at 98; *Wilson*, 96 A.D.2d at 96, 94 N. Y.S.2d at 94. Rather, lying on the grass is consistent with picnicking, which is the intended use of state parks.

Of course, the prosecution could argue that Mr. Andrews was sleeping within the meaning of the statute because he was observed snoring, with his eyes closed, for five minutes. Like Mr. Andrews, the defendant in *Matthews* was observed lying down, with his eyes closed, and snoring, for five minutes. *Matthews*, 100 A.D.2d at 100, 98 N.Y.S.2d at 98. Since the defendant's conviction in *Matthews* was affirmed, arguably, Mr. Andrews could be convicted under the statute as well. However, although Mr. Andrews was actually sleeping, prosecuting him does not seem consistent with the legislative intent behind the statute. As the Fourth Department noted, "New York State sought to ensure that its parks would be used only for the purpose for which they were intended: The picnic areas of parks are designed as a place where people can picnic, play, and relax and not as a place for people to sleep." *Wilson*, 96 A.D.2d at 96, 94 N. Y.S.2d at 94. Mr. Andrews ate his lunch in the park in the middle of the day, after which he happened to take a nap, which is entirely consistent with the legislative intent of protecting picnicking and relaxing. In this case, the overall purpose of the statute is more significant than whether he was actually sleeping at the time of arrest.

CONCLUSION

Mr. Andrews was not "sleeping in the park" in violation of Penal Law § 10.10.10. A nap in the middle of the day is completely distinct from sleeping in the middle of the night under a blanket or sleeping bag. Specifically, Mr. Andrews' behavior differs from that of the *Matthews* defendant and the *Wilson* defendant because he was napping in the middle of the day, not at night, and because he had no blanket or sleeping bag. Because his nap was casual and connected to the recreational use of picnicking, Mr. Andrews was not using the park as a place to sleep, which is what the New York legislature sought to avoid when it enacted Penal Law § 10.10.10.

SLEEPING IN THE PARK MOTION

The People of the State of Oz

                                        Index No: 11211

v.   MOTION TO DISMISS

Mark Andrews, Defendant

INTRODUCTION

Pursuant to Criminal Procedure Rule 10, the defendant requests a dismissal of the criminal charge for violating Penal Law § 10.10.10, which prohibits sleeping in the park, because the evidence cannot support a finding beyond a reasonable doubt that Mr. Andrews was violating the true purpose and intent of the statute. The purpose of Penal Law § 10.10.10 is to prohibit people using the park as a place to sleep at night. Mr. Andrews was not using the park as a place to sleep, but rather, was taking a short nap during the day after his lunch. Mr. Andrews' use of the park was consistent with the purpose of the park to provide a place for people to enjoy nature and relax.

STATEMENT OF FACTS

At approximately 1:08 p.m. in the afternoon on May 4, 2018, Officer James Cricket issued Mark Andrews a ticket for sleeping in City Park. (Police Report dated 1/1/16.) According to the Police Report, Cricket noticed Mr. Andrews lying down, with his eyes closed, sleeping, in the picnic area. (Police Report dated 1/1/16.) Mr. Andrews was not charged with any other crime, and there is no evidence of any inappropriate conduct such as public drunkenness or lewd behavior.

ARGUMENT

The charge against Mr. Andrews should be dismissed in the interest of justice and because the prosecution has failed to state a proper offense under the true meaning of the statute. Although Mr. Andrews was observed sleeping in the picnic area of City Park, he was hardly using the park as a place to sleep. He was not making a nuisance out of himself by napping in the middle of the day, nor was he substituting the park for a home or a camping site by using it as a place to spend the night.

Penal Law § 10.10.10 does prohibit sleeping in the park when it states: " "It is unlawful for any person to sleep in the picnic areas of a state, county or city owned park." However, the statute has been applied only to itinerants who set themselves up to spend the entire night in the park. For example, in *People v. Matthews*, 100 A.D.2d 99, 98 N.Y.S.2d 97 (4th Dep't 2000), the defendant was convicted because he was discovered by the police officer in the early morning hours—at 1:00 a.m.—and observed snoring and sleeping in a sleeping bag. Likewise, in *People v. Wilson*, 96 A.D.2d 95, 94 N.Y.S.2d 93 (4th Dep't 1997), although the defendant was found with his eyes open, he was also found by the police officer in the early morning hours—at 3:00 a.m.—lying down, under a blanket, using a knapsack as his pillow. The court stated that the defendant "was using the park as a place to sleep," *id.* at 96, 94 N.Y.S.2d at 94, which is unlawful under the statute.

A person napping during the lunch hour should not be guilty of violating the same statute as defendants who are camping out in a public park with sleeping materials. Unlike the defendants in *Wilson* and *Matthews*, Mr. Andrews did not have a blanket, sleeping bag, or pillow, and he was not found by a police officer in the early hours of the morning. Mr. Andrews was simply napping, while the *Wilson* and *Matthews* defendants were spending the night. Mr. Andrews was not using the park as a place to sleep, unlike those defendants; he was just taking a casual daytime nap.

Additionally, by enjoying a mid-day nap, Mr. Andrews was using the City Park in a way that is consistent with the legislative purpose behind Penal Law § 10.10.10. According to the Fourth Department, the purpose behind the statute is to protect state parks and ensure they are used for recreation so people can "picnic, play, and relax." *Matthews*, 100 A.D.2d at 101, 98 N.Y.S.2d at 99. A daytime nap is consistent with relaxing, while sleeping at night with a blanket and a pillow is consistent with sleeping in violation of the statute.

Pursuing this prosecution of Mr. Andrews is in opposition to the basic protective purpose of the statute, and the violation of the statute cannot be proven beyond a reasonable doubt. Therefore, the charge should be dismissed.

CONCLUSION

Based on Criminal Procedure Rule 10, this Court can dismiss the pending charge against Mr. Andrews because it is outside the scope of the statute and cannot be proven beyond a reasonable doubt at trial. Rule 10 allows dismissal of criminal charges when there is "insufficient basis in fact or law" and the charges could not be successful at trial. If an arrest is entirely inconsistent with the meaning of a statute established by the Fourth Department, then the basis is "insufficient" under the rule and the charges should not be sustained. Mr. Andrews was not using the park as a place to sleep, but rather, was using the park in a way that is consistent with the purpose of the Penal Code—for rest and relaxation.

Databases and Resources for Legal Instruction and Legal Research

LEGAL SUBSCRIPTION DATABASES

Bloomberg Law

https://www.bloomberglaw.com/

Fastcase

https://www.fastcase.com/

HeinOnline

https://home.heinonline.org/

Lexis Advance

https://advance.lexis.com/

Westlaw

https://www.westlaw.com/

OTHER ONLINE SOURCES

Agile Law, "13 Free Sites to Do Your Legal Research"

https://www.agilelaw.com/blog/13-free-sites-to-do-your-legal-research/

CALI (Computer Assisted Legal Instruction)

https://www.cali.org/

FindLaw for Legal Professionals

https://lp.findlaw.com/

Government publishing office:

https://www.govinfo.gov/help/tutorials-handouts

Justia

www.justia.com

Legal System Basics: Crash Course Government and Politics (Episode 18) (see also episodes on court structure, due process, how a bill becomes a law, etc.)

https://www.pbs.org/video/crash-course-government-18/

National Conference of State Legislatures

http://www.ncsl.org/

Oyez

https://www.oyez.org/

Supreme Court of the United States

https://www.supremecourt.gov/

U.S. Congress

https://www.congress.gov/

USA.gov

https://www.usa.gov/laws-and-regulations

US Legal

https://system.uslegal.com/administrative-agencies/

* Check your state government websites for court, legislative and agency information!

HELPFUL LAW SCHOOL LIBRARY GUIDES

UCLA

http://libguides.law.ucla.edu/c.php?g=183340&p=1208896

(According to the UCLA law school library guide at http://libguides. law.ucla.edu/onlinelegalresearch: "These "one stop shopping" sites provide users with a myriad of links to law-related materials on the Internet. They provide users with a catalog of Web sites, a search engine or both.")

- HG.org
- WashLaw
- vLex
- Internet Legal Research Group's PublicLegal
- American Law Sources Online
- Public.Resource.org
- Google Scholar
- OpenJurist

Georgetown

http://guides.ll.georgetown.edu/c.php?g=181233&p=1192870

Harvard

https://guides.library.harvard.edu/c.php?g=309942&p=2070277

University of Washington

https://lib.law.uw.edu/

Index